P

"Of the raft of books about the calamitous mismanagement of the intervention in Iraq, Patrick Cockburn's is probably the most readable . . . he displays exemplary courage in continuing to travel the country." Christopher Hitchens, *Slate*

"Cockburn's laconic prose is marinated in scorn when recounting the remarkable mix of incompetence and corruption that attended the occupation . . . a necessary book." *Guardian*

"The lurid, heartbreaking story of how the first Iraq war begat the second is brilliantly told in Patrick Cockburn's *The Occupation*, one of the most concise readable books to emerge out of the conflict. No Western reporter knows the country better . . . *The Occupation* breaks new ground in the way it puts these events on a timeline with terrific on-the-ground reporting." John Freeman, *The Plain Dealer*

"A wealth of telling detail illustrates how poorly Iraq is understood by its occupiers." Editor's Choice, *New York Times*

"Patrick Cockburn tells us so consistently and bravely how it really is." Jacqueline Rose, *Observer* Books of the Year

"From the front line itself, the brilliant and brave Patrick Cockburn has produced one of the books of the year." James Naughtie, *The Herald* Books of the Year

"All the richer for capturing Iraqi points of view – and noting the grim humour that survived in the most depressing of situations." *Metro* Books of the Year

"A quietly angry book about the foreseeable disaster of the Iraq War that everyone ought to read. Cockburn is a superb, courageous reporter. He writes with the clear simplicity that can be achieved only by those who really know what they are talking about." Peter Hitchens, *i*

"Required reading, especially for those who still believe that the invasion might have done some good, or actually did. It is a masterpiece of journalism which will surely scoop all the prizes. It certainly deserves to." A.N. Wilson, *Evening Standard* Books of the Year

"The anecdotal epiphanies and clear-sighted analysis offered up by Cockburn offer small jewels of insight into a situation of increasing ugliness, brutality and hopelessness. Cockburn offers an authoritative analysis often revealed through sharp detail [and] gift for strong but subtle understatement." *Toronto Globe and Mail*

"This isn't a book of cheap and easy questions . . . It is a sober piece of accurate, on-the ground reporting by one of the wisest men in the business. By God it makes you angry to read it." *The Oldie*

"Patrick Cockburn tells us in the restrained and elegant prose of his brilliant new book why we should forget US discomfiture and concentrate on the war crimes committed against the Iraqis – as civilised and humane people of any nationality should do." *Tribune*

"A lively and highly informative book on the American war in Iraq and the follies of occupation . . . informed by [Cockburn's] keen personal observations and understanding of the complexities and horrors of daily life in Iraq." Starred review, *Library Journal*

15 FEB 2020

THE OCCUPATION

WAR AND RESISTANCE IN IRAQ

Patrick Cockburn

VERSO

London • New York

For Janet, Henry and Alexander

First published by Verso 2006
© Patrick Cockburn 2006
This edition published by Verso 2007
© Patrick Cockburn 2007
All rights reserved

1 3 5 7 9 10 8 6 4 2

Verso
UK: 6 Meard Street, London W1F 0EG
USA: 180 Varick Street, New York, NY 10014-4606
www.versobooks.com

Verso is the imprint of New Left Books

ISBN-13: 978-1-84467-164-9

British Library Cataloguing in Publication Data
A catalogue record for this book is available from the British Library

Library of Congress Cataloging-in-Publication Data
A catalog record for this book is available from the Library of Congress

Printed in the USA by Quebecor World, Fairfield

Contents

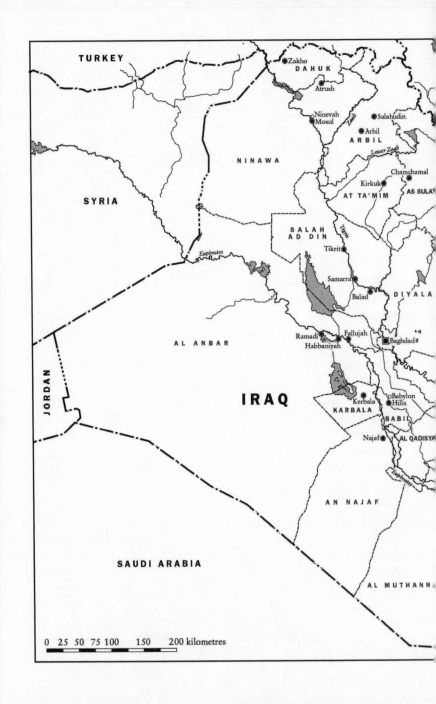

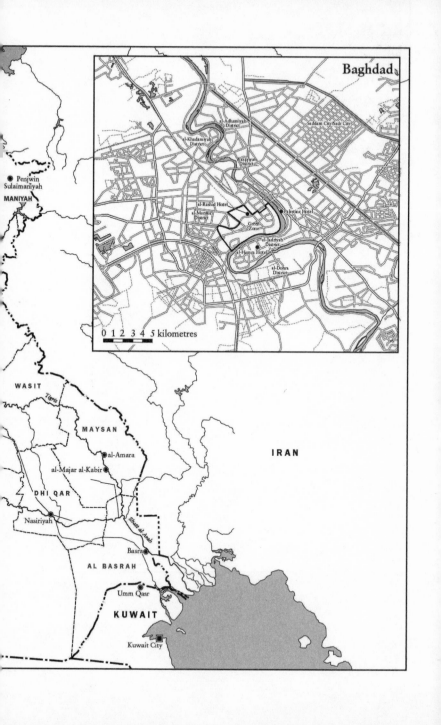

Acknowledgements

I did the reporting on which this book is based for the *Independent*, to which many thanks are due for its support over the years. In the months after the invasion I started writing a regular diary on Iraq for the *London Review of Books*. This enabled me to take a somewhat longer view of current events. Thanks are due to my editors on the *Independent* and the *LRB* and also to the Iraqis, many of whom appear anonymously in these pages, who have helped me try to understand their country.

The Surge

At 3 a.m. on January 11 2007 a fleet of American helicopters made a sudden swoop on the long-established Iranian liaison office in the city of Arbil in northern Iraq. Their mission was to capture two senior Iranian security officials, Mohammed Jafari, the deputy head of the Iranian National Security Council, and General Minojahar Frouzanda, the head of intelligence of the Iranian Revolutionary Guards. What made the American raid so extraordinary is that both men were in Iraq at the official invitation of the Iraqi President Jalal Talabani who held talks with them at his lakeside headquarters at Dokan in eastern Kurdistan. The Iranians had then asked to see Massoud Barzani, the president of the Kurdistan Regional Government, in the Kurdish capital Arbil. There was nothing covert about the meeting which was featured on Kurdish television.

In the event the US attack failed. It was only able to net five junior Iranian officials at the liaison office that had existed in Arbil for years issuing travel documents, and which was being upgraded to a consular office by the Iraqi Foreign Ministry in Baghdad. The Kurdish leaders were understandably furious asking why, without a word to them, their close allies the Americans had tried to abduct two important foreign officials who were in Iraq at the request of the Iraqi president. Kurdish troops had almost opened fire on the American troops. At the very least the raid showed a contempt for Iraqi sovereignty which the US was supposedly defending. It was three months before officials in Washington admitted that they had tried and failed to capture Jafari and General Frouzanda. The US state department and Iraqi government argued for the release of the five officials as relative minnows, but Vice-President Cheney's office insisted fiercely that they should be held.

If Iran had undertaken a similar venture by, for example, trying to kidnap the deputy head of the CIA when he was on an official visit to Pakistan or Afghanistan then Washington might have considered the attempt a reason for going to war. In this instance the US assault on Arbil attracted bemused attention inside and outside Iraq for only a few days before it was buried by news of the torrent of violence in the rest of the country. The US understandably did not reveal the seniority of its real targets – or that they had escaped.

The Arbil raid is important because it was the first visible sign of a string of highly significant American policy decisions announced by President George W. Bush in an address to the nation broadcast in the US a few hours earlier on January 10. There have been so many spurious turning points in the war – such as the capture of Saddam Hussein in 2003, the hand over of sovereignty to an Iraqi government in 2004 or the elections of 2005 – that truly critical moments are obscured or underrated. The true importance of Bush's words took time to sink in. In the months prior to his speech the US seemed to be feeling its way towards an end to the war. The Republicans had lost control of both houses of Congress in the November 2006 elections, an unexpectedly heavy defeat blamed on the Iraq war. Soon afterwards the bipartisan Iraqi Study Group of senior Republicans and Democrats, led by James Baker and Lee Hamilton, spelled out the extent of American failure thus far, arguing for a reduced US military commitment and suggesting negotiations with Iran and Syria.

President Bush did the exact opposite of what the Baker-Hamilton report had proposed. He identified Iran and Syria as

America's prime enemies in Iraq, stating that 'These two regimes are allowing terrorists and insurgents to use their territory to move in and out of Iraq.' Instead of reducing the American commitment, Bush pledged to send 20,000 extra troops to Iraq to try to secure Baghdad. In other words the US was going to respond to its lack of success in the conflict by escalating both the war in Iraq and America's confrontation with Iran in the Middle East as a whole. The invasion of 2003 had destabilized the whole region; now Bush was about to deepen that instability.

The raid on Arbil showed that the new policies were not just rhetoric. Iraqis were quicker than the rest of the world to pick up on what was happening. 'People are saying that Bush's speech means that the occupation is going to go on a long time,' the Iraqi political scientist Ghassan Attiyah told me soon after the president had stopped speaking. Although the new US security plan for Baghdad, which began on February 14, was sold as a temporary 'surge' in US troop numbers it was evident that the reinforcements were there to stay. In April the Pentagon announced it was increasing US army tours in Iraq from twelve to fifteen months. Without anybody paying much attention, American officials stopped talking about training Iraqi army troops as a main priority. This was an important shift in emphasis. Training and equipping Iraqi troops to replace American soldiers so they could be withdrawn from Iraq had been the cornerstone of US military planning since 2005. Now the policy was being quietly downgraded, though not abandoned altogether.

Could the new US strategy succeed? It seemed very unlikely. The US had failed to pacify Iraq between 2003 and 2007. Now, with much of the US public openly disillusioned with the war, Bush was to try for victory once again. Common sense suggested that he needed to reduce the number of America's enemies inside and outside Iraq. But his new strategy was only going to increase them. The US army was to go on fighting the 5 million-strong Sunni community as it had been doing since the capture of

Baghdad. The Sunni demand for a timetable for US withdrawal was not being met. At the same time the US was going to deal more aggressively with the 17 million Shias in Iraq. It would contest the control over much of Baghdad and southern Iraq of the Mehdi Army, the powerful Shia militia led by the nationalist Shia cleric Muqtada al-Sadr, who is regarded with cult-like devotion by many Shia Iraqis. Not content with this, Washington was also more openly going to confront Iran, the most powerful of Iraq's neighbours.

As with so many US policies under Bush the new strategy made sense in terms of American domestic politics, but in Iraq seemed a recipe for disaster. Iran was easy to demonize in the US, just as Saddam Hussein had been blamed four years earlier for everything that was wrong in Iraq and the Middle East. The *New York Times,* which had once uncritically repeated White House claims that Saddam possessed weapons of mass destruction, now ran articles on its front page saying that Iran was exporting sophisticated roadside bombs to Iraq that were killing American soldiers. There was no reference to the embarrassing discoveries of workshops making just such bombs in Baghdad and Basra. Above all the Bush administration was determined to put off the day, at least until after the Presidential election in 2008, when it had to admit that the US had failed in Iraq.

I was in Baghdad soon after Bush had spoken. I had never known it so bad. My driver had to take a serpentine route from the airport, driving along the main highway and then suddenly doing a U-turn to dart down an alleyway. He was trying to avoid checkpoints that might be manned by Police Commandos in their mottled uniforms who often acted as Shia death squads. The journey to the al-Hamra Hotel in Jadriyah, a district built in a loop of the Tigris river, took three times as long as normal. In the following days I could see Mehdi Army checkpoints, civilians with guns and a car slewed across the road, operating almost within sight of the heavily guarded 14 July Bridge that leads to the Green Zone.

The extent of the military failure over the previous three-and-a-half years was extraordinary. The foreign media never quite made clear how little territory the US and the Iraqi army fully controlled even in the heart of Baghdad. It was astonishing in early 2007 to look out from the north-facing windows in the Hamra and see columns of black smoke billowing up from Haifa Street on the other side of the Tigris river. This is a two-mile-long militant Sunni corridor less than a mile from the northern end of the Green Zone. Since the early days of the fighting the US army, supported by Iraqi army troops, had been unsuccessfully trying to drive out the insurgents who ruled it.

Sometimes US commanders persuaded both themselves and embedded journalists that they were making progress. On this occasion I looked up and read a long, optimistic article about Haifa Street in an American paper claiming that there were signs that 'the tide was turning on Iraq's street of fear'. It was no longer an arrow pointing at the heart of the Green Zone: rebel leaders had been arrested or killed; large weapons caches had been discovered; insurgent attacks were less intense and less frequent; Iraqi troops were at last being effectively deployed. Having finished reading the piece I was reflecting on whether or not the US military and its local allies was at last achieving something in Haifa Street when I glanced at the date of the piece and realized, with a groan, that it was dated March 2005, almost two years earlier.

American commanders often genuinely believed that they were in command of towns and cities which Iraqis, including the local police, told me were dominated by Sunni insurgents or Shia militia. On one occasion in early 2007 senior US and Iraqi officers were giving a video press conference from Diyala, a much fought over province north-east of Baghdad, confidently claiming that they were winning the fight against the Sunni rebels. Even as they were speaking an insurgent squad attacked and captured the mayor's office in Baquba, the capital of Diyala. It only withdrew after blowing up the building and kidnapping the mayor. The government announced that it was dismissing 1,500 policemen in Diyala because of their repeated failure to resist the insurgents. When I checked with a police commander a few months later he threw up his hands in disgust and said not a single policeman had been fired.

The addition, promised by Bush, of five extra brigades to the US forces in Baghdad made, at least at first, some difference to security in the capital. The number of bodies of people, tortured, shot in the head and dumped in the street, went down from the horrific levels of late 2006. These death-squad killings were mostly of Sunni and were the work of the Mehdi Army or of army and police units collaborating with them.

A few days before the security plan began Muqtada al-Sadr stood down his militiamen, telling them to dump their arms and move out of Baghdad. He was intent on avoiding direct military confrontation with the US reinforcements. But while the Shia were killing fewer Sunni, the Sunni insurgents were still slaughtering Shia civilians with massive suicide bombs, often vehicle-borne, targeting crowded market places. These did not stop, and improved security measures made little difference. On February 3 a truck delivering vegetables blew up in the Shia Kurdish Sadriya quarter in central Baghdad killing 135 people and wounding 305. Ten weeks later, long after the security plan had been launched, another vehicle bomb blew up in the same market, killing 127 people and wounding 148. Not surprisingly local people jeered and threw stones at American and Iraqi soldiers who turned up after the explosion. The main failing of the security plan for ordinary Iraqis, many of whom had initially welcomed it, was simply that it did not deliver security for them or their families.

There was a central lesson of four years of war which Bush and Tony Blair never seemed to take on board though it was obvious to anybody living in Iraq: the occupation was unpopular and becoming more so by the day. Anti-American guerrillas and militiamen always had enough water to swim in. The only community in Iraq that fully supported the US presence was the Kurds and Kurdistan was not occupied. It is this lack of political support that has so far doomed all US political and military actions in Iraq. It makes the country very different from Afghanistan where foreign troops are far more welcome. Opinion polls consistently show this trend. A comprehensive survey of Iraqis has been conducted by ABC News, USA Today, BBC and ARD annually over the last three years. Its findings illuminate the most important trends in Iraqi politics. They show that by March 2007 no less than 78 per cent of Iraqis opposed the presence of US forces, compared to 65 per cent in November 2005 and 51 per cent in February 2004. In the latter year only 17 per cent of the population thought that violence against US forces was acceptable while by 2007 the figure had risen to 51 per cent. This pool of people sympathetic to Sunni insurgents and Shia militias was so large as to make it difficult to control and impossible to eliminate them.

Again and again assassinations and bombs showed that the Iraqi army and police were thoroughly infiltrated by militants from all sides. Nowhere was safe. Some incidents are well known. In April 2007 a suicide bomber blew himself up in the café of the Iraqi parliament in its heavily defended building in the Green Zone. The bomber had somehow circumvented seven or eight layers of security. Earlier, on March 23, the deputy prime minister Salam al-Zubaie, was badly injured by a bomber who got close to him with the connivance of his bodyguards. There were lesser unknown incidents indicative of the divided loyalties of the security forces. On March 6 militants from the Islamic State of Iraq movement of which al-Qaeda in Iraq is part stormed Badoush prison north-west of Mosul. In the biggest jailbreak since 2003 they freed 68 prisoners, of whom 57 were foreign. Of the 1,200 guards at the prison, 400–500 were on duty at the time but did nothing to stop the Islamic militants breaking in or the prisoners breaking out. Some American soldiers see that the problem is not about a few infiltrators. 'Any Iraqi officer who hasn't been assassinated or targeted for assassination is giving information or support to the insurgents,' one US marine was quoted as saying. 'Any Iraqi officer who isn't in bed with the insurgents is already dead.'

Some problems facing the US and Britain in Iraq have not changed since Saddam Hussein invaded Kuwait in 1990. Getting rid of the Iraqi leader was far easier than finding a successor regime that would not be more dangerous to American interests. It is a dilemma still unresolved more than four years into the occupation. A prime reason why the US supported Saddam Hussein during his war with Iran in 1980–1988 is that it did not want a Shia clerical regime, possibly sympathetic to America's enemies in Tehran, to come to power in Iraq. It was the same motive that stopped President Bush senior pushing on to Baghdad and overthrowing Saddam after defeating the Iraqi army in Kuwait in 1991. After 2003 Washington was in the same quandary: if elections were held the Shia, comprising 60 per cent of the population that had long been excluded from power, were bound to win. The nightmare for Washington was to find that it had conquered Iraq only to install black-turbaned clerics in power in Baghdad, as they already were in Tehran. At first the US tried to postpone elections, claiming that a census had to be held. It was only on the insistence of the Shia Grand Ayatollah Ali al-Sistani that two elections were held in 2005, in which the Shia religious parties triumphed. Washington has never been comfortable with these Shia–Kurdish governments. It demanded that they try to reconcile with the Sunni, though exactly how Shia and Kurdish leaders are supposed to do this, given that the main Sunni demand is a timetable for an American withdrawal, has never been clear.

For their part, the Shia have become increasingly suspicious that the US and Britain do not intend to relinquish real control over security to the elected Iraqi government. There were many examples of this. For instance, in the Middle East the most important force underpinning every government is the intelligence service. In theory, as I explain later in this book, the Iraqi government should get its information from the Iraqi National Intelligence Service (INIS) that was established in 2004 by the US-run Coalition Provisional Authority. But a peculiarity of the INIS is that its budget is not provided by the Iraqi Finance Ministry but by the CIA. Over the next three years they paid $3 billion to fund its activities. During this time it was run by General Mohammed Shahwani, who had been the central figure in a CIA-run coup in 1996 against Saddam Hussein that had failed disastrously. For long periods he was even banned from attending Iraqi cabinet meetings. A former Iraqi cabinet minister who was a member of the country's National Security Council complained to me that 'we only get information that the CIA wants us to hear'. Iraqis did not fail to spot the extent to which the power of their elected government was being trimmed. The poll cited above showed that by spring 2007 only 34 per cent of Iraqis thought their country was being run by their own government; 59 per cent believed the US was in control. The Iraqi government had been robbed of legitimacy in the eyes of its own people.

In the course of 2006 and 2007 Baghdad disintegrated into a dozen hostile cities at war with each other. There were fewer and fewer mixed Sunni and Shia neighbourhoods. Terror engulfed the city like a poisonous cloud. There was a lot to be frightened of: Sunni insurgent groups; the Shia militias, Mehdi Army and the Badr Organization; police and police commandos; the Iraqi army and Americans. One day I received an e-mail message from an old friend. He wrote: 'Yesterday the cousin of my step-brother (as you know my father married twice) was killed by Badr troops three days after he was arrested. His body was found in the trash in al-Shula district. He was one of three other people who were killed after heavy torture. They did nothing, but they are Sunni people among the huge numbers of Shia people in the General Factory for Cotton in al-Khadamiyah where they were working. His family couldn't recognize his face [and only knew it was him] because of the wart on his arm.'

Most of my Iraqi friends had fled Iraq to Jordan or Syria or, when they could get a visa, to Western Europe. Soon I could not enter the coffee shop of the Four Seasons hotel, where I usually stayed in the Jordanian capital of Amman, without seeing several Iraqis I knew sitting at other tables. These were the better-off. The poor often had to choose between staying in jobs where they were at risk, becoming permanently unemployed or taking flight. I was in contact with a Sunni family called al-Mashadani who lived in the west Baghdad district of Hurriya. It was under attack by Shia militiamen. Khalid, the father, worked as a mechanic in the railway station. He was forced to leave his job when the repair yard was taken over by the militiamen. He stayed away and asked a Shia fellow worker to pick up his salary. This worked until the Shia militias found out what was happening and threatened to kill any Shia who passed on the salary of a Sunni.

Khalid was forced to leave for Syria where he found work. He left behind his wife Nadia, and four children, the eldest of whom was eight years old. Living with them in the house was Nadia's sister Sarah, whose husband had been an ordinary guard at the Oil Ministry building. He was killed by the resistance who considered that his job made him a collaborator with the government. On December 25 2006 this whole family group was told by the Shia militia to get out of their house immediately, without taking any possessions, or be killed. They fled into the night and sat beside the road until a charitable minibus driver picked them up. Eventually they found refuge in a school. Nadia recalled that 'we stayed twenty-nine days in a dark and damp room and we couldn't go out of it when the students were studying'. Her husband in Syria offered to return, but she told him to stay because the family could not afford for him to lose his job.

Nadia blames the Americans for the sectarian civil war that had engulfed her family. She says: 'We were living together, Sunni and Shia, and there was no sign of sectarian differences between us in Iraq until the Americans came and encouraged sectarianism and let in foreign terrorists.' Many Iraqis similarly see sectarianism as the work of the Americans. This is not entirely fair. Sectarian differences in Iraq, as I explain below, were deeper under Saddam Hussein and his predecessors than many Iraqis now admit. But in one important respect foreign occupation did encourage and deepen sectarianism. Previously a Sunni might feel differently from a Shia but still feel they were both Iraqis. Iraqi nationalism did exist though Sunni and Shia defined it differently. But the Sunnis fought the US occupation, unlike the Shia who were prepared to cooperate with it. After 2003 the Sunni saw the Shia who took a job as a policeman not only as a member of a different community, but also as a traitor to his country. Sectarian and national antipathies combined to produce a lethal brew.

The war in Iraq that started in 2003 has now lasted longer than the First World War. Militarily the conflicts could not be more different. The scale of the fighting in Iraq is far below anything seen in 1914–1918. But the political significance of the Iraq war has been enormous. America blithely invaded Iraq to overthrow Saddam Hussein and show its great political and military strength. Instead it demonstrated its weakness. The vastly expensive US war machine failed to defeat a limited number of Sunni Arab guerrillas. International leaders such as Tony Blair, who confidently allied themselves to Washington at the start of the war convinced that they were betting on a winner, are either discredited or out of power.

At times President Bush seemed intent on finding out how much damage could be done to the US by the conflict in Iraq. He did so by believing a high proportion of his own propaganda about the resistance to the occupation being limited in scale and inspired from outside the country. By 2007 the administration was even claiming that the fervently anti-Iranian Sunni insurgents were being equipped by Iran. It was a repeat performance of US assertions four years earlier that Saddam Hussein was backing al-Qaeda. In this fantasy world constructed to impress American voters, in which failures were sold as successes, it was impossible to devise sensible policies.

The US occupation has destabilized Iraq and the Middle East. Stability will not return until the occupation has ended. The Iraqi government, penned into the Green Zone, has become tainted in the eyes of Iraqis by reliance on a foreign power. Even when it tries to be independent it seldom escapes the culture of dependency in which its members live. Much of what has gone wrong has more to do with the US than Iraq. The weaknesses of its government and army have been exposed. Iraq has joined the list of small wars, as France found in Algeria in the 1950s and the Soviet Union in Afghanistan in the 1980s, that inflict extraordinary damage on the occupiers.

Baghdad and Arbil
April 2007

I

IT HAS BEEN the strangest war. It had hardly begun in 2003 when President George W. Bush announced on May 1 that it was over: the American mission had been accomplished. Months passed before Washington and London realized that the conflict had not finished. In fact, the war was only just beginning. Three years after Bush had spoken the US military had suffered 2,000 dead and injured in Iraq, 95 per cent of the casualties inflicted after the fall of Baghdad.

Almost without thinking, the US put to the test its claim to be the only superpower in the world. It spurned allies inside and outside Iraq; in invading Iraq Tony Blair was Bush's only significant supporter. The first President George Bush led a vast UN-backed coalition to complete victory in the Gulf War in 1991 largely because he fought a conservative war to return the Middle East to the way it was before Iraq's invasion of Kuwait. It was a status quo with which the world was familiar, and restoring it was therefore supported internationally – and in the Middle East. The war launched by his son, George W. Bush, twelve years later in 2003 was a far more radical venture. It was nothing less than an attempt to alter the balance of power in the world. The US, acting almost alone, would seize control of a country with vast oil reserves. It would assume quasi-colonial control over a nation which fifteen years previously had been the greatest Arab power. Senior American officials openly threatened to change the governments of states neighbouring Iraq.

The debate on why the US invaded Iraq has been over-sophisticated. The main motive for going to war was that the White House thought it could win such a conflict very easily and to its own great advantage. They were heady times in Washington in 2002, as the final decisions were being taken to invade Iraq. It was the high tide of imperial self-confidence. The US had just achieved a swift victory in Afghanistan. The Taliban forces had evaporated after a few weeks of bombing by B-52s and the withdrawal of Pakistani support. Their strongholds in Kabul and Kandahar fell with scarcely a shot fired. To Tony Blair, believing that the US was about to fight another short and victorious war, support for Bush must have looked like a safe bet.

There was no reason why Saddam Hussein should not be defeated with the same ease as the Taliban. His army was a rabble, his heavier weapons, such as tanks and artillery, obsolete and ill-maintained. Iraq was exhausted by its eight-year war with Iran between 1980 and 1988, the humiliating defeat in Kuwait three years later and the thirteen long years of UN sanctions. If Bush and Blair had truly believed that the Iraqi leader possessed the military strength sufficient to pose a threat to the Middle East through weapons of mass destruction, they would probably not have attacked him.

They were right to suspect he could not put up much of a fight. A few years earlier I had watched a military parade in Baghdad from a distance. A well-disciplined column of elite infantry marched past Saddam, standing on a raised platform near the Triumphal Arch made of crossed swords that commemorated victory over Iran. All the soldiers appeared to be wearing smart white gloves. Only when I got closer did I realize that the Iraqi army was short of gloves, as it was of so many other types of equipment, and that the soldiers were wearing white sports socks on their hands.

Few governments can resist the temptation to fight and win a war that will boost their standing at home. It enables them to stand tall as defenders of the homeland. Domestic political opponents can be portrayed as traitors or lacking in patriotism. The Bush administration had been peculiarly successful in wrapping the flag around itself after September 11 and later during the war in Afghanistan. It intended to do the same thing in Iraq in the run-up to the 2004 presidential election.

It was evident to very few in the US or the rest of the world that Bush was engaged in an extraordinary gamble. Even opponents of the war mostly cited moral objections to the invasion. For supporters of the attack on Iraq this was the moment that the US would lay the ghosts of Vietnam and Somalia. But history is full of examples of wars launched by great powers against weaker opponents in the mistaken expectation of an easy victory. The Duke of Wellington, warning hawkish politicians in Britain against ill-considered military intervention abroad, once said: 'Great nations do not have small wars.' He meant that such supposedly insignificant conflicts can inflict terrible damage on powerful states. Having seen what a small war in Spain had done to Napoleon, he knew what he was talking about.

The US failure in Iraq has been even more damaging than Vietnam because the opponent was punier and the original ambitions were greater. The belief that the US could act alone, almost without allies, was quickly shown to be wholly false. By the summer of 2004 the US military had only islands of control. The failure was all the worse because it was self-inflicted, like the British invasion of Egypt to overthrow Nasser in 1956. But by the time of the Suez crisis the British empire was already on its deathbed. The disaster only represented a final nail in its coffin. Perhaps the better analogy is the Boer War, at the height of British imperial power, when the inability of its forces to defeat a few thousand Boer farmers damagingly exposed both Britain's real lack of military strength and its diplomatic isolation.

In many ways the guerrilla war in Iraq resembled Vietnam. A year after it started I talked to US sappers with the highly dangerous job of looking for buried bombs, known as IEDs

(Improvised Explosive Devices), usually several heavy artillery shells wired together and detonated by a long wire or by remote control. These so-called 'convoy killers' were to prove a devastating weapon, causing half of US fatal casualties. The sappers explained they had received no training for the job. 'I never heard of an IED before I came to Iraq,' remarked one soldier. A sergeant said that he had with difficulty obtained an old but still valid US army handbook, printed during the Vietnam war, about this type of bomb and the lethal booby traps often placed nearby to kill unwary sappers. He believed the army had not reissued the handbook, useful though it was, because doing so might appear to contradict the official line from the Pentagon that Iraq was not like Vietnam.

There should be no doubt about the extent of the US failure. General William Odom, the former head of National Security Agency, the largest US intelligence agency, called it 'the greatest strategic disaster in American history'.[1] Back in the US it took time for this to sink in. Right-wing commentators claimed that the good news about Iraq was being suppressed. US network news programmes were edgy about reporting the bad news because they feared being accused of lack of patriotic zeal. The same inhibition hamstrung the Democrats during the presidential election in 2004. The sharpest denunciations of the US debacle in Iraq came first from the US army or its political allies. 'Many say the army is broken,' said Congressman John Murtha, former Marine and veteran of Vietnam, in a stirring philippic on the war in November 2005. 'The future of the country is at risk. We cannot continue in our present course . . . It's a flawed policy wrapped in an illusion.' He added that the very presence of US soldiers was fuelling the uprising and referred to a leaked British Ministry of Defence poll showing that 80 per cent of Iraqis opposed the presence of foreign troops in Iraq.[2]

It was the overwhelming unpopularity of the occupation among the five million Sunni Arabs in Iraq which led to the speedy start of guerrilla warfare. The Shia leaders were also hostile to the occupation but were not going to oppose it in arms if they could take power through the elections. But neither Sunni nor Shia were ever going to provide reliable allies for the US. All this became evident during the first year of the war. Less obvious was the failure of the US to give most Iraqis a better life at the most basic level. For instance, before the overthrow of Saddam Hussein 50 per cent of Iraqis had access to drinkable water, but this figure had dropped to 32 per cent by the end of 2005. Some $4 billion was spent by the US and Iraqi governments on increasing the electricity supply, but in April 2006 this fell to 4,100 megawatts, below pre-invasion levels, which represents half the 8,000 megawatts needed by Iraq. Oil production touched a low of 1.4 million barrels a day.[3] These figures meant that most Iraqis lived on the edge of destitution, surviving only because of cheap government rations. At least 50 per cent of people who could work were unemployed.[4] Violence was not going to end so long as there were millions of angry young men so desperate for work that they were prepared to fight in any militia or join any criminal gang.

It was not only the poor – the vast majority of Iraqis – who were alienated. One friend, a highly educated businessman, described listening to a US officer solemnly lecturing half a dozen Iraqis with PhDs and the command of several languages on the future of their country. One place where the US might have hoped for a sympathetic hearing was among the brokers on the Baghdad stock exchange. But in 2003 control of the exchange was given to a 24-year-old American whose main credential for the job was his family's contributions to the Republican Party. He allegedly failed to renew the lease on a building housing the exchange, which consequently stayed shut for a year.

After six months the brokers' frustrated fury at the US occupation made them sound more like Islamic militants from Fallujah than the highly conservative businessmen they were.

* * *

Once, after surveying a battlefield during the American Civil War, the great Confederate General Stonewall Jackson turned to an aide and asked: 'Did you ever think, sir, what an opportunity a battlefield affords liars?'[5] He meant that the pace and complexity of events in war makes it very difficult to distinguish truth from falsehood. This is true of all armed conflicts, but the efforts of US political and military officials in Baghdad to deny or play down bad news went beyond parody. The main forum for press conferences and briefings in Baghdad was the cavernous Convention Center in the heavily fortified US enclave in the Green Zone. Over three years the upbeat tone of military briefings never wavered. For the officials who briefed the media a US victory was always just over the horizon as the US military closed in on a small gang of al-Qaeda terrorists and die-hard survivors of Saddam Hussein's regime, both desperately and vainly seeking to prevent the birth of a free and democratic Iraq. Inside the Convention Center nothing changed as the years went by, but outside the military was always adding new fortifications. By early 2006 anybody entering the Green Zone on his or her way to the Convention Center had to pass through eight separate checkpoints, each defended by concrete blast walls, sandbags and razor wire. Documents were repeatedly checked by a bewildering array of Iraqi, Georgian, Peruvian and American guards. The spokesmen inside the Centre saw no contradiction between the daily doses of optimism they dispensed and the need for these ever more elaborate defences.

My favourite military spokesman was Brigadier General Mark Kimmit, who specialized in steely-eyed determination. He liked to illustrate his answers with homilies drawn from the home life of the Kimmit family. One day, during the first year of the occupation, an Iraqi journalist complained that US helicopters were scaring children in Baghdad by roaring low and fast over the rooftops. In fact, the pilots had started flying so low to make it more difficult for guerrillas to shoot them down after several had been hit, mostly around the town of Fallujah, by shoulder-fired heat-seeking ground-to-air missiles. But in answering the Iraqi's question General Kimmit wanted to draw a deeper moral. The general said he had spent most of his adult life 'either in or near military bases, married to a woman who teaches in the schools', and that on these bases 'You often hear the sound of tanks firing. You often hear the sound of artillery rounds going off.' Yet Mrs Kimmit, the general continued proudly, had been able to keep her pupils calm despite the constant thundering of the guns by 'letting them understand that those booms and those guns were simply the sounds of freedom'. General Kimmit urged the Iraqi journalist to go home and explain to his children that it was only thanks to the thundering guns, those sounds of freedom, that they were able to enjoy a free life.

Of course, General Kimmit's target audience was in the US not in Iraq. Nevertheless, Iraqis watched his performances on television with the same sort of revulsion and fascination as the British once listened to Lord Haw-Haw's broadcasts from Berlin in World War Two. Probably the White House and US officials in Baghdad truly believed their own propaganda. As late as June 2005 Vice President Dick Cheney claimed that the insurgency was in its 'last throes'. The Green Zone in which all the American civilian officials lived was a macabre place, as cut off from the rest of Baghdad as if it had been built on a separate planet. Ghazi al-Yawer, briefly president of Iraq in 2004–5 and not a man notable for expressing critical views of the US and its allies, once remarked that the Green Zone bore 'the same relationship to the rest of Iraq as a safari park does to the real jungle'.

Paradoxically Iraq became so dangerous that journalists, however courageous, could not rebut claims that most of Iraq was safe without being kidnapped or killed themselves. Even with armed guards it was difficult to move. In the spring of 2006 I was in Mosul in northern Iraq, the largest Sunni Arab city, with a 3,000-strong Kurdish brigade of the Iraqi army. Even so it was considered too dangerous for them to go on patrol in daylight (night-time was safer because a rigorously enforced curfew started at 8 p.m., after which the soldiers shot at any person or vehicle moving on the streets). To cover the referendum on the constitution in October 2005 I got a special correspondent's pass from the Interior Ministry permitting me to drive around during the day-time curfew. 'I wouldn't use it if I were you,' warned the friendly official who handed it to me. 'Obviously if one of our policemen or soldiers suspects that you are a suicide bomber he'll open fire immediately, long before you can show him your little pass.'

After the invasion I stayed for two and a half years in suite 106 on the first floor of the al-Hamra Hotel in the Jadriyah district of east Baghdad. At first when I heard a bomb go off, shaking the window frames of my room, I would take the lift up to a flat roof on the sixth floor of the hotel. From there I scanned the horizon for oily black smoke rising above the green palm trees. But one column of smoke looks much like another and soon I began to stay in my room unless the bomb was very close.

Every day brought its bombs, assassinations and ambushes, and it was easy to become numb to violence. I felt most sympathy for friends who had known all about the dangers of remaining in Iraq but stayed in order to help people. I had met Margaret Hassan, the Irish-Iraqi aid worker and head of the charity CARE in Iraq five years earlier when readers of the *Independent* donated money to buy medicine to be sent to the country. In an amateur way I was annoyed when the arrival of the medicine in Baghdad, which she was organizing, was long delayed. I went to see her and she patiently explained the technical and legal problems in importing medicines. As I listened I found myself liking more and more this calm, unsentimental and efficient woman working to keep people alive in a society which was visibly collapsing. I met her last in the coffee shop of the Hamra in 2004. She had left Iraq briefly and then come back. She sounded and looked nervous and it turned out she had reason to be. Within a few weeks she was kidnapped, held hostage and then murdered. Her body was never found.

As the years passed I went less often to the scenes of bomb attacks or ambushes. More and more people I knew were being kidnapped, wounded or killed. I loaned the *Independent*'s spare room to a striking young Californian woman with long blonde hair called Marla Ruzicka. Opposed to the US invasion when it happened, she felt it was her duty to do something for its victims. She tried to get the US military to tell her how many civilians they had accidentally killed though they insisted they kept no count. There was some meagre compensation available but bureaucratic obstacles deterred the Iraqis most in need from claiming it. Marla would help these impoverished and frightened people to get some money, seldom more than a few thousand dollars but enough for their survival. Early in the morning she would disappear into the Green Zone to go jogging with American officers whose signatures she needed for compensation claims to be met.

When Marla or I were away from Baghdad we exchanged e-mails. Their nervous tone gives a sense of the atmosphere in the city at the time. One of the last I received from her was on February 23 2005. I had warned her that the situation was getting worse. 'Don't be mad but going to Baghdad around the 12th [March],' she wrote back. 'Just going to stay in the Hamra for a week and conduct interviews there. I know it is dangerous. You just got out right? I am doing a book and it is going well. I miss you. I know everyone is going to be mad at me for going but I have something really pressing. X, Marla.' I was in England and about to travel to Iraqi Kurdistan but I was worried and replied immediately in telegraphic style: 'Do be very careful in Baghdad. Get people to come to the Hamra. I really am not an alarmist but it is dangerous – particularly from commercial kidnappers. Don't make appointments with people outside the hotel. The *Il Manifesto* woman – so the Interior Ministry told me – spent four hours with the Fallujan refugees waiting for an appointment with a sheikh. Kidnappers turned up instead. The *Libération* reporter the same sort of thing.' Marla was determined to return to Iraq. (It turned out later that she believed she had discovered how to find out how many Iraqis had been killed by US soldiers.) She wrote back: 'Don't tell anyone in Baghdad I am coming. I just don't want them to tell me not to. I know how bad it is and plan only to be in the hotel – only – and for five days.'

Of course she stayed much longer than five days and not just in the hotel. I was in Arbil in Iraqi Kurdistan on April 16 when I saw a wire story saying an American aid worker had been killed. It was Marla. She was driving with her translator to the giant American base at Baghdad airport when a suicide bomber in a truck attacked a US convoy. Burned over 90 per cent of her body, she awoke for a few seconds in hospital and murmured 'I am alive', and then she died.

By 2005 the Hamra was one of the few well-known buildings in Baghdad where foreigners lived which had not been attacked. I did not think that our immunity would last forever. I often looked down from my balcony at the grey concrete blast wall sixty yards away thinking it was too close to the hotel to protect it adequately. There was a car park just on the other side of the wall which anybody could enter. This seemed to be the one weak point in the defences of the heavily fortified hotel. Somebody else thought so too. Fortunately for me I left Iraq after the October 15 referendum on the constitution. At 8.25 a.m. on November 18 two vehicles entered the car park. The first suicide bomber blew himself up to try to breach the concrete blast wall so the second vehicle, with a 1,000 kg bomb on board, could pass through the gap, get close to our building and destroy it. The plan just failed. The second bomber was not able to drive across the deep crater made by the first explosion. He blew himself up where he was, killing half a dozen people and tearing the building apart.

II

THERE IS AN old joke by the humorist Stephen Potter which explains how to confound an expert on a country, say China or Peru, about which one is ignorant. Potter says one should listen politely while the expert expounds on the country about which he knows everything. When he has concluded, the listener simply asks: 'All very true, no doubt, but surely conditions are different in the south?' They always are. The expert, his reputation for omniscience torpedoed, will be instantly forced to retreat in embarrassment from his sweeping and supposedly authoritative generalizations.

In no country is this truer than in Iraq. It is different not only in the south but in every other quarter of the compass. Iraqi society has a complex web of loyalties superior to any allegiance owed to the state. First, there are the three great communities of Sunni and Shia Arabs and the Kurds. But Iraqis may also feel intense loyalty to tribe, clan, extended family, city, town and village. Saddam Hussein's regime was too brutal and its security forces too efficient to be overthrown, but his power was always contested. He was never able to suppress the Kurds, who were in permanent rebellion for almost half a century. They were repeatedly able to destabilize the country.

Washington made scant effort in 2003 to understand the strange nature of the country it was about to invade. The White House and the Pentagon felt that no great knowledge was necessary. The State Department, which did know something of Iraq, was pushed aside and ignored. Among US policymakers there was a mood of extraordinary arrogance. Had they looked at Iraq more closely they would have noticed that it had an unnerving resemblance to Lebanon. The country is a mosaic of communities. There is an old Iraqi proverb that says: 'Two Iraqis, three sects.'

At first sight, Iraq under Saddam Hussein looked like an East European autocracy during the zenith of Communism. A brutal state machine appeared to monopolize power – but this was never the case. It was not just the Kurds who had the means to resist the power of the government. When US troops began to spread out into Iraq after the fall of Baghdad in 2003 they made a surprising discovery. Most people were armed, often with high-powered modern weapons. Saddam Hussein was reduced to introducing a buy-back scheme in the early 1990s to cut down on the number of heavy weapons on the streets. Even so, his officials in south-east Iraq were astonished when a tribe turned up with three tanks – presumably purloined during the Iran–Iraq war – which they were prepared to turn over for a sizeable sum of money.

The politics of an Iraqi city or town are determined by the differing ethnic and religious ingredients contained in each. For instance, in September 2005 the government in Baghdad was trumpeting the capture by the Iraqi army, backed by US forces, of the northern city of Tal Afar, west of Mosul, from the insurgents. From a distance it sounded simple: the government has won, the resistance has lost. The reality was more complex. The 200,000 people of Tal Afar are mostly Turkmen, distantly related to the Turks. The area in which the city stands is predominantly Kurdish. Furthermore the Turkmen of Tal Afar are 70 per cent Sunni, sympathizing with the Sunni Arab insurgents, and 30 per cent Shia Turkmen who support the Shia and Kurdish-dominated government in Baghdad. The Iraqi army units which captured the city were predominantly made up of Shia Arabs and Kurds. The Sunni Turkmen, making up most of the 683 people detained by the US and the Iraqi army in the city, claimed that the US forces were being manipulated by the Kurds and the Shia Turkmen backed by Shia Arabs from the rest of Iraq, all anxious to assert their power in this contested region.

In defence of the officials taking the crucial decisions in the White House and the Pentagon before the war, they were not alone in underestimating the ethnic and sectarian divisions in Iraq. Exiled Iraqi opposition leaders who advised them sincerely believed that Saddam Hussein had fomented such antagonisms. Deprived of the dictator's malign leadership, so they argued, Iraqis would peaceably work out an understanding with each other. I always noticed, however, that optimistic Iraqi friends who downplayed sectarianism in Iraq knew who was a Shia and who was a Sunni, just as accurately as people in Belfast, however liberal, are aware of which of their neighbours is a Protestant and which a Roman Catholic.

Relations between Sunni, Shia and Kurd have always shaped Iraqi politics. In 1919, two years after the British capture of Baghdad from the Turks, a far-sighted British official called Arnold Wilson, the civil commissioner, warned that the creation of a new state out of Iraq was a recipe for disaster. He said it was impossible to weld together Shia, Sunni and Kurd, three groups of people who detested each other. Wilson told the British that the new state could only be 'the antithesis of democratic government'. This was because the Shia majority rejected domination by the Sunni minority, but 'no form of government has yet been envisaged which does not involve Sunni domination'. The Kurds in the north, whom it was intended to include in Iraq, 'will never accept Iraqi rule'.[6] These calculations were still largely true when American troops entered Baghdad over eighty years later. By this time the Shia Arabs numbered approximately 15–16 million, and Sunni Arabs and Kurds, 5 million each, out of the 26 million population.

Wilson's insight did him little good. He argued that Iraqis

were so divided that the only solution was direct imperial rule as in India. But he underestimated the desire of Iraqis to be in control of their own country and the strength of Iraqi nationalism. The year after he wrote the perceptive passage cited above, the tribes in the centre of the country, mostly Shia, rose in revolt. By the time it was suppressed the British and Indian troops had lost 2,269 dead and wounded – and the Iraqis an estimated 8,450 dead. The uprising created a potent myth for Iraqi nationalists. It saw tentative combined action by Sunni and Shia; they even held joint religious services. Wilson and several other highly placed British officials in Baghdad at the time had underestimated the fact that, however much Shia and Sunni disliked each other, they hated the British even more. The point is important because the fragmentation of Iraq is so evident today that it is easy to forget that Sunni and Shia Arabs, even when on the verge of civil war, also see themselves as sharing an Iraqi identity, though they differ violently in their definition of what this is.

Saddam had been able to appeal to Iraqi patriotism during the Iran–Iraq war. In the years after he launched his disastrous invasion of Iran in 1980, some 70,000 Iraqi soldiers, mostly Shia, surrendered on the battlefield. But when the Iranian army advanced towards Basra in 1982 and invaded Iraq, the mass surrenders stopped. Saddam was able to fight on for another six years although most of the officer corps were Sunni Arab and the great majority of the lower ranks were Shia. Despite this there were always tensions between the two communities just below the surface. When the Shia uprising started in southern Iraq in 1991, Saddam was quick to publicize the fate of Baath party members killed by the insurgents in the Shia holy city of Kerbala. Their mutilated bodies were presented as proof by the government that if Shia rebels captured Baghdad, Baathists and Sunni Arabs alike would share the same grisly fate. The tactic worked. I had one friend, a well-educated Sunni journalist, who frequently told me how much he detested the regime and prayed for its downfall. But within twenty-four hours of this massacre in

Kerbala he was saying he was terrified of what would happen to him and his family if the Shia insurgents captured Baghdad.

Stephen Potter or one of his acolytes would have found it all the easier to dumbfound an expert on Iraq because the strength of different allegiances influencing Iraqis is not static. It is an ever-changing kaleidoscope. In the 1970s and 1980s, for instance, the power of the tribes was weakening because the government and the Baath party had jobs and money to give to their supporters. But after Saddam Hussein's defeat in the First Gulf War in 1991 his oil revenues were much curtailed. He looked to favoured tribes and tribal leaders for support. In the government-owned al-Rashid Hotel in Baghdad in the early 1990s these were known as the 'flying sheikhs' because the more rustic among them were entranced by the hotel lifts, to them an exciting novelty, which they and their heavily armed bodyguards enjoyed riding up and down in for hours at a time. But these sheikhs were often not quite what they seemed. Many had been appointed by Saddam Hussein from among several contenders for tribal leadership. The regime even commissioned a police colonel in the early 1990s to write a ten-volume *Encyclopaedia of the Iraqi Tribes*. Only sheikhs loyal to Saddam Hussein were given the official imprimatur by the colonel while the names of those whose loyalty was suspect were ignored.[7]

Iraq on the eve of the invasion was not only a country divided by religion and ethnicity. These divisions had been deepened and complicated by a quarter of a century of war and deprivation. Iraq was a broken society. Its standard of living had fallen from that of Greece to that of Burundi. The economy had collapsed under the weight of UN sanctions. Much of the middle class had been pauperized. In the great slums of Baghdad and across Iraq there were the urban poor, crushed by the misery of their lives, willing to turn their hands to any job legal or illegal, prepared to loot or protect a building against looters, to join a charismatic religious leader or become the foot soldiers in a militia force.

Unemployment may have been as high as 70 per cent. These young men had no skill other than knowing how to use a gun, which they had been trained to do in the army or the government-sponsored militia. It was these people, often living in total poverty, who poured into the streets across Iraq in an orgy of theft and destruction as the old government collapsed in 2003.

I first went to Iraq in 1978 and have watched the country disintegrate over twenty-eight years. It was a slow but inexorable process. The first time I arrived in Baghdad the country was at peace. The long-running Kurdish rebellion had been crushed three years earlier when Iran, supported by the US, had signed the Algiers agreement with Saddam Hussein, treacherously abandoning the Kurds, whom it had previously supported, in return for territorial concessions from Iraq. Oil revenues were soaring after the oil price increase in 1973. I was working for a magazine called the *Middle East Economic Digest* based in London. I did not know much about Iraq, but I had seen a lot of sectarian warfare having spent the previous five years in Belfast, Beirut and Nicosia. Iraq seemed orderly and peaceful by comparison. We drove to Basra and stayed in the Shatt al-Arab hotel, an ageing relic of British rule. My uncle Terry Arbuthnot had commanded the RAF airbase nearby in the 1930s. The main complaint locally was that Kuwaitis in their white robes would pour across the border at the weekend and drink the city dry of beer. In the Kurdish north we spent a day in the mountaintop town of Salahudin, which had been in the past and would in the future be the headquarters of Kurdish guerrillas. Local officials spoke lyrically of the chances of turning the town into a tourist resort, to which end they had constructed a number of hideous chalets on a steep hillside, variously coloured red, yellow or green.

Iraq did not yet have a picture of Saddam Hussein decorating every street since in theory he was only number two in the government, though he was already referred to as 'the strong man' of Iraq. But I got a foretaste of the new leader's style and growing megalomania when I visited Iraq a few months later. I was summoned along with other correspondents to a press conference which he was supposed to address. It took place in a former royal palace. We waited for an hour. An official appeared on stage, jiggled the microphone in irritation and disappeared. There was no visible sign of Saddam Hussein though frightened-looking officials occasionally disappeared behind a curtain to confer with somebody. It turned out that the microphone was not working. Although Saddam was on the premises and could easily have raised his voice to address the journalists, he refused to do so, harried officials explained to us, on the grounds that this would be an admission that Iraq did not have the technical wherewithal to fix a simple mike. He kept us waiting five hours. I asked if I could leave and was told that the palace was surrounded by Saddam's guards, who would shoot anybody who tried to get out. Finally, after work by some agitated technicians, Saddam appeared and delivered a few anodyne and forgettable remarks.

It would be wrong to say that I got Saddam Hussein's number or plumbed the full extent of his villainy at once. He seemed to be one more Arab nationalist leader underpinned by violent security services, but otherwise not much different from President Hafez al-Assad in Syria or Algerian President Houari Boumedienne. Perhaps the most important point I missed in those early visits to Iraq was that in many ways Saddam Hussein was a man who, while not actually a fool, had such an exaggerated idea of his own abilities that he could easily commit an act of folly. His opponents compared him to Stalin, and certainly both men were characterized by extreme violence. But Saddam's character, unlike Stalin's, contained a touch of Inspector Clouseau, an ability to blunder repeatedly without learning from his mistakes or denting his own self-confidence. I was in Iraq in early 1980 and later spent the summer in Tehran before being expelled. Ayatollah Khomeini was at the height of his popularity, regarded as semi-divine by millions of Iranians. I did not believe that Saddam Hussein, who so far had shown a certain caution in dealing with foreign powers, would be foolish enough to attack a country with a population three times larger than Iraq's and able to mobilize vast and fanatical armies. When asked what was going to happen I downplayed the danger of war.

I woke up on September 22 1980 to find Saddam had invaded Iran. Ever since I· have had a certain sympathy for intelligence services like the CIA, when they are criticized for failing to predict just when a leader like Saddam Hussein will take a decision so obviously against his own best interests. In attacking Iran he made an extraordinary miscalculation which ruined Iraq. A whole generation of Iraqis was traumatized by this war, which achieved nothing. In eight years of bloody fighting some half a million Iraqis were killed, wounded or taken prisoner out of a population which then numbered an estimated nineteen million. Some of the thousands of prisoners were held captive in Iran for almost a quarter of a century. I once met an Iraqi general who had been taken prisoner as a lieutenant in 1982 and only released in 2003. His rise through the ranks had all taken place while in Iranian prison camps. He was distraught because he was owed twenty years' back pay but Saddam Hussein had just been overthrown, the Iraqi army was dissolved and the newly installed US authorities were not acknowledging the debts of the old regime. Every Iraqi family lost one or more members. All the country's oil revenues were poured into paying for the war with Iran so no new hospitals and few schools were built. Young Iraqis were trained solely for war.

The conflict ended in a stalemate, though it was Iran which sued for peace in 1988. Ayatollah Khomeini, advised that the US was more and more openly entering the war on the Iraqi side, said Iran must 'drain the poisoned cup'. Iraq had gained nothing and was burdened by huge debts, but it did have a powerful army. Saddam Hussein's conviction of his own genius had grown. He compared himself to the great heroes of the Meso-potamian past such as Sargon of Akkad, Nebuchadnezzar, Saladin and even the Prophet Muhammad. In the middle of the war, when resources were short, Saddam even started to rebuild the ancient city of Babylon, its ugly mustard-coloured bricks imprinted with his name. For the Iraqi leader the conquest of Kuwait in 1990 was the pay-off for the long war just finished that had brought Iraq so few benefits. When Iraqi armoured divisions massed south of Basra, and the world waited to see if they would invade Kuwait, I remembered what had happened ten years earlier when Saddam attacked Iran. Once again he was taking on opponents – this time the whole world – which Iraq did not have the strength to defeat, but I did not think that would deter him.

I flew to Baghdad a few weeks after the invasion. In the streets people were reacting with jubilation and trepidation to what was being portrayed as the recapture of Iraq's 19th province, long sundered from the motherland by British imperialist schemes (this allegation was not wholly false). But ordinary Iraqis did not want to pay a price for it. The country was utterly war-weary; men who had spent their youth in the army would weep when they were recalled to the colours. The invasion was conducted like a Bedouin raid, with mass looting officially sanctioned. I watched large yellow cranes and bulldozers, stolen in Kuwait, making their way along the highways to Baghdad. In the al-Rashid Hotel lobster suddenly appeared on the menu. The waiters giggled as they told diners that it had been freshly liberated from the deep freeze of a hotel in Kuwait.

It soon became clear that Saddam did not know what to do with his new conquest. His best plan was to withdraw his army immediately in return for concessions, such as the two islands in the north of Kuwait which Iraq had previously claimed. As the weeks went by he was bound to get weaker as President George Bush sent the American army to Saudi Arabia and put together a powerful coalition. This was obvious to many Iraqis, all of whom obsessively listened to foreign radio broadcasts on the BBC in Arabic, Voice of America or Radio Monte Carlo. Saddam alone thought he could cling on to his prize. It was only in the last days of the crisis, on the eve of the US-led coalition counter-attack, that he desperately sought a compromise; by then it was far too late.

At the start of the crisis, Saddam had decided that the situation was so serious that he needed somebody competent at the Information Ministry, a powerful institution controlling the domestic media and also in charge of the foreign press. He appointed as director-general Naji Sabri al-Hadithi, whom I had known when he was a rising diplomat in London in the 1970s. He later fell from grace after his uncle was tortured and executed, accused of involvement in a plot against Saddam. Typically, Saddam balanced an expert like Naji with a proven loyalist at the top of the ministry. The latter, in this case, was a Baathist thug called Latif Nassif Jassim, who had been made Information Minister. I asked him what would happen to American airmen who might be shot down. This was a moment when Iraq was trying to impress the outside world with the idea of the essential moderation of its views. 'We will cut off their legs,' shouted the minister in reply. Naji, swallowing hard, rushed forward to say that in Iraqi Arabic, 'to cut off somebody's legs' did not mean literal amputation and the words might be better translated as 'being extremely angry'. It was no use. 'Cut off their legs,' Jassim bellowed again, making a chopping motion with his hand towards his thighs.

There had been a strange 'phoney war' atmosphere in Baghdad in the months up to the start of the bombing on January 17 1991. Nobody quite believed it was going to happen. 'We didn't expect a war,' said a general who later fled into exile. 'We thought it was all a political manoeuvre.' They soon learned differently. The troops in Kuwait, aside from the large numbers who had already deserted, were pounded by US bombers. In Baghdad the power stations were hit and the lights went out. Some Iraqis had stocked up on food but had not counted on the lack of electricity to power their deep freezes and fridges. In a few days the air in the better-off districts of Baghdad stank with the smell of rotting meat which householders could no longer freeze and had been forced to throw out. It lay on the ground as there were no garbage trucks to collect it because Iraq had run out of fuel. It was a sign of how the government had failed to make the simplest preparations for war: it had failed to stockpile any fuel before the bombing and could produce no more once the refineries were hit.

Humiliating defeat in Kuwait provoked uprisings by Shia and Kurds. Saddam Hussein was caught by surprise. Even in Shia cities like Najaf which were known to detest the regime the troops had been sent to the front. All the southern provinces fell to the rebels. Much of the army had mutinied or simply gone home. The Shia insurrection was followed by a further rebellion in Kurdistan. The Kurdish armies were able to capture Kirkuk, only two hours' drive from Baghdad. But the Sunni centre of the country held firm. There was no uprising in Baghdad. It also became clear that the US was not going to help the rebels. Whatever his other failings Saddam had good nerves and fully grasped the intricacies of Iraqi sectarian and ethnic politics in a way he never understood the rest of the world. Swift counter-attacks and savage vengeance rapidly restored Saddam's rule across the country.

The regime was eager to prove that it had survived and was in control. It allowed a few journalists like myself to visit newly recaptured Shia cities such as Basra, Kerbala and Najaf in the south, and Sulaimaniyah in its green plain below the Kurdish mountains. It knew we would report on the terrible destruction but did not care so long as we said who had won the civil war. In the holy city of Kerbala the yellow-and-blue tiles on the outer gate of the shrine of al-Abbas, the warrior martyr, had been smashed by a rocket-propelled grenade. All around the shrine tank guns and artillery had reduced the small shops to piles of ruins. As I walked past surviving houses I could hear terrified voices from behind closed doors saying: 'Help us. Help us.' In the courtyard of the other great Shia shrine in Najaf Iraqi soldiers marked their victory by placing a peculiarly inappropriate picture of Saddam Hussein on a chair amid the rubble. In it, the Iraqi leader looked like an extra from *The Sound of Music*: dressed in tweeds, he was bending down to pick a blue flower as he climbed up an alpine slope, and was apparently about to burst into song.

The grim-faced government minders took us on to a house in Kufa. Here, lying on a divan, was the venerable Shia Grand Ayatollah al-Khoie, effectively under house arrest. The minders wanted him to condemn the uprising. They were in a position to pressure him because 102 of his followers and students had disappeared into Iraqi jails, never to reappear. Instead he would only say ambiguously: 'What happened in Najaf and other cities is not allowed and is against the will of God.' He went on, 'Nobody visits me. I don't know what is happening. I have difficulty breathing.'

Iraq had been devastated by the war with Iran in 1980–88, the defeat in Kuwait in 1991 and the Shia and Kurdish uprisings the same year. But for ordinary Iraqis the nightmare was not over. 'We have got the worst of all possible outcomes,' an Iraqi friend lamented to me in 1992. 'We have been completely defeated and we still have Saddam Hussein in power.' Iraqis now had to endure UN economic sanctions, first imposed in 1990, whereby the UN controlled Iraq's oil revenues and how they were spent. After the fall of Saddam Hussein the UN was caught up in a scandal over bribes paid by the Iraqi regime in order to get as much of its oil revenues as possible into its hands. But the real scandal was that for thirteen years Iraqis were subjected to a close economic siege which caused intense suffering but did nothing to remove Saddam Hussein and the clique around him.

The signs of the new poverty were everywhere in Iraq in the 1990s. The currency collapsed during the war in Kuwait. In 1990, one Iraqi dinar was worth $3.20. Five years later a single dollar bought 2,550 dinars. Money changers provided black plastic bags in which to carry the weighty bundles of notes out of their shops. As a result of inflation, professors at the universities found they were being paid $5–10 a month. School-teachers and doctors were making even less. Baghdad was soon full of open-air markets where the pauperized middle class were selling off their possessions. It became common to see dignified-looking men standing for hours in the heat of the day beside a heap of dinner plates they were trying to sell. Some people were close to starvation. Garbage collectors noticed that Baghdadis were no longer throwing away scraps of food like old melon skins but keeping them to eat. In 1998 a nationwide health survey of Iraqi children under five years old showed 9.1 per cent as being acutely malnourished, 26.7 per cent chronically mal-nourished and 22.8 per cent underweight.[8]

People went to extraordinary lengths to earn a little money to stay alive. This was true in the three Kurdish provinces, after 1991 no longer under Saddam's control, as it was in the rest of Iraq. In 1996 I visited a village called Penjwin, a parrot's beak of territory sticking into Iran. To survive, its inhabitants had developed a unique and highly dangerous skill. Penjwin had been in the front line during the Iran–Iraq war. Its fields were full of mines. These included a peculiarly lethal jumping mine called the Valmara, with horns sticking out of the top. Touch any of these and a small charge would hurl the Valmara into the air to waist height where a larger explosion would spray lethal ball bearings in all directions. To prevent their families starving, men in Penjwin would defuse these mines. Their aim was to obtain a small piece of aluminium containing the explosive and sell it for a few dollars. The village main street was full of men without a hand or a leg – though the Valmara usually killed those who made the slightest mistake while trying to defuse it.

Imposing sanctions on all ordinary Iraqis was a cruel collective punishment, one of the great man-made disasters of the last half-century. The UN Oil-for-Food programme of 1996 was sup-posed to alleviate suffering. It led to some limited improvement in living standards. But when Denis Halliday, an Irish Quaker and career UN official sent to oversee the Oil-for-Food programme, resigned in disgust in 1998, he said the economic blockade of Iraq caused 'four or five thousand children to die unnecessarily every month due to the impact of sanctions because of the breakdown of water and sanitation, inadequate diet, and the bad internal health situation'.

Everywhere there were signs of distress. The health service was collapsing. In one Baghdad hospital a team of western doctors 'witnessed a surgeon trying to operate with scissors that were too blunt to cut the patient's skin'. When I visited the countryside farmers thought I was a doctor and chased after me with ageing dusty X-rays of their children, taken years before when there was a local X-ray centre, asking for a diagnosis. Clean water became a luxury. There was a permanent shortage of electricity.

In the past Iraq had once possessed a cadre of highly educated doctors, engineers and academics. Now they were leaving the country whenever they could. Soon in New Zealand alone there were 30,000 Iraqi immigrants, many of them highly trained. The regime tried to stop professionals resigning from government service. But by the mid-1990s a bribe could do almost anything in Iraq. I had a friend who was a professor of engineering at Baghdad University who, because he was paid so little, needed to resign to search for work in the private sector. 'Eventually I bribed a doctor to say I had a serious heart condition,' he explained later. 'Even so I had to spend two weeks in the hospital, where they gave me medicine I didn't need. They even hung fabricated charts at the end of my bed showing I was really ill.' He laughed bitterly as he added: 'What a way to finish twenty-five years of service.'

Many people took to crime. Taxi drivers started carrying guns in case they were robbed by their passengers. Bandits ambushed a party of foreign journalists going to Basra under the auspices of the Information Ministry and left them and their minders on the main road stripped to their underpants. The government struck back by amputating the hands of thieves on television as a warning.

The impact of sanctions was devastating for the Iraqi people but it did nothing to help bring down Saddam Hussein. His real skills were as a secret policeman. He trusted nobody and took endless precautions against conspiracy. He was never in real danger of being brought down by an internal coup between the end of the uprising in 1991 and 2003. The US and Britain systematically downplayed for years the sufferings of ordinary Iraqis resulting from sanctions. Ironically they were about to pay a heavy and unexpected price for this policy and the destruction wrought on Iraq. After the overthrow of Saddam Hussein they found themselves presiding over a society in a state of collapse, full of bitter and dangerous people with very little left to lose.

III

I N THE MIDDLE of December 2002 people attending Christmas parties in the Metropole Hotel on London's Edgware Road were surprised by a strange invasion. Women in off-the-shoulder dresses suddenly found themselves nervously rubbing shoulders with Iraqi Muslim clerics in turbans and long robes. It was the largest meeting of the Iraqi opposition for years. The mullahs, along with some 350 assorted Kurdish leaders, former generals, long-exiled party leaders, intellectuals, and members of the Iraqi diaspora had gathered in London to discuss the imminent overthrow of Saddam Hussein by the US. There was an air of barely suppressed excitement as they sipped mint tea in the Metropole coffee shop. 'Do you think the Americans are really going to do it?' asked one delegate edgily, as if he could not quite take on board what was going to happen. But most of the exiled Iraqis at the meeting believed that the US was going to destroy the old regime in the next few months. As the conference began, Sayid Muhammad Bahir al-Aloum, a religious and political leader, raised his hands above his head and cried: 'For thirty years Iraqis have lived in a great prison. Shame on you Saddam!'

If any of the Christmas partygoers draining their margaritas in the Metropole had understood Arabic and were curious about what their strangely dressed fellow guests were discussing in the coffee shop they would rapidly have learned that the Iraqi opposition was far from united. One delegate to the conference laughingly described how he had overheard one life-long opponent of Saddam shout at another: 'Just you wait until we have democracy in Iraq and I'll throw you in jail.' The conference had already been postponed twice after furious arguments about who should be represented. At the time the differences seemed pettifogging, but there was a simple and compelling reason why the in-fighting was so intense. Here, beside the rain-swept Edgware Road in the murk of pre-Christmas London, we were seeing the first round in the struggle for power in post-Saddam Iraq. 'Why should they all be here if they did not want a share in the new administration?' asked one of the delegates now filling the lobby of the hotel.

Hoshyar Zebari, a leading member of the Kurdistan Democratic Party (KDP), had spent many frustrating days trying to organize the meeting. I had always thought of him as an optimist in even the direst situations – and for Kurdish leaders dire situations had been all too common over the previous twenty years – but in the run-up to the London meeting even he was looking downcast. Slumped in a chair in the lobby of the Sheraton Tower Hotel he complained wearily: 'If we can't discuss things democratically between us now, what will it be like when we are part of a [post-Saddam] government?'

There was one feature of the conference which I suspected at the time did not bode well for the future. One delegate later complained that decisions 'were being taken in smoke-filled rooms'. But in fact there was very little smoke because few of the delegates were smokers aside from the Kurdish leaders. This was ominous because people inside Iraq almost always have a cigarette in their mouth, not a surprising habit given the nervous tension in which so many live. The absence of clouds of smoke at the London meeting could only mean that a high proportion of delegates had been in exile and out of Iraq for a very long time. They had become used to smoke-free offices in Los Angeles, Boston or London. This would have mattered less if the parties had been united by common objectives, but the delay in convening the conference showed that they were not. Some viewed the prospects for an agreement gloomily. Dr Mahmoud Othman, a respected and independent-minded Kurdish leader, believed that any real chance for the opposition to combine had long passed. He said: 'They have had twelve years to combine on common aims. Instead they have looked to the US, Iran, Turkey or Syria. It is too late now to do in two months what they should have been doing since 1990.'

By the time the conference got underway on December 14 most of the men – there were few women present – who would rule Iraq in the years after the invasion were gathered in the Metropole. It was they who would provide the presidents, prime ministers, ministers and senior officials in the post-Saddam era. A year later Zebari had become Iraq's highly effective foreign minister and Dr Othman a member of the Iraqi Governing Council. A grimmer fate awaited other delegates. Striding into the conference hall looking resplendent in his long clerical robes and beaming at fellow delegates was Sayid Majid al-Khoie. He was the liberal-minded son and political heir of Grand Ayatollah al-Khoie, whom I had seen under house arrest in Kufa after the Shia uprising twelve years earlier. Within four months he was dead, murdered by political opponents outside the golden-domed Shrine of Ali in the Shia holy city of Najaf.

The driving force behind the conference was the so-called Group of Four. These were the KDP led by Massoud Barzani, its short, intense, unsmiling leader, and the Patriotic Union of Kurdistan (PUK) of Jalal Talabani, its rotund and mercurial leader who was to become president of Iraq. They were working with the Supreme Council for Islamic Revolution in Iraq (SCIRI), the most important Shia party, supported by Iran and led by Ayatollah Muhammad Baqr al-Hakim. He was dead in less than a year, assassinated when a massive bomb exploded near his motorcade in Najaf in August 2003. The fourth party in the group was the Iraqi National Accord (INA), a shadowy group of former Baathists and Iraqi soldiers, led by Iyad Allawi. His one attempt to stage a military coup in Baghdad in 1996 had collapsed but he was still very popular with the CIA and MI6. When the US and Britain supposedly handed sovereignty back to Iraq in June 2004 it was Allawi who became prime minister.

The most interesting figure at the conference was probably Ahmed Chalabi, the leader of the Iraqi National Congress and the man who had done most to persuade the US to get rid of Saddam Hussein. He moved purposively across the hotel lobby in the middle of an entourage of aides and supporters. Chalabi was a man with many friends – and many enemies. He had cultivated officials, politicians and journalists in Washington for many years and was notoriously close to the neo-conservatives and the civilian leadership of the Pentagon. But he was detested by the CIA and the State Department. A previous attempt to hold the opposition conference in Brussels had foundered because Chalabi refused to attend, claiming that the Group of Four were seeking to marginalize him.

The Iraqi opposition was later to be attacked inside and outside Iraq as corrupt and incompetent carpetbaggers who were pawns of the Americans. They were unable, certainly, to stop Iraq being plunged into a new war or to reverse the economic misery of the previous quarter century. Ali Allawi, one of the ablest of the new leaders, who served successively as Trade, Defence and Finance Minister between 2003 and 2006, told me: 'At the end of the day the opposition to Saddam completely failed.' But a total condemnation of the opposition is unfair and simple-minded. Their task was never easy. Many lost family members to the firing squads and torture chambers of Saddam. In the case of Massoud Barzani no less than 7,000 of his tribe had been murdered in 1983. American and British journalists and officials often had a romantic idea about the feasibility of anti-government resistance within Iraq. Ahmed Chalabi said to me several years earlier, 'American officials often don't realize that it is almost impossible to organize an effective underground opposition movement in Iraq in the face of pro-active and violent security services.'

Chalabi was important in the opposition movement because of his influence with the White House. But the Kurds were at the heart of the resistance to Saddam Hussein to a degree which was never understood in the rest of Iraq or abroad. Their dominance was significant for the future because it meant the Kurds were the most effective part of post-war governments in Baghdad. The ministries they ran worked visibly better than those controlled by Shia or Sunni Arab ministers. This is not surprising. It was the Kurds, 20 per cent of the Iraqi population, who had been in revolt against Baghdad for almost half a century. They had seen over 180,000 of their people killed by the regime in 1987–8 alone in revenge for their rebellion during the Iran–Iraq war. The Kurdish countryside was bleakly empty because 3,800 of their villages had been destroyed. But the Kurdish leaders very sensibly wanted to present the opposition to Saddam as pan-Iraqi and not just Kurdish. If they presented themselves as a Kurdish resistance movement this would make it difficult for them to find allies among the 80 per cent of Iraqis who are not Kurdish. It would also frighten the US and those neighbours of Iraq with large and restive Kurdish minorities such as Turkey, Iran and Syria. In the longer term the greater experience and better organization of the Kurds had the bizarre consequence that the most impressive people at the core of the post-Saddam Iraqi government wanted to have their own independent country and not be part of Iraq.

The leading role of the Kurds in the opposition was inevitable because their resources were greater than anybody else's. They had an able and experienced cadre of leaders, well-armed soldiers and money. Unlike the Iraqi Shia they had retained important gains from their uprising in 1991. After the Iraqi army retreated from Kurdistan and the US started military over-flights there sprang into being a quasi-independent Kurdish state with a population of three million. Divided in two – the KDP controlled the west and the PUK the east of the Kurdish enclave – the Kurds commanded a more powerful state than many countries represented at the UN.

I expected to see divisions at the London conference, and there were signs of rancour even before it officially opened. Just as delegates and the media were collecting their accreditation on the first day, the British public relations company retained by Ahmed Chalabi, the INC leader, announced a press conference. Many of the numerous journalists attending thought this was the official opening. Rushing off to the King's Suite in the hotel, they discovered Chalabi and Kanan Makiya, a noted Iraqi intellectual, presenting a weighty plan for 'the building of a democratic system of government and a thriving civil society' in Iraq. Makiya, author of *The Republic of Fear*, a denunciation of Saddam published when the US, Britain and most of the rest of the world still supported him in his war with Iran, spoke eloquently of the virtues of his own plan. He appeared to believe that it would be feasible, once the Baathist regime had been eliminated, to unite Iraqis around a common pluralist and federalist platform, and to create a stable democracy. He was soon disabused. All these issues were going to be painfully negotiated between Arabs and Kurds, Shias and Sunnis. No sooner had Makiya finished speaking than Zebari, his normally benign face frozen with anger at what he saw as an attempt to hijack the conference, appeared on the platform to announce curtly, 'The conference has not yet begun. These are just personal views.'

There were other suspicions. What did the US really want? It was Washington, after all, which was expected to overthrow the regime in Baghdad. Obviously it was in the interest of the US to see a gathering of influential Iraqis support the attack. But would it cede them any real power? Zilmay Khalilzad, the US envoy to the Iraqi opposition, was in the hotel to paper over public disagreements but avoided any real commitments to the opposition. The US did not want an Iraqi provisional government formed which might cramp its style after the war and might, in any case, alienate more Iraqis than it attracted. Right up to the last moment the opposition leaders were worried that the US would just get rid of Saddam Hussein but keep the rest of his Sunni-dominated regime, by now pro-American, intact. Khalilzad, an astute and softly spoken diplomat, said that the US target was Saddam Hussein and not the Iraqi army, but denied the US aim was 'Saddamism without Saddam'.

In the event it turned out that the US was going to see if it could rule Iraq on old-fashioned imperial lines and without sharing power with anybody in Iraq. It was always hoping to find a pro-American constituency of liberal, secular, middle-class, nationalist people – preferably English-speaking. At the London conference it was already becoming plain that the US was uncomfortable with the likelihood that the main beneficiaries of the overthrow of Baathist rule would be Shia religious parties with close links to Iran like SCIRI and Dawa, though Dawa took the more nationalist line and looked to the Iraqi religious leaders for guidance. Over the next three years American officials tried many alternatives to these parties, but the Iraqis most acceptable to Washington usually turned out to have little support in, or knowledge of, their own country. The US found that the divisions among the Iraqi opposition stemmed not solely from the egotism and greed of its leaders but truly reflected the real religious and ethnic fragmentation of Iraq. Some Iraqis had a shrewd idea of what the US was getting itself into, but they were careful not to discourage American officials by emphasizing the risks of their Iraqi venture. Had less arrogant and better-informed people been in charge in Washington in 2003 they might possibly have paused at the edge of the quagmire before jumping in. As the London conference came to an end – it was agreed to reconvene in Kurdistan on January 15 – an Iraqi friend attending it said: 'I have only one fear. It is that the Americans will realize at the last moment that attacking Iraq and overthrowing Saddam Hussein is not in their own best interests.'

*   *   *

There was little need for my Iraqi friend to worry. By now an American invasion to overthrow Saddam Hussein was inevitable. I wanted a perch in Washington to watch America's final steps towards war, and the Center for Strategic and International Studies, a think tank on K Street in downtown Washington, gave me a three-month visiting fellowship with the brief of writing and talking about Iraq. The mood among supporters of a war was over-confident. It stemmed primarily from the unexpectedly swift American success in Afghanistan. Victory over the Taliban appeared to show, as the Republicans had long suspected, that American military power alone, untroubled by fractious allies, was all that was needed to win. Questions about the complexities of Iraqi politics and society were polite and sometimes genuine, but I sensed that people making policy in Washington did not really believe these intricacies were going to be of much relevance. The Iraqi people were expected to play a spectator's role in forthcoming events. President Bush had reportedly expressed surprise and interest when told that there were two sorts of Muslim in Iraq, Sunni and Shia. Arrogance was not confined to politicians and officials. An influential American journalist told me over dinner of America's radical plans for reshaping Iraq and I responded mildly that ordinary Iraqis might object. 'Who cares?' he replied contemptuously. 'Who cares?'

Ironically, there was one point on which Baghdad and Washington were publicly agreed. This was that Saddam Hussein was a powerful leader at the helm of a state with real military muscle. In Iraq the official media had repeated this message ad nauseam for a quarter of a century. People feared arrest if they accidentally spilled their coffee over the front page of their newspaper, invariably featuring a picture of Saddam Hussein, because they might then be deemed by watching secret policemen to have insulted their great leader. In the US the exaggerations were all in the opposite direction. The Iraqi dictator was demonized as a modern-day dictator not only the moral equivalent of Hitler or Stalin, but with power equal to theirs, capable of menacing the Middle East and possibly the entire world. Bush and Blair must have known from briefings by their military staff that the Iraqi army was a wreck, degraded even from what it was in 1991 when it failed to put up much of a fight. There was clearly going to be little resistance. But the propaganda had one unfortunate side-effect. In their single-minded focus on Saddam Hussein, American and British propagandists convinced themselves that he alone was the source of Iraq's problems, which could be easily resolved once he and his regime were eliminated.

Of course many perceptive people in Washington were sceptical that the US would have such an easy ride. There were experts, several of them at CSIS, who recalled the disastrous US entanglements in Lebanon and Somalia. I remember Judith Kipper, with long experience in the region and her office next to mine, hammering her desk so hard that her coffee mug jumped into the air as she expressed her frustration at the bovine wrong-headedness of the administration. Jon Alterman, more softly spoken, wondered if 'the US might not be heading for its very own Suez crisis'. But then he had written a study of how Britain had over-extended its strength by invading Egypt to overthrow Nasser in 1956, when military success was followed by political disaster. But few in official Washington in January 2003 knew much about the history of the Middle East or, if they had, would have seen the relevance to themselves of such ominous precedents.

Not that dissent was getting much of an airing anywhere in the US at that time. The mood of super-patriotism engendered in reaction to 9/11 meant that newspapers and above all television were nervous of carrying critical comments. The administration was successfully playing up threats to the homeland and tying them to the regime in Baghdad. If evidence of such threats was lacking it could be exaggerated, manipulated or manufactured. Many stories exposed as false several years later were known to be fake at the time. The *New Yorker* published an article based on an interview with a gunman imprisoned by the Patriotic Union of

Kurdistan in which he detailed links between Baghdad and al-Qaeda. He claimed to have spoken to senior lieutenants of Saddam Hussein who made surprisingly damaging admissions about their terrorist connections to this gun-for-hire. 'I don't know a single opposition leader who believes a word of this,' chuckled a well-informed Kurdish friend long resident in London. 'If I was in a PUK prison I'd confess to trying to assassinate Queen Victoria if they asked me.'

I spent the first six weeks of the year in Washington and was struck by how little the intense private doubts about Iraq and the war on terror, expressed by even the most establishment figures at dinner parties, ever made it into the papers and almost never on to television. Washington has always been notoriously inward-looking. But the cumulative picture created by the mass of misinformation and disinformation about Iraq and al-Qaeda and the terrorist threat in general had produced a picture of the outside world that was close to fantasy. I was reminded, listening to Bush or Donald Rumsfeld, of the famous scene in Joseph Conrad's *The Secret Agent* when Mr Verloc, a revolutionary in the pay of a foreign embassy, listens with consternation as a diplomat called Mr Vladimir, for whom he is working, gives his confused and ignorant vision of the terrorist world: 'He confounded causes with effects more than was excusable; the most distinguished propagandists with impulsive bomb throwers; assumed organization where in the nature of things it could not exist,' writes Conrad in words which could be applied to many a speech by George W. Bush. The diplomat spoke of the revolutionaries at 'one moment as of a perfectly disciplined army, where the word of chiefs was supreme, and at another as if it was the loosest association of desperate brigands that ever camped in a mountain gorge'.

The personality of George W. Bush explained much of the lack of knowledge of, or interest in, what was really happening in Iraq. Iraqi leaders who got as far as the Oval Office said they found him more intelligent than they expected but 'very, very

strange'. A more immediate impact of Bush being president was
that divisions within bureaucracy were more unrestrained than
ever before. This was not at first obvious because power is
invariably more fragmented between the great departments of
state in Washington than it is in Europe. The State Department
was at war with the Pentagon. 'I thought that we were divided,
but they are even worse than us,' said an Iraqi friend mirthlessly
after doing the rounds among senior officials. Access to the
administration would mysteriously appear and disappear. Laith
Kubba, an eloquent and veteran opponent of Saddam, was about
to see Bush when the meeting was abruptly cancelled at the last
moment. Hoshyar Zebari, a senior emissary of the KDP, even
found it difficult to obtain a visa to enter the US. Ahmed Chalabi
and the Iraqi National Congress, having long cultivated the neo-
conservatives and the Republicans, had the greatest access, a fact
which created much jealousy among other Iraqis. Although
eager to see Bush and thereby establish themselves as players
in post-Saddam Iraq it was never clear that Iraqi opponents of
Saddam had much new to tell the Americans. All wanted them
to invade. All said it would be easy. At a meeting with Bush in
early 2003 Kanan Makiya, whose draft constitution had so
annoyed the Kurds in London, assured the president that
'The Iraqis will welcome US forces with flowers and sweets
when they come.'

I had a more immediate and personal worry than the future of
American power in the Middle East as I sat in my office in CSIS. I
wanted to get to Iraq before the war began but the way was full
of obstacles. The Ministry of Information in Baghdad was
handing out visas to journalists but I did not think they would
give one to me. I knew they had strongly resented *Out of the
Ashes*, the book on Iraq written by my brother Andrew and
myself in 1999. It contained too many disobliging stories about
Saddam, Uday and the rest of his family, and had a full account of
the Shia and Kurdish uprisings in 1991. Iraqis told me that even if

I did get a visa I would be unwise, until I was quite sure that the furore over the book had died down, to visit Baghdad. I wondered at the time if they were over-dramatizing the risks, but in fact the regime's ferocious security services turned out to have taken an unnerving interest in our book, possibly because it had sold well on the black market.

The only alternative way to cover the war while keeping out of reach of the Iraqi security services was to travel to the three Kurdish provinces in the north. These had been a quasi-independent enclave since 1991. They were also highly inaccessible. I knew the Kurds themselves would be welcoming but Iran, Turkey and Syria all kept a tight grip on their border with Iraqi Kurdistan. They were suspicious of its quasi-independence and feared its impact on their own Kurdish minorities. Turkey, through which I used to travel to Kurdistan, had long forbidden journalists to pass through its closely guarded frontier. The PUK historically had good relations with Iran and the KDP with Syria. Both tried hard to extract from their patrons permission for me to travel overland. At one point the PUK, though inured to Iranian equivocation, were so optimistic that a visa was about to be issued that I even paid for it in advance. Then, as the days slipped by alarmingly, the required permit never arrived at the Iranian consulate, though expected by the hour. Finally, as I was beginning to despair, Hoshyar Zebari called to say the Syrian *mukhabarat*, the secret police, had agreed to let me to cross the Tigris river unofficially from Syria into KDP-controlled territory. The KDP had persuaded the Syrians that the presence of a few foreign journalists in Kurdistan would help deter Turkey from sending its army into northern Iraq, something the Syrians and Kurds both wanted to avoid.

My travel difficulties were still not entirely solved. A problem of dealing with security services in the Middle East is that they seldom tell the rest of the government for whom they are working what they are up to. I still had to get a tourist visa to Syria, a country deeply suspicious of journalists. I went to the

Syrian consulate in Belgravia in London and filled in an application form for a tourist visa claiming that I worked for a publisher, as in a certain sense I did. A fellow applicant to whom I mentioned this said: 'For God's sake don't mention anything to do with books or they'll never let you in.' I hastily tore up the form and substituted 'executive in egg processing plant' as my job.

My journey was harrowing, not so much because of any physical difficulty but because, having come so far, I feared some small last-minute piece of ill-luck would sabotage my plans. One difficulty arose as soon as I got to Damascus in the middle of the Id al-Adha feast, when every Muslim likes to eat with his or her family. My KDP contacts, their help essential for dealing with the *mukhabarat*, did not answer their phones for 24 hours during the festivities. I did not dare leave my dingy room in the Sheraton Hotel in case they should call. Finally the phone rang and a few hours later I started for the border across the rain-swept plains of north-eastern Syria. Middle Eastern borders have a nasty habit of closing at unexpected and deeply inconvenient moments. But there, on the west bank of the Tigris, swollen by winter rains, was a tin boat with a rickety outboard motor and single oar. A few minutes later I was back in Iraq. I was just in time. Soon afterwards the Syrians, responding to complaints from Baghdad, took away the tin boat and sent soldiers to patrol the riverbanks with orders to stop anybody crossing.

IV

THE FIRST AMERICAN soldiers to arrive officially in Iraq did not want to leave anybody in doubt about who was in charge. 'Stop filming and friggin' listen to me,' shouted one of them at a small band of journalists. He was wearing black wraparound aviator glasses and was protected by full body armour. Clutching a machine gun in one hand and with a pistol strapped to his thigh, he and the other soldiers were in Salahudin, the mountaintop headquarters of the Kurdish leader Massoud Barzani, to guard Zilmay Khalilzad, the suave and soft-spoken Afghan-born US envoy to the Iraqi opposition, who had just arrived from Turkey on this cold late February morning in 2003. The war was still three weeks away but the public appearance of a senior American diplomat and his bodyguards on Iraqi soil, even if it was in practice controlled by the Kurds, showed how far we had come since the conference in London in December. The invasion was clearly imminent. Inside the small conference hall Khalilzad reassured the sceptical opposition delegates that 'The US has no desire to govern Iraq. The Iraqis should govern their own country as soon as possible'.

I suspected that the aggressive actions of the soldiers standing outside the conference hall might prove a better guide to future American behaviour in Iraq than the emollient words of the US envoy. Standing in the driving snow, they were trying to martial the group of foreign journalists who had made their way to

Salahudin. 'This is non-negotiable and anybody who doesn't like it can leave,' yelled a soldier as he explained the stringent search procedures for anybody entering the conference hall. Journalists were not alone in being singled out. The Americans seemed to regard all Iraqis with equal suspicion as they prodded and patted veteran Kurdish opponents of Saddam Hussein and venerable Shia clerics in their search for concealed weapons. Kurdish officials looked a little embarrassed by the swift takeover of their headquarters by these burly and heavily armed Americans, but did not protest. Half a dozen *peshmerga* – Kurdish soldiers – peered with expressionless eyes as the sudden blizzard covered journalists, delegates and bodyguards alike with a coating of white.

I had arrived in Arbil, the largest city in Kurdistan, a fortnight earlier on February 15 after driving through the rain from the Syrian border. The narrow road, full of water-filled potholes, skirted the Iraqi front line which had sealed off the three Kurdish provinces of Dohuk, Arbil and Sulaimaniyah from the rest of the country since 1991. But the border had long been quiet and my driver looked unworried by the proximity of Iraqi army sentry posts. He took me to a ramshackle hotel in Arbil called the Dim-Dim. I knew there were better hotels in the city but I was too tired and relieved to be inside Iraq to argue. In the event the hotel staff were friendly, the food dull but edible and, of critical importance for a journalist, I was able to get a room facing south. This was the direction in which I had to point the dish of my phone if it was to connect with a satellite. If there was a clear view to the south I could transmit articles to London without having to clamber on to the roof. I ended up staying in the Dim-Dim for two months.

I never really liked Arbil. It is the oldest continuously in-habited city in the world, built 5,000 years earlier on the rich plain below the Kurdish mountains. Its skyline was dominated by an enormous mound or Tel built from the ruins of more ancient cities. Once this artificial hill, its sides covered in green grass, had been the citadel of Arbil. Ottoman officials and merchants built mansions with delicately painted reception rooms and airy courtyards on it. From the balconies of these houses they had a fine view of the rolling grasslands of the Assyrian plain. But by now the citadel was a close-packed slum. Paint and plaster was flaking off the walls of the grand houses. The view from the wooden balconies, dangerously rotted and difficult to walk on, had become more dismal over the years. In the 1980s the Iraqi army had destroyed 3,800 Kurdish villages in their anti-guerrilla campaigns. The villagers had fled to Arbil after their houses were demolished, their flocks of sheep slaughtered and concrete was poured into the village wells. Their houses now stretched to the horizon. Most were miserably poor, eking out a living as part-time labourers and surviving on government rations paid for by the UN's Oil-for-Food programme.

Even so, the last time I had seen Arbil in 1996 conditions were worse. It had just been the scene of heavy fighting. In one of the complex and bloody manoeuvres of the Kurdish civil war in the 1990s the PUK, which held Arbil and was backed by Iran, had tried to wipe out the KDP. But their offensive had backfired. The KDP had cynically called in Saddam Hussein, whose tanks swiftly captured the city, killed several hundred of his opponents and then withdrew before the US could react. It was one of Saddam Hussein's few military campaigns in which he did not overplay his hand, and had consequently been his most success-ful. Seven years later the wreckage of the old Sheraton Hotel in the centre of the city was still pock-marked with bullet holes from the fighting, but by now it was no longer tactful to talk to the newly reconciled Kurdish leaders about their past disputes.

Arbil might not be an attractive city but I decided to stay there. It was the KDP's capital and it was they who had persuaded the Syrians to let me reach Kurdistan; I felt I owed it to them to cover what they were doing. They were also the Iraqis I knew best and to whom I felt closest. In 1979 I was in Tehran for the *Financial Times* and had driven to the Iranian border with Iraqi

Kurdistan to meet Massoud Barzani, later to be the KDP leader. He was an intelligent man, cautious in action but ruthless when necessary, who always sounded as if he suspected, almost invariably with good reason, that his ally of the moment was about to betray him. I had been a friend of Hoshyar Zebari, the spokesman and in effect the foreign minister of the KDP, since he came to London at the beginning of the Iran–Iraq war. In 1980 the KDP was taking advantage of this to restart the guerrilla war. Zebari was trying to run the KDP office in London, revive international interest in the plight of the Kurds and do a degree at Essex University at the same time. One day he wrote a statement announcing that the KDP had launched a series of attacks on the Iraqi army. He delivered it to the offices of all the main newspapers and read them next morning to see if they had taken notice of the Kurds' return to war. With increasing gloom he discovered that his statement had been wholly ignored until he came to the pink pages of the *Financial Times*, where I was one of the Middle East staff and had run everything he had written in full, adding a few words of commentary about the restarting of the guerrilla campaign. Zebari was the best propagandist I ever met. He knew, unlike most public relations experts, what would make a news story. He was highly informed and knew how, when and to whom to pass on his information. He was also very good company and I thought that if I stuck close to him in the weeks leading up to the war I would know most of what was happening in Kurdistan.

I also hoped to learn what the Kurds knew about the rest of Iraq. The KDP had a good intelligence service. It covered the whole country because there was hardly a town or city in Iraq where Kurds did not live. Some were there by choice, others because they had been deported by Saddam Hussein, as part of his campaign to control and Arabize Kurdistan. The development of satellite phones made it easy for them to communicate (it was also extremely dangerous because the regime in Baghdad executed anybody caught with an unauthorized satellite phone as a spy). When the British Army claimed a few weeks later to have captured Umm Qasr, the port south of Basra at the other end of Iraq, a Kurdish leader told me within hours that this was not true: 'Our people there say fighting is still going on.' A day later the British admitted that they were premature in their claim of victory.

Arbil was well placed geographically for covering the war. The US was expected to open a northern front, sending 62,000 soldiers supported by 310 aircraft across the border from Turkey into Iraq. The attack would be led by the 4th Infantry Division, whose equipment was already arriving in Turkey. The US targets were likely to be Mosul, the largely Sunni Arab capital of northern Iraq, and Kirkuk, claimed by the Kurds, at the centre of the northern oilfields. If the Iraqi front line collapsed as expected I could reach each city quickly from Arbil. I would then be able to follow the US troops south as they fought their way down the Tigris river towards Baghdad.

Other journalists had the same idea, though many had not succeeded in reaching Kurdistan. The Turks remained unrelentingly hostile to giving safe passage, the Iranians were evasive and the Syrians were furious that a television correspondent had filmed himself crossing the Tigris into Iraq from their territory. They closed their frontier. When two intrepid British journalists later tried to cross the river on an improvised raft made out of inflated inner tubes they were promptly arrested by a Syrian army patrol.

A trickle of correspondents and television crews were nevertheless arriving in Arbil. The print journalists noted with some envy that the television correspondents were not stinting themselves in either accommodation or protection. CNN had taken over an entire hotel in the centre of Arbil. Its forecourt was protected by red-and-white painted barrels filled with concrete to prevent a car bomb getting too close. In what had been the lobby of the hotel was a birdcage with a canary called Diehard 2 which was expected to provide early warning of a poisoned gas attack by dutifully expiring at the first whiff, thereby giving his CNN employers the vital few seconds necessary to don their gas masks. In the Arbil Tower Hotel Fox Television had taken over an entire floor – I think it was the seventh – and fortified it as if they expected imminent infantry assault. Anybody opening the lift door was immediately faced with a sandbag emplacement and an alert-looking armed guard. Their defences did not end there. A crane lifted more sandbags to the seventh floor and these were placed along every wall and window. Other hotel guests became worried that the whole shoddily constructed building was going to collapse into the street under the weight of sandbags. At the time we other journalists wrote derisively about the paranoia of Fox and CNN but a year later, as suicide bomb attacks escalated, their fortifications began to seem a sensible and modest precaution.

Over the next month the Kurds and the Americans were each to have a nasty surprise. The Kurdish leaders discovered that US preparations to overthrow Saddam Hussein had, from their point of view, a very major catch in them. The priority for the US was to invade Iraq from the north as well as the south and thus open up a second, northern front against Saddam Hussein. To do this it needed the use of military bases in Turkey from which to launch its offensive. To their horror the Kurds learned that the Turkish price for this cooperation was for the US to agree to a Turkish army numbering up to 40,000 men crossing the border into Iraqi Kurdistan alongside the Americans. This would mean the end of the quasi-independent Kurdish enclave. The Turkish army had spent years fighting a bloody war against Kurdish separatists in Turkey. It wanted to make sure that in future they would not receive support from their fellow Kurds in northern Iraq. Ankara was also eager to stop the Kurds capturing Mosul and Kirkuk when the war came. 'Turkey is adamant that it wants a foothold inside Iraq,' said a Kurdish leader after talks in Turkey. 'Once they are in it will be very difficult to get them out.'

This was a nightmare for Kurdish leaders, particularly for the KDP whose territory shared a 200–mile-long common border with Turkey. The Turks claimed ingenuously that their purpose was solely humanitarian and they simply wanted to stop Kurdish refugees fleeing to Turkey as they had done in 1991. They added that, since their purpose was humanitarian and not military, their forces would not be under direct US command. Nobody took the Turkish protestations too seriously because in the First Gulf War the Kurds had fled from the vengeance of the advancing Iraqi army. This time round the situation was entirely different since Iraqi troops were likely to be in full retreat. The US made chillingly clear that it needed Turkey a lot more than it needed the Kurds. Khalilzad issued a statement saying: 'It is important now for our Kurdish friends to work with us and our ally Turkey.' An angry Kurdish official immediately placed his finger on this passage, pointing out to me the distinction between 'friends' and 'allies'.

Fear of Turkish attack terrified ordinary Kurds. Karim Sinjari, the powerful Kurdish Interior Minister, said: 'Only a week ago the main topic in the streets among Kurds was Saddam and the fear of chemical attack. Now the only thing people talk about is Turkey and the Turkish advance.' There were anti-Turkish demonstrations in the streets. They chanted 'Yes to Liberation! No to Occupation!' I went to watch a football match between an Arbil club and one from Baghdad at the local stadium. When the supporters of the 10,000-strong Kurdish club were not cheering for their own side they chanted: 'Fuck the Turks.' There were no chants against Saddam. Kurdish demonstrators in Zakho, on the border with Turkey, even promised a naked protest against the threatened Turkish invasion. They had apparently got the idea from nude Australian anti-war protestors they had seen on television. This seemed to be such a radical departure from the Kurds' traditional antipathy to male nudity that I drove to Zakho to see how far they would go. In the event the protestors lost their nerve at the last moment and stripped only to their underpants. One of them played Kurdish patriotic songs on a violin.

The Kurdish leaders were in a delicate position. They had hoped to become the Americans' main ally inside Iraq. The Kurds would then try to emulate the Northern Alliance, the anti-Taliban coalition in north-east Afghanistan, which had teamed up with the US in 2001. Washington did not like them much – they had formerly been supported by Iran and Russia – but it needed local military forces otherwise it would have to send its own soldiers. In the end the US grudgingly had to accept the Northern Alliance as its military ally on the ground, backed by US airpower. But if the Turks, with their powerful army, became America's regional ally in Iraq then the Iraqi Kurds would be marginalized. Their position in a post-Saddam Iraq might be worse than it currently was.

I went to see Sami Abdul-Rahman, the KDP deputy prime minister, a 72-year-old veteran of the Kurdish struggle, whom I thought would be forthright about the American plans. He was looking gaunt after a serious illness. (He was to live another year and then died in a suicide bomb attack during a religious festival on February 1 2004 in Arbil which killed 104 people.) He was particularly furious not only because of the planned Turkish invasion but because American officials had just told the Kurds at a meeting in Ankara that plans to introduce democracy to Iraq immediately after the fall of Saddam Hussein had been shelved. Instead the country would be run by US military officers. 'Conquerors always call themselves liberators,' said Abdul-Rahman scathingly, referring to a speech by Bush the previous week saying US troops were going to liberate Iraq.

The Kurds did not dare to quarrel too openly with the Americans, whom they were still trying to cultivate. Their independent enclave had only existed because it was protected by US military over-flights since 1991. But the Kurdish leaders hinted obliquely that if the Turks invaded there would be fighting with local Kurds. 'Any intervention under any circumstances will lead to clashes,' said Hoshyar Zebari. 'It will be bad for the reputation of the US and the UK to see two of their allies – the Turks and the Kurds – at each other's throats.' This, of course, was the reason why the KDP had taken such trouble to bring myself and other journalists to Kurdistan. They hoped it would prove embarrassing for President Bush to allow the only truly pro-American community in Iraq to be crushed by another US ally at the beginning of the war to overthrow Saddam Hussein and introduce democracy to Iraq.

I was taken along with Dan Williams of the *Washington Post* – we travelled together for two months before and during the war – to see the Kurdish *peshmerga* train for war. The KDP claimed to have 50,000 combat troops, though this was probably an exaggeration. The main constraint was not lack of armed men but money to pay and feed them. Nevertheless the Kurds were keen to impress the outside world with the idea that if the Turks invaded they would fight them. Military exercises made few concessions to military reality. At Atrush, high in the mountains, we watched twenty-five *peshmerga* in green-and-brown camouflage uniforms storm a rocky hilltop in the face of machine-gun fire. Enemy soldiers emerged with their hands in the air and were taken prisoner as the yellow KDP flag was raised over the captured bunker. The triumphant *peshmerga* formed a column and marched down the hill singing a Kurdish song of victory. I was standing beside General Aziz Hamas, commander of the Kurdish special forces, who spoke of the operation with a certain cynicism. 'We don't have enough ammunition for real exercises,' he said. 'But, all the same, whoever fights us will regret it, especially Turkey.'

In the event, in the first of many unpleasant surprises for the US during the Iraq conflict, Turkey refused to allow America to invade Iraq from its territory. The Turkish parliament spurned a US offer of $30 billion in aid and loan guarantees in return for letting the US army use Turkish bases. I had visited Turkey many times but I was always perplexed, politically speaking, as to what 'made the country tick'. I asked every expert on Turkey I knew what was going to happen and without exception they gave convincing reasons why Turkey could not afford to stay out of the war. All were dumbfounded by the Turkish stand. The KDP leaders were delighted. They gleefully reported how the jaws of American diplomats staying in Salahudin had dropped in surprise and consternation on hearing of the Turkish refusal to allow the US to invade Iraq from Turkey.

The importance of the collapse of the northern front – the absence of a second military pincer aimed at Baghdad – was swiftly forgotten in the coming weeks because Saddam Hussein's regime collapsed so easily. The absence of the Turkish army did not seem militarily important. But in the longer term the Turkish decision had immense significance. The US had lost its only ally in the Middle East capable of sending well-trained troops to Iraq in large numbers; instead it would have to rely on the Iraqi Kurds as the one significant American friend inside the country. The vote by the Turkish parliament underlined the unpopularity of the impending US invasion across the region. The US-led coalition in 1991 was regarded with hostility at street level in many Middle Eastern countries and beyond but their governments had in general supported Washington. In 2003, by contrast, governments and people were both against the war. One Kurdish leader said to me: 'Do not underestimate the importance of the fact that none of Iraq's neighbours, with the possible exception of Kuwait, will want a US occupation of Iraq to succeed.'

I hoped Kurdistan would prove a good listening post to find what Iraqis in the rest of the country thought about the war, which now seemed inevitable, and the overthrow of Saddam Hussein. It was still possible for people to move between Saddam-controlled Iraq and the northern provinces. They would be more willing to talk there than in Baghdad. In the past I had always found that Iraqis were politically astute, as indeed they needed to be to survive in a country where everybody under the age of thirty-five had lived their entire lives in a society in a state of permanent crisis. Since the Baath party came to power in 1968 Iraqis had been the victims of brutal repression, two disastrous wars and, for the last thirteen years, a severe economic blockade in the shape of UN sanctions as well as periodic American and British air attacks.

I visited Kurdish checkpoints on the roads leading from Kirkuk and Mosul to Arbil to talk to people arriving from further south. They all looked deeply relieved as they arrived on Kurdish territory. Some had come because they feared arrest, a call-up to the army or simply thought Kurdistan would be the safest place to be in the next few weeks. They all said that the mood in their towns and villages was increasingly fearful as the war approached. Women were stocking rice, oil and sugar. A Shia shopkeeper from Baghdad said: 'If there is any sign of weakness on the part of the government there will be an uprising.' Kurds from Kirkuk said they were frightened of being forced to join the government-run militia and then used as cannon fodder. On the other hand if they refused to join the militia they might be arrested for disloyalty to the regime. Many men were no longer sleeping at home, but had taken refuge in the local cemeteries. In retrospect an uprising was never likely. It had started in 1991 because of a mutiny in the defeated army units returning from Kuwait. This time Iraqi security was prepared and ready to crush any uprising. Iraqi security men had large-scale maps with the houses of possible dissidents marked on them in dark ink. In any case, why should any Iraqi risk his life to overthrow Saddam Hussein if the American army was going to dispose of him in the next few weeks?

Iraqis already in the army could not similarly stand on the sidelines, but from the accounts of deserters few soldiers had any intention of dying for a regime they did not like in a war it could not win. Four days into the war I interviewed two wary and exhausted Iraqi army soldiers, Haidar Abdul Hussein and Abdul

Hassan Ali, who had dodged Iraqi army patrols before crossing the front line into Kurdish controlled territory. They said that in the last days before the war, morale was rock bottom in their units. It was so bad that even the formal outbreak of hostilities made no difference. Haidar said: 'Breakfast was lentils and tea. At 10 a.m. the soldiers received stale bread and poor quality dates that you would not feed to animals in the south. Lunch was rice and soup. Every two days there was a small piece of chicken in it. The only rations that were increased recently were the breadloaves. They started to give us four small loaves instead of three.' Abdul added that there was not enough kerosene for the lamps at night.

Most of the soldiers' time was spent digging trenches outside their camps, which their officers assumed would soon be bombed. Haidar explained: 'We dug a deep trench about 100 metres from our camp and camouflaged it with soil from somewhere else so nobody could see that there had been fresh digging.' He was a commando, but this did not mean much since every brigade had such a unit for quick reaction in the event of an emergency. The government banned soldiers from owning radios. Haidar said: 'I heard the war had started on a little radio the size of a cigarette packet we had smuggled into my unit, although radios were forbidden. I did not want to die for Saddam.' Soon after Haidar and Abdul were on sentry duty one night and, having checked there were no mines in front of them, they deserted together and headed for Kurdistan. They were sceptical about an uprising of the Shia of southern Iraq or mass desertion of soldiers. Haidar said: 'Unless Baghdad surrenders, they have to fight because they don't know if Saddam will really be toppled.'

Deserters and refugees were hardly an unbiased sample of Iraqi opinion but what they said rang true. For years people I knew well enough in Baghdad for them to trust me had been telling me the same thing. They were desperate for a normal life free of Saddam and sanctions. My friend the engineering professor who had faked an illness to resign from the university had asked me if I could find him a job at the UN. 'I will do anything, drive a car, whatever they want,' he said desperately. Finally he got a job as consultant working on the giant mosque Saddam was building at the site of Muthana municipal airport in Baghdad. The Iraqi middle class had been ruined. The working class was living on the edge of starvation. Even the Sunni Arabs from country towns, the supposed core support of the regime, were wretchedly paid. Those who truly benefited from Saddam's regime were by now confined to a corrupt coterie in his entourage.

In the months before the invasion people in the rest of the world disputed the case for or against war, but Iraqis felt they had effectively been in a state of war since at least 1980. They wanted to live normal lives. 'What we want is simply a dose of stability,' explained a student at Mosul University. 'We have suffered enough due to our leaders' mistakes.' In September and October 2002 the highly-regarded Brussels-based International Crisis Group carried out dozens of covert interviews in Baghdad, Mosul and Najaf. It confirmed what I was being told by Iraqis three months later. The majority wanted an end to the regime even if this involved an American-led attack. 'We do not particularly want a US military strike, but we do want a political change,' said a young architect in Baghdad. 'We are even ready to live under international tutelage. We have nothing to lose, and it cannot be any worse than our present condition.' There was also a sense in Baghdad that the Americans owed it to Iraqis to rebuild what had been destroyed by sanctions. Most Iraqis wanted to see the back of Saddam Hussein, but they already viewed their liberators – the Americans and the Iraqi exile parties – with suspicion. A civil servant in Baghdad said of the latter: 'The exiled Iraqis are the exact replica of those who currently govern us . . . with the sole difference that the latter are already satiated since they have been robbing us for the past thirty years. Those who accompany the American troops will be ravenous.'[9]

V

THE SECOND US-LED war against Iraq in 2003 was militarily very much a re-run of the first war in 1991. In both cases the US army and its allies swiftly won a complete victory. The Iraqi army scarcely fought at all. US casualties were minimal. In the reconquest of Kuwait, at a time when Saddam Hussein claimed to have one million men under arms, the US military lost just 376 men killed by accident and in battle during the whole campaign. The allied unit to suffer the heaviest losses proportionate to its size was a Romanian medical detachment, stationed far behind the front line in Saudi Arabia, which had set up an illicit still. Through some error in its construction the Romanians made methanol rather than alcohol, with horrendous results for those who drank the poisonous brew. In the second American-led war against Saddam Hussein, this time to overthrow him and his regime, only 122 American soldiers died up to the fall of Baghdad.

The lack of serious fighting was not immediately obvious to television viewers across the world who saw clouds of black smoke billowing up from air strikes or Iraqi tanks ablaze beside the road. The battlefield looked much as people had come to expect from watching films about El Alamein, Stalingrad or the Normandy landings. But American soldiers found few dead bodies in the tanks they destroyed, the great majority of which were hit after these elderly Soviet-made vehicles had been sensibly abandoned by their crews. Shortly after the first US–Iraq war I met an Iraqi medical general on a plane flying from Baghdad to Basra. I asked him why, so far as I could see from visiting hospitals, Iraqi military losses had been very low in the recent conflict despite Iraq's complete defeat in Kuwait. After being reassured that I would never publish his name the general explained: 'Our men may not be very professional soldiers but after fighting for eight years against Iran they have military experience. They know a lost battle when they see one so they ran away before they could be killed.'

Iraqi soldiers knew it was hopeless to fight against such a powerful enemy which had full control of the air. But there was more to it than that. As the deserters I interviewed some days after the beginning of the second war had told me, few Iraqi soldiers wanted 'to die for Saddam'. This was understandably true of half-starved Shia conscripts but it turned out that the same applied to the 70,000 Republican Guard troops and the even more elite 15,000 Special Republican Guards, whose men were recruited from Sunni Arab tribes known to be loyal to the regime. They too went home without fighting. The evaporation of these forces showed the extent to which Saddam's government in 2003 was discredited among all Iraqis, even those closest to the regime.

Saddam Hussein was always a secret policeman first and a soldier second (as a youth he had been turned down by the military academy in Baghdad). The lesson he learned from disaster in Kuwait and the Kurdish and Shia uprisings was to supervise the military even more closely. His priority had always been to prevent the army staging a coup like the one which he had used to climb to power in 1968. To this end armoured units based near Baghdad were issued with only a few rounds of ammunition for their guns. Security men monitored officers and men to detect any sign of dissent. In the wake of 1991, when the regime had almost lost power, greater effort was put into preventing desertion from the army using savage punishments, such as cutting off the ears of offenders. Soldiers were not only forbidden radios to prevent them listening to foreign radio stations but they were also threatened with severe punishment if they were found with civilian clothes, which was taken as evidence that they planned to desert.

The effect of Saddam's inept tactics was to hasten the American military victory. In the longer term it left the US army, as it began to occupy Iraq, with an exaggerated idea of its own powers. It came to believe that it did not matter what Iraqis thought about the occupation because there was nothing they could do about it. 'Because the Americans won so easily against Saddam they don't take us seriously,' said one Iraqi friend. 'We have to fight them just to get them to take us seriously.' The next few years were to show that the American army was far more vulnerable than it imagined to an intelligent enemy which exploited its weaknesses.

There was a further simple misconception about the war which was to affect the occupation which followed. Journalists were often unwittingly responsible for this misunderstanding. Reporting from the front line, we often gave the impression that the fighting in Iraq was on a heroic scale, like Vietnam or World War Two. But it never quite measured up. It was difficult for a reporter on the ground, under attack and frightened of being blown apart, to play down the significance of what he was seeing. In the First Gulf War I was in Baghdad when it was under air attack. I described the thunderous boom and blaze of intense white light as bombs and missiles detonated. I was struck by the strange beauty of the curtains of anti-aircraft fire sparkling in the night sky. It seemed very like pictures of the Blitz in London in 1940–41 when my mother was working in Air Raid Precautions from a bunker deep under Paddington. It only occurred to me at the end of the war in Iraq that, given the great size of Baghdad, the bombardment was not very heavy and could not be compared to the Blitz.

These unintentional exaggerations about the scale of the

fighting in the second war misled many Americans into believing afterwards that Iraq had been solidly defeated, like Germany and Japan in 1945. If those countries could accept foreign occupation peacefully, why shouldn't the Iraqis? But the Germans and the Japanese had both largely supported their governments in World War Two. They had fought very hard and suffered terrible losses on the road to defeat. They had given the war their best shot and were willing to see their societies remodelled by the victor. The attitude of Iraqis in 2003 was very different. They had not, as President Bush and Tony Blair never tired of pointing out, identified with Saddam Hussein. They had not fought for him except under compulsion. They did not see why their future should be determined over their heads by foreign conquerors. They did not want and would not accept the colonial-type occupation the US was now going to try to impose. Hoshyar Zebari, normally sympathetic to the US, told me: 'If the US wants to impose its own government, regardless of the ethnic and religious composition of Iraq, there is going to be a backlash.'

The fighting in Iraq was not as intense as the outside world supposed but for correspondents this did not make it a safer place. In some respects the messy skirmishing in Kurdistan, the way the front line gyrated backwards and forwards, was more dangerous than conventional warfare. Much of Iraq was a no-man's land where nobody was in control. I wondered, it turned out with good reason, if the pilots of American bombers flying overhead could really tell friend from foe, intermingled as they were on the ground far below. The Iraqi army was not the only or even the most dangerous enemy. There were also looters and Arab villagers lying in ambush on the flat roofs of their houses, who fired at any vehicle with number plates indicating it was from a Kurdish province.

I was particularly wary because I had nearly been killed in the aftermath of the Kurdish uprising and successful Iraqi counter-attack in 1991. I went with two Swedish diplomats working with the UN in a convoy of cars to see if supplies were being prepositioned to feed Kurdish refugees returning from the mountains near Sulaimaniyah. I did not notice that the cars we were using had no number plates, which to a Kurd meant that they belonged to the detested *mukhabarat*. The drivers took a wrong turn and drove at speed along a narrow glen past the Iraqi army's forward positions and up to a PUK checkpoint. All would have been well had we stopped and explained who we were. Instead our drivers panicked, reversed the cars and tried to escape by driving away at speed. The PUK *peshmerga*, thinking we were hated police agents, responsible for torturing and murdering their relatives, opened fire from the checkpoint and a hill overlooking the road. They hit the car I was in seven or eight times. Miraculously, none of us were killed or seriously injured, but I was left streaming blood from wounds in the face where I had been struck by pieces of metal from the bodywork of the car sent flying by the bullets. Doctors in Kurdistan and later in London extracted these small pieces of shrapnel from around my eyes and told me I was lucky not to be blind.

The US and British invasion started on March 19 but for the first few weeks there was only a phoney war in the north. The US had been caught by surprise by the refusal of the Turkish parliament to allow US forces to use bases in Turkey. But the atmosphere was far from peaceful. The Kurds were terrified that Saddam Hussein would use chemical weapons against them. After a few days Arbil and other cities were deserted as families fled to villages, rebuilt since 1991, where they had relatives. Usually they left one man behind in their houses to protect them. A whole row of shops in the bazaar sold nothing but rolls of multi-coloured plastic to seal up windows against poison gas. Noticing that most businesses were closing, I went to a money changer to get some money while I still could. He said anxiously: 'All my friends are frightened of a gas attack and have left. I am going soon myself.' The mobile phone system stopped working because the foreign engineers who maintained it, mostly Turks and Iranians, had fled the country. On the roads shepherds were prudently herding great herds of sheep from the pastures close to the front line into the mountains.

Dan Williams and I wanted to reach Mosul and Kirkuk as soon as they were captured. Every day we reconnoitred the different roads leading to the cities. To the west there was a direct road across an old bridge over the Zaab river, now a broad brown torrent of water as snow melted in the mountains. We could see Iraqi army trenches on the green ridge on the other side of the river. These soon became the most-filmed military positions in Iraq because, directly opposite them on the Kurdish-held side of the river in the town of Kalakh, numerous foreign television companies had rented houses and set up their cameras. Very occasionally they were rewarded by a bomb landing among the Iraqi bunkers and sending up a billowing cloud of dust and smoke, pictures of which were instantly transmitted around the world.

The Kurdish strategy was subtle. They would edge towards Mosul and Kirkuk, their prime targets, while denying they were doing so. They would not attack until the Iraqi army had been thoroughly softened up by US bombers. In advancing they would emphasize that these were joint Kurdish–American operations, thus making it very difficult for the Turkish army to intervene without shooting at American troops. The US was getting an early lesson in what was to be a recurring theme for the American intervention in Iraq over the next three years. Each Iraqi ethnic and religious community as well as every political faction sought to lure their American occupiers into aiding them in fulfilling a purely communal agenda. Given America's chronic lack of international, regional or local allies they often succeeded. The Kurds in particular became expert in these manoeuvres. I suspected that the Kurds would try to capture Kirkuk and probably Mosul. They had always considered the former, surrounded by the northern oilfields, as their natural capital. It was from Kirkuk that so many Kurds had been ethnically cleansed by Saddam Hussein and forced to live in the slums of Arbil. Control of Kirkuk oil and the oil revenues was essential if the Kurds were going to win national independence or a degree of autonomy which was close to it. Any doubts I had about Kurdish intentions towards Kirkuk disappeared when I ran into a police colonel, resplendent in a new uniform which I did not recognize. He explained he was to be the new head of traffic police in Kirkuk and would take up his duties just as soon as the city had been captured.

The sudden retreats by the Iraqi army came suddenly and were perplexing. Could they be a ploy by Saddam Hussein to lure the Kurds forward and thereby provoke a Turkish invasion? There was nothing much to prevent the Iraqi army returning as swiftly as they had gone. They could easily brush the Kurdish militia-men aside (though not the US planes overhead). The KDP and PUK claimed to be able to put 100,000 *peshmerga* into the field, but we seldom saw bands of more than a few hundred lightly armed and raggedly dressed men.

Old frontiers were dissolving. For twelve years the Iraqi front line between Kirkuk and Sulaimaniyah had run along a ridge of hills halfway between the two cities overlooking the town of Chamchamal. Then one day the troops were gone. Their retreat back to Kirkuk was well-organized. Possibly it was the American bombers that persuaded them to go. 'They have pulled out because of the air raids so they will be in populated places where the planes cannot be used,' said Shamal Ali, a *peshmerga* we met who was manning a light machine gun on top of a pick-up truck. The Kurdish commanders tied themselves into knots in order to explain away their advance. Mam Rostam, a leader of the PUK, was standing in the road saying: 'None of our official forces have gone beyond this point. Anybody further down the road is irregular *peshmerga*, they don't belong to us. We are definitely not on the edge of Kirkuk.' In the abandoned Iraqi army camp looters were already at work. The soldiers had not left much behind. But Iraqi looters are nothing if not thorough and soon they were hacking window frames out of the concrete walls.

One man had even dug up a small tree and, when we saw him, had already dragged it five or six miles down the road towards his home.

Changing sides in Iraq is a delicate art: a day too early or too late could prove fatal. Iraqis generally have a well-honed sense of personal survival but in the chaotic week before the fall of Baghdad this was being severely tested. One Kurdish village in particular was terrified that it had made a fatal miscalculation as to the timing of the end of the regime in Baghdad. Villagers in Dubardan, an unexceptional collection of flat-roofed build-ings north of Mosul, had rebelled too early and were frightened that the Iraqi army would return and kill them all. We had arrived by chance outside the village, overlooked by a mountain still held by the Iraqis, and started talking to a local teacher called Sheikh Shamsadani Dubardani. He explained the uprising had taken place after American air-strikes killed and wounded a number of Iraqi soldiers camped near Dubardan. He said: 'When the US planes bombed the Iraqi positions we thought it was a good chance to rise up.' The villagers, mostly armed with sub-machine guns, as was usual in the Iraqi countryside, shouted slogans against Saddam Hussein, ran up the yellow flag of the KDP and put up posters of its leader Massoud Barzani. Within a few hours, however, the people of Dubardan, numbering about 600, discovered to their horror that they had switched sides prematurely. Some *peshmerga* entered the village but then re-treated, probably on American insistence. The villagers them-selves had only seventy armed men. 'Our position is very dangerous,' said Sheikh Shamsadani. 'We are afraid the Iraqi army will occupy the village again and kill everybody.' He explained that the nearest Iraqi troops were only 200 metres away from Dubardan.

The Kurdish leaders had placed their *peshmerga* under the operational control of the Americans and were eagerly seeking to establish their credentials as reliable military partners. We had first learned of the dangerous situation in Dubardan from a *peshmerga* commander in dark glasses called Commander Said, standing beside the mangled remains of two Iraqi military trucks hit by an American air-strike near the bridge close to the village. We did not see any American Special Forces but they were certainly about.

On a wrecked truck one of them had stuck a sticker advertising his local rifle range in the US: 'I Shot My Loads at Range One.' Commander Said explained his military dilemma. He knew that the people in Dubardan were in danger of a counter-attack but 'we have to cooperate with US air support'. Shahab Ahmed, the local political leader of the KDP, also admitted that the Kurdish fighters could not do anything without American permission and support. 'The *peshmerga* cannot fight the Iraqi army alone because it has artillery and tanks and we do not,' he said. 'We are able to fight in the mountains for 100 years, but not in open country.'

In the event the Iraqi army commanders had other things on their mind than ordering the slaughter of the people of Dubardan. But before we left we discovered an interesting fact about the original uprising and the village's premature attempt to change sides. Sheikh Shamsadani and three leaders of the revolt sitting with him had mentioned in passing that local members of the Baath party had joined the uprising. We asked if we could meet these Baathist rebels. 'Actually we are them,' said one of the four men shyly. They explained why even though they were Kurds they had joined the Baath, which had between 500,000 and 800,000 members. Sheikh Shamsadani explained that he could not have held his job as a teacher without a party card. A truck driver called Abdul Qarim Kassim said: 'I had to join the Baath so I could pass through checkpoints on the road.' Perhaps the four former Baathists had started their last-minute uprising specifically in order to make sure that their past relationship with the regime was forgotten and to establish their Kurdish nationalist credentials.

The next day we found that our fear that the American

bombers circling high above us had only a vague idea of what was happening on the ground was well based. We heard on the radio that a convoy carrying Kurdish leaders and the BBC World Affairs Editor John Simpson along with his television crew had been hit by an American missile by mistake. Seventeen people had been killed. Minutes after the attack, Simpson, himself wounded in the leg, reported: 'This is a scene from hell. All the vehicles are on fire. There are bodies burning around me, there are bodies lying around, there are bits of bodies on the ground. This is a bad own goal by the Americans.' A piece of shrapnel cut off the legs of Kamran Abdurazaq Muhammad, the BBC translator, who bled to death before he could be brought to hospital. The commander of the Kurdish special forces Wajy Barzani, a brother of Massoud, had been critically wounded. We arrived a few hours later. There were pools of dried blood on the road and the heat of the explosions, which had ripped apart the vehicles of the convoy, was so intense that it had melted the zinc of their batteries. The disaster had happened on a bare ridge above the village of Dibagah, from which the Iraqi army had just withdrawn. The convoy had stopped at a point from which one could see the plain below through a dusty haze. A US Special Forces commander apparently saw an Iraqi tank firing about a mile away. He called for an air-strike. About fifty yards from the remains of the convoy I saw an elderly Soviet T-54 tank with its round turret lying abandoned in a deep ditch beside the road. I wondered if the American pilot had been trying to attack the wrong tank.

The final collapse came suddenly. On April 10, the day after the fall of Baghdad, we drove to a small dishevelled town to the west of Kirkuk called Mahmour which the *peshmerga* had just captured. At midday news began to spread that Kirkuk itself had fallen. We swiftly drove east down a long straight road towards the oil city, but noticed with alarm that there was no traffic coming in the opposite direction. This is always a bad sign in war zones because it means there is some obstacle ahead stopping oncoming cars and trucks. It also meant that there were no drivers to flag down and ask about approaching dangers. As we drove towards Kirkuk, *peshmerga* we met were uncertain if the city had really fallen. Villages of Arab settlers, who had replaced Kurds in the region over the previous twenty years, stood empty apart from a few ducks and stray dogs. There were empty Iraqi army posts, but, ominously, no looters. Since Iraqi thieves will usually go to work while a battle is raging in order to get to the choicest pickings first I thought they could only have been deterred by something very dangerous.

At this point our car stopped because our translator and driver had mutinied. They said we were all going to get killed if we went on. Dan Williams, who was as usual contemptuous of danger, saying it almost invariably turned out to be exaggerated, wanted to push on towards Kirkuk. He threatened to get out of the car and walk if the rest of us would not come along. I was also eager to reach Kirkuk but only if we could find somebody to tell us what was happening. We turned off the main road, north into the oilfields. As we did so we spotted a single car coming towards us. 'It is finished, the way to Kirkuk is open,' the driver shouted. Saddam had guarded the oilfields well. Every few miles there was a little grey concrete fortress, looking like a medieval castle, which had once been held by the Iraqi army; all were now abandoned. We soon discovered why we had seen no looters before. I was wrong to think they were too frightened to practice their trade; instead they were engaged in stripping the oil company offices, more likely to contain items worth stealing than Iraqi army barracks. Soon the road was filled with trucks carting away stolen goods, the drivers in such a hurry that they did not even pause to smash the portraits of Saddam Hussein still standing beside the road.

By the time we reached the centre of Kirkuk there were only intermittent bursts of machine-gun fire. The Kurds in the street – the Arabs and Turkomans, each making up a third of the city's population, were keeping a low profile – were astonished at the speed with which the Iraqi army had fled. 'At 8 a.m. I went to my work and heard the B-52 aircraft making strikes in the hills,' said Ahmed Rasul, a Kurdish resident. 'It was after that that the Baath party and the army escaped and I saw the *peshmerga*.' In theory the latter had rushed to Kirkuk to restore order after the army fled. In reality, as my gaudily dressed traffic policeman had revealed, the capture of Kirkuk had been planned for weeks. In a PUK office, outside which a man was trying to smash a ceramic portrait of Saddam with his rifle butt, officials were distributing safe conduct passes to people frightened because of their membership of the Baath party or close association with it. The quiet efficiency with which they were doing so showed that they had been preparing to occupy Kirkuk for weeks. A PUK official – the PUK was always much stronger in Kirkuk than the KDP – conceded that they might have 'gone beyond the programme agreed between us and the Americans' but suggested everybody get used to what had happened.

The Kurdish leaders claimed piously that they had only advanced to prevent an orgy of looting, but if that was their objective they were not having much success. Within the space of five minutes I saw looters steal a fire engine, an agricultural thresher and an Iraqi Airways bus. Not that stopping the mass theft was easy or safe. Two *peshmerga* waved a large yellow bulldozer to the side of the road and stood in front of it waiting for it to stop. At the last moment they realized that whoever had stolen the enormous vehicle had no such plans, forcing them to jump aside just in time before they were crushed under its wheels.

In the newly appointed governor's office there were triumphant-looking Kurds and a few harassed-looking American officers. We spoke to Pavel Talabani, the son of the PUK leader Jalal Talabani who, playing down what had happened, said: 'We came to control the situation. There will be a US presence here and we're expecting to withdraw some of our men within forty-five minutes.' Some but not all: three years later the PUK was still firmly in control of Kirkuk.

The fall of Mosul came the following day and was much more violent. The entire Iraqi army V Corps had surrendered with its commander. The Americans did not have many men in the north and of these 2,000 had been rushed to secure the oilfields near Kirkuk that we had seen being looted. The welcome for the liberators of this great Sunni Arab city with a population of 1.7 million lasted only a few hours. In the morning there was a sense of jubilation as people realized that Saddam's iron rule was finished and the war almost over. Scores of young men were smashing down the imposing doors of the Iraqi Central Bank building, emerging minutes later with bundles of newly printed bank notes in their arms. A small yellow KDP flag floated from one end of the Iraqi governor's office and an Iraqi flag from the other, but inside the looters were in charge. I was fascinated by one determined man who was trying unaided to drag a hideously ornate gold and purple sofa, which had decorated the governor's inner sanctum, down the stairs into the street. He would go to one end of the sofa and move it a couple of feet. Then he would go to the other and repeat the process. I kept running into him in the course of the day as he and his giant sofa slowly made their way across the main square of the city towards his home.

By the afternoon Arabs in Mosul were frightened and angry. A young priest from Mosul's sizeable Christian minority said: 'A few months ago Saddam amnestied everybody in prison in Iraq, so there are plenty of criminals and even convicted murderers able to take advantage of the present situation.' Others wondered why the Americans, if they had won the war, weren't in Mosul to stop the looting. The museum was attacked and the hotels ransacked and set on fire. Outside the governor's office an angry man called Amir, a geologist who said he had deserted from the Iraqi army at the start of the war, shouted: 'Why do you let these people steal the public belongings? Those murderers should be shot.' He went on to suggest that the Americans do the shooting and then added cautiously: 'But the Americans must not enter our houses or interfere with our lives.' Others in Mosul were also resentful at the Americans' arrival. At a checkpoint into the city US soldiers had raised the Stars and Stripes. Suddenly a man popped from behind a wall nearby and vigorously waved a large Iraqi flag. The soldiers, fearing he might lob a grenade at them, opened fire but he dodged down and escaped.

By evening most Arabs in Mosul had concluded that the real problem was not the criminals but the Kurds. We went to the Republic hospital in Mosul where Dr Ayad Ramadani, the hospital director, had no doubt about the source of the problem. 'The Kurdish militias are looting the city,' he explained. 'The main protection is from the civilians organized by the mosques.' As we spoke to Dr Ramadani, there was a deafening chatter of machine-gun fire near the hospital gates, forcing us to duck down. Four men had been lifting the body of a dead relative, wrapped in a white shroud, into the back of a pick-up truck. At the sound of gunfire the driver panicked and suddenly accelerated away, leaving the mourners with the body, shaking their fists at the departing vehicle. As we cautiously drove out the back gate of the hospital we could see the vigilantes of whom the doctor had spoken at work building rudimentary barricades of rocks to seal off their streets from looters. The loudspeakers on top of minarets were calling for more volunteers to help restore order. As the Saddam government dissolved it was the local religious leaders who were emerging as the new authority.

Almost immediately we saw another unnerving example of how the mosques could be the centre for spontaneous political mobilization. We had gone to the medieval heart of Mosul and walked up an ancient street in a mostly Christian quarter looking for a safe house in which to stay for the night. When we got back to our car, which we'd had to leave behind because the streets were so narrow, we found that our driver Yusuf, normally taciturn, was looking shaken. He said that while we were gone,

100 people who had been at prayers in a nearby mosque came and surrounded his car. The number plates revealed it was from Arbil. They wanted to know what a Kurd from outside Mosul was doing in their city. Yusuf said: 'One of them yelled, "Let's kill him and burn the car."' Wiser counsels prevailed but some men in the crowd warned him to go at once if he wanted to stay alive. Bravely, Yusuf waited for us to return, but, having heard his story, we drove rapidly back to Arbil.

In those first dangerous days of the US occupation the weaknesses of America in Iraq were already becoming evident. Saddam Hussein had been overthrown but the violence was getting worse not better. The US evidently had no settled policy for ruling Iraq but was making up its plans day-by-day. A few days after the fall of Mosul and Kirkuk we drove south to Baghdad. Just north of Kirkuk we saw an American checkpoint at which two American soldiers were holding up placards, each of which bore a message written in Kurdish. One read: 'Drivers must get into one lane', the other: 'Carrying weapons is forbidden'. The problem was that the soldiers, being unable to read Kurdish, had mixed up the placards so one was angrily waving his sign – forbidding weapons – in front of a car which had tried to jump the queue, while a hundred yards down the road a confused-looking officer was asking drivers in English, which they did not speak, if they were armed, and was receiving benign smiles and enthusiastic thumbs-up signs in return.

VI

T HERE USED TO be a mosaic of President George Bush on the floor at the entrance to Baghdad's al-Rashid Hotel. It was placed there soon after the First Gulf War in 1991 and was a good likeness, though the artist gave Bush unnaturally jagged teeth and a slightly sinister grimace. The idea was that nobody would be able to get into the hotel, where most foreign visitors to Iraq stayed in the 1990s, without stepping on Bush's face. The mosaic did not long survive the capture of the city on April 9 and the takeover of the al-Rashid by US officials and soldiers. One American officer, patriotically determined not to place his foot on Bush's features, tried to step over the mosaic. The distance was too great. He strained his groin and had to be hospitalized. The mosaic was removed.

I liked the story because it seemed like a parable about the failings of the US occupation. There was the officer seeking, like his army, to carry out a task beyond his strength. When he failed and suffered injury this was blamed on the legacy of the old regime. The British diplomat who told me about the fate of the mosaic with amused disapproval, said he had tried to convince his American colleagues to preserve it as a memento of Iraqi history 'but they insisted on destroying it'. Compromise with Iraqi sensitivities was not high up on the agenda of the new rulers of Baghdad.

The American presence in those first self-confident weeks of the occupation seemed to sit on top of Iraqi society like a film of oil on water. Later it became too dangerous for Americans to move around Baghdad without an armed escort, but even at this early stage they lived in extraordinary isolation, seldom meeting Iraqis who had lived in Iraq under Saddam Hussein. Often, the Iraqis they did talk to had been out of the country for decades, the non-smoking English-speaking exiles I had seen at the London opposition conference in London in December. The self-confidence of the new regime grated on the nerves even of the Iraqis most sympathetic to it. Once an Iraqi friend of mine spotted a group of visitors from the US holding a party in a hotel at which the waiters were all wearing turbans reminiscent of the British Raj in India. He went up to one of them and said: 'I would like to shake you by the hand.' Gratified, the American did so. 'Now,' my friend said, 'you can go home and say you met at least one real Iraqi.'

The assurances about Iraqis ruling Iraq were soon forgotten. Everything was to be controlled by US advisers with a few British assistants. Iraqis were to play a secondary role. The reason for the American change of tack was that the war had been so easy. The US thought it had no need for friends or allies. There was also a strategic reason for keeping all power in its own hands. The US had hesitated to advance on Baghdad and overthrow Saddam Hussein in 1991 because it feared he would be succeeded by a Shia regime, probably highly Islamic in direction and close to Iran. Twelve years later Washington faced the same dilemma. Some 60 per cent of Iraqis were Shia. Their demand was for elections which they were bound to win. The US reaction was to announce that a poll could not be organized for several years. Washington felt it had the strength in Iraq to move pieces around on the Iraqi political chessboard as it wished. Democracy was on the agenda but only if it produced a government supportive of Washington. Asked at the end of April 2003 about the visibly growing influence of the Shia clergy, a senior member of the US administration said: 'We don't want

Persian fundamentalism to gain any foothold. We want to find more moderate clerics and move them into positions of influence.' He assumed that members of the Shia hierarchy, far and away the most influential leaders in their community, could be promoted and demoted at the whim of the US.

When Baghdad fell Iraqis were divided down the middle between those who thought they had been liberated and those who said they were being occupied. The polls taken at the time are a little dubious but they seemed to reflect what people said to me. Saddam Hussein, who had ruined and impoverished his country, should not have been a hard act to follow. But within weeks Iraqis found they were being ruled by a classic colonial occupation. Young Americans, whose only credentials were their links to the administration, poured into Baghdad. The country became a feeding trough for politically well-connected American companies and individuals. No money could be spent without an American counter-signature. In one mental asylum patients did not eat for a day because the appropriate American could not be found to permit the spending of $360 on food.

L. Paul Bremer III was the head of the occupation administration, known as the Coalition Provisional Authority (CPA), for the next disastrous year.[10] Lauded at the beginning by Washington, he later became its chosen scapegoat for everything that went wrong. He was a former career State Department official and ambassador to the Netherlands, who claimed no knowledge of Iraq – presumably the White House thought that none was necessary. Flying into Baghdad on May 12, he became dictator of Iraq as soon as he landed. Neither then nor in his memoirs does he reveal much understanding of the country he was meant to govern. At press conferences I found his smug appearance, crisp dark suit and purple tie even more irritating than his absurdly upbeat assessments of developments in Iraq. As guerrilla attacks escalated he would claim week after week that they were the last throes of a small number of 'desperate men' still loyal to Saddam. 'Those who refuse to to embrace the new Iraq are clearly panicking.' One day he assured his audience that Baghdad was receiving twenty hours of electricity a day. 'It simply isn't true,' said an Iraqi journalist, shaking his head in disbelief. 'Everybody in Baghdad knows it.'

By the time Bremer left Iraq just over a year later there were few, either among the Iraqis or the Americans who dealt with him, who had a good word to say for him. The White House and the Pentagon blamed him for everything, conveniently forgetting they once shared his imperial hubris and misconception that Iraq was a *tabula rasa* they could reconstruct as they wished. Bremer had many faults but they were not without precedent. He may not even have been, as some believed, the worst American proconsul in history. Towards the end of Bremer's tenure in Baghdad I reread *Naples '44*, the fascinating account by Norman Lewis, then a low-level member of British intelligence, of the US occupation of Naples in World War Two. I wanted to see if American rule in Baghdad sixty years later was uniquely incompetent and corrupt or if American occupations were always like this. Naples sixty years earlier and Baghdad in 2003 were both dangerous cities. Each was inhabited by destitute and desperate people equally willing to work as a gunman or a labourer. The US viceroy in Naples, General Mark Clark, left behind an even murkier reputation than Paul Bremer. On his first night in the city Clark dined on exotic fish looted from the Naples aquarium and appointed Lucky Luciano, the head of the New York mafia, as his senior security adviser.

Probably Luciano knew a lot more about Naples than some of Bremer's American-Iraqi advisers did about Iraq. They encouraged him to dissolve the Iraqi army and purge former members of the Baath party belonging to its four upper ranks. This was supposedly going to affect only 20,000 people or 1 per cent of all party members. In fact it left many more people unemployed. Doctors in hospitals and head teachers in schools were sacked. Most were Sunni Arabs. Without quite knowing what it was doing the CPA was trying to force through a revolutionary change in social and ethnic relations in Iraq. Later in 2003 I was in Hawaija, a strongly Sunni Arab district in the west of Kirkuk province, where the pro-American mayor (he had survived several attempts to assassinate him) confessed that he might have to close down the local hospital because so many of its doctors were Baathists within the prohibited degree. The popular head-master of a secondary school had been fired for the same reason. One of his pupils told me that he and other pupils had gone to him and told him they were planning to burn the school down by way of protest. He was able to dissuade them. A Turkoman was appointed headmaster by the local authorities in Kirkuk but was too frightened to take up his new job.

Loss of employment was so important because the over-whelming political and economic fact in Iraq – central to understanding the past defeat of Saddam Hussein and the coming failure of the occupation – was the misery in which most people lived. Some 70 per cent of the labour force or twelve million people out of a population of twenty-five million in 2003 were unemployed, according to the Ministry of Labour. Other figures were lower but there is no questioning the mass destitution. Engineers would try to make a little money selling glasses of tea to passers-by from a table on the pavement. Men stood all day in the markets trying to sell a bunch of blackened bananas or a few cracked plates. As under Saddam Hussein, it was only the ration of basic foodstuffs provided almost free by the state that fended off starvation. There was a horrible desperation in the hunt for work. A Russian company asked a man who was trying to get a job as a driver about his qualifications. He said he felt he should be given a job because, quite apart from his great experience as a driver, he had a live grenade in his pocket. He then showed the grenade to the Russian interviewing him and threatened to remove the pin unless he was immediately taken on.

One day, a month after the army had been dissolved, I saw several thousand men marching along Abu Nawas Street on the east bank of the Tigris. They were ex-officers demonstrating against the break-up of the army and demanding compensation. I joined the demonstration. Walking beside me was a distraught man who said his name was Ryad Abdul Wahab, who drew up his shirt to show the stump of his right arm as he marched and said: 'I was wounded . . . in the fighting at the airport during the war and now I can get no pension. How can I survive?' Other officers chimed in, saying they were being punished though they had refused to fight for Saddam Hussein. As we approached the so-called Assassin's Gate, an entrance into the Green Zone, the mood of the crowd became angrier. 'We did not fight for Saddam, but we will fight for our children,' said Major Kassim Ali, formerly an artillery officer. He said they wanted back-pay, pensions and the re-establishment of the army. He added: 'If a country has no army it cannot be independent.' Other officers threatened suicide attacks on American soldiers. It was an angry but by no means vengeful demonstration which posed no threat to armed US soldiers in flak jackets and helmets. But as I walked away I heard the sound of shots. A US military police convoy had driven up and demonstrators banged on the side of vehicles. A US spokesman claimed that stones were thrown and the military police had reacted by shooting two officers dead and wounding two others.

There was something dysfunctional about the occupation from the beginning. It could not carry out important projects even when its own most crucial interests were involved. A friend of mine called Ali, long in exile but a specialist in broadcasting, was hired to help create a pro-American satellite television station. This was very important for the CPA, which complained continually that the al-Jezeera satellite channel was biased against it. Ali rapidly found that his task was made more difficult because the well-connected American company which had won the contract to establish the television station had never done so before. Experienced Iraqis who had previously worked in television in Baghdad could not be hired because they had been in the top ranks of the Baath party. 'The only person I was allowed to hire from the old Iraqi television was the man who looked after the parking lot,' lamented Ali. Desperately though the CPA needed the channel it was months before it got off the ground. (Though Bremer may also have been lucky; one Iraqi friend said: 'If more Iraqis had been able to hear his broadcasts about dissolving the army and purging the Baath party there would have been a revolution.')

There was a seedy gold-rush atmosphere in Iraq in the early summer months of 2003. Word had spread across the world that there was quick money to be made. I was staying in the al-Hamra Hotel in the Jadriyah district in east Baghdad. Every day there were more former soldiers, many of them South Africans speaking Afrikaans, arriving to work for the security companies. The Pentagon was trying to keep down the number of US soldiers in Iraq by hiring vastly expensive mercenaries from all over the world. All claimed to be former members of elite military units like the SAS. Their motive for being in Iraq was to make as much money as quickly as possible. Ali, conscious that his attempt to set up a pro-American TV channel would make him a target for assassination, had been allocated a house in the Green Zone where he was protected by members of a foreign security company. At first they were assiduous in their duties. Then he noticed that his guards were less and less interested in his safety and were furtively moving large quantities of weapons and ammunition into his villa. He discovered that his security men had found several arsenals of high-value arms secreted by the former regime in the Green Zone, and were storing them in his house before secretly flying them out of the country and selling them abroad. 'I can't even smoke a cigarette in my own house because I am afraid of detonating all the explosives the guards have left lying about there,' complained Ali, who invariably had a cigarette in his mouth.

I accidentally ran into Ali, whom I knew from London, at

dusk one evening as I was leaving the al-Rashid Hotel. He was hardly recognizable because he had put on a lot of weight. 'I am getting fat because it is too risky for me to go for a walk outside the Green Zone,' he said. 'At least you're safe here,' I replied. 'Not as safe as you might think,' he said and gave details of a recent incident which I thought very funny but he thought highly dangerous. He had been talking to an American soldier of Iraqi origin who spoke Arabic and was on guard duty at one of the entrances to the Green Zone. The soldier told Ali that the Green Zone might not be as well protected as it seemed, adding: 'If you don't believe me go and look in the bathroom of the house over there.' It turned out that under Saddam Hussein, whose family and lieutenants lived in the enclave which became the Green Zone, a group of prostitutes had set up a brothel close to the Republican Palace. Under the CPA the girls continued their work unaffected by the change of regime. They had somehow obtained all the right papers to enter this impregnable American fortress. Ali went to the house, found its door invitingly open and located the bathroom. He saw that on the large mirror over the washbasins the Iraqi prostitutes had written in their lipstick anti-American and pro-Baathist slogans in Arabic which their new American clients were unable to read.

'The Iraqi criminals have been quicker to organize than the CPA,' said an international aid official long resident in the southern port city of Basra ten weeks after the fall of Saddam. 'It is rather like the rise of the Russian mafia after the collapse of the Soviet Union.' Three months earlier 100 giant statues, cast in copper, of Iraqi military heroes had stood on plinths on the quay in Basra. Their right arms were raised and their fingers pointed in a threatening gesture across the Shatt al-Arab waterway towards the Iranian border a few miles away. But this striking war memorial was too tempting a target for looters, eager to sell the copper. All were torn from their plinths and, with one exception, sold for scrap. The sole surviving statue was of

General Adnan Khairallah Tulfah, a cousin of Saddam Hussein and a former minister of defence, whom the Iraqi leader is widely believed to have murdered. It is a rare example of Iraqi looters showing discrimination in what they stole.

The failure of the US military to deal with the looters convinced many Iraqis that Washington did not care what happened to them. 'If they had shot a few of them at the beginning it would have stopped,' remarked one young Iraqi doctor. 'Instead I saw American soldiers standing by, taking photographs, cheering them on.' In the confusion surrounding the sudden fall of Baghdad the US military had some excuse for not restoring order; but as the weeks passed scruffy white pick-ups were still taking loot out to markets in Fallujah and Ramadi. Security was never truly restored over the next few years. The word 'looting' does not convey the extra atmosphere of fear created by the savage ransacking to which Iraqis were subjected for days on end. Dr Ayad al-Dahwi, a distinguished neurosurgeon in Baghdad, believed that the spontaneous ferocity of the looters, mostly from the working-class Shia suburb of Saddam City (soon to be renamed Sadr City) with a population of 1.5 million, was 'like a social revolution after thirty-five years of humiliation'. But not all the looting was spontaneous; sometimes it required chillingly careful preparation. The aid official to whom I had spoken in Basra pointed out that only nine large masts carrying electric cable had been destroyed during the war but no less than 120 had been stolen in the ten weeks after it was over. He said: 'It requires organization and special equipment to take down these masts. Looting has not ended. It has just become more professional.'

Systematic looting is an Iraqi tradition. Bedouin and Kurdish raiders had for centuries swooped down on towns and villages to steal what they could. In the First World War the British and Turks had both complained furiously about scavengers on the battlefield who stole weapons and slit the throats of the wounded, often while the fighting was still raging. The Iraqi army plundered Kuwait in 1990. During the uprising the next year all the museums in the south of the country were emptied by thieves. In the civil war in Kurdistan in 1996 some 5,000 cars were stolen in Arbil in a single day. But all previous incidents were dwarfed by the prolonged thievery after the fall of Saddam Hussein. Stolen cars were openly on sale in Saadoun Street in the centre of Baghdad from mid-afternoon onwards. The thieves expected transactions to be swift and to be in cash. Many cars were immediately driven to Iraqi Kurdistan and then, using unguarded smugglers' roads, across the border into Iran. One man spotted his own car, just stolen at gunpoint, on sale in Saadoun Street but said: 'I did not dare demand it back myself, of course, because I saw that the car thieves all had pistols hidden in their belts and there were no police I could ask to help me.'

Sometimes the destruction wrought by the looters seemed to have had no particular objective. I visited the Iraqi Natural History Museum in the Wazariyah district of Baghdad where the looters had even decapitated the gigantic model dinosaur in the forecourt. In the middle of one ground-floor gallery almost the only exhibit still intact was a stuffed white horse which, when living, belonged to Saddam. Wahad Adnan Mahmoud, a painter who also looked after the gallery, told me that the horse had been given to the Iraqi leader in 1986 by the King of Morocco. The King had sent a message along with it saying he hoped that Saddam would ride the horse through the streets of Baghdad when Iraq won its war with Iran. Before this could happen, however, a dog bit the horse, and it died. Saddam issued a Republican decree ordering the dog to be executed, which may have been his idea of a joke.

'I don't know why the looters didn't take the horse – they took everything else,' complained Mahmoud, who was sitting in the wreckage of his office at work on a painting of Baghdad in flames. 'It isn't even stuffed very well.' The horse, he added, was not the only dead animal which had been sent from Saddam's Republican Palace to be stuffed by the museum. One day an official from the palace arrived with a dead dolphin in the back of a truck. He said the leader wanted it stuffed. The museum staff protested that this was impossible because a dolphin's skin contained too much oil. Mahmoud laughed as he remembered the terrified expression on the official's face when told that Saddam's order could not be obeyed.

A week after I had been to look at Saddam's stuffed horse I had a shocking reminder of the insecurity of life in Baghdad. A young British freelance journalist called Richard Wild had gone like me to the Natural History Museum to get a story about its destruction by looters. He was a tall man with close-cropped blond hair and he was wearing a white shirt and khaki trousers. To an Iraqi he might have looked as if he was working for the CPA. As he stood in a crowd outside the museum near the headless dinosaur a man walked up behind him and shot him in the back of the head, killing him instantly.

Iraqis jokingly called those who had done well out of the collapse and occupation *hawasimi* or 'finalists'. This was a reference to Saddam's pre-war claim that Iraqis were about to witness 'a final battle with the Americans'. In a bid to curtail the rampant crime the CPA started to recruit policemen; these were known as *hawasimi*, said with a slight sneer. The word was especially used to describe those who were obviously better off following the looting.

There was a brief lightening of the atmosphere across Iraq as Baathist appointees disappeared or were removed. In Basra I attended by chance a meeting of the local branch of the Iraqi Red Crescent Society (IRCS), whose volunteers heroically braved the bombing to help victims of the war. They were voting to appoint a new local leader because his predecessor was too closely linked to the Baath party. 'The old leaders are not acceptable to the people,' said Dr Jamal al-Karboli, the head of the IRCS in Baghdad. There were other examples of local democracy. In the main neurological hospital in the capital

Dr al-Dahwi said: 'I have just been re-elected to run the hospital, though in fact I've already being doing it for thirteen years.' He added, gently, that he wondered if it had really been necessary for the hospital's chief matron also to run for election, but he appeared happy at the outcome.

I thought that a good place to look for optimists in Baghdad in the early days of the occupation would be among the booksellers of al-Mutanabi Street, the centre of the book trade in Baghdad. They would not exactly be *hawasimi*, the term carrying with it an implication of dirty dealing, but they had traditionally been a focus for intellectual dissent and had consequently been censored and persecuted. They should have benefited from the destruction of Saddam Hussein's ferocious security apparatus. I also had a more personal reason for talking to the booksellers. I knew that the history of Iraq after the First Gulf War written by my brother Andrew and myself, entitled *Out of the Ashes: The Resurrection of Saddam Hussein*, had been much disliked by the old regime. I learned later that a copperplate longhand translation into Arabic had been made of the book by the *mukhabarat*. A copy with a soft green binding had been found in the house of Sabawi, Saddam's half-brother who was once head of the al-Amn al-Amm, the General Security Service.

I had been visiting al-Mutanabi for years and always found it a relief from the oppressive atmosphere in the rest of the city. The street runs between the Tigris river and al-Rashid Street, now shabby and decayed but once the commercial heart of Baghdad. The bookshops are small and open all the time; on Fridays there is a market, when vendors lay out their books in Arabic and English on mats on the dusty and broken surface of the road, which is closed to traffic. Most books are second-hand. In the 1990s, after the First Gulf War, I used to walk around the district looking at books, often English classics once owned by students. Difficult words were underlined and translated into Arabic in the margin. There was plenty of stock as the Iraqi intelligentsia, progressively ruined by sanctions, sold off their libraries.

The market was carefully monitored by a section of the al-Amn al-Amm led by Major Jammal Askar, a poet who used to write poems in praise of Saddam. He oversaw the banning of books on modern Iraq, mostly histories and memoirs written by exiles, and works by Shia and Sunni clerics. Even so, books, often printed in Beirut, were smuggled in through Jordan, Syria and Turkey. 'You could bribe the officials at the border to let in religious books, but not political books,' one bookseller told me. 'We used to take off the covers and replace them with the jackets of Baath party books which they approved of.' Often only one copy was brought in, photocopied a hundred or more times and then sold covertly. The Amn al-Amm, its operations on the street led by a certain Captain Khalid, launched repeated raids to find out who was selling them.

It turned out that the booksellers in al-Mutanabi knew all about *Out of the Ashes*. It had sold well on the black market – mainly, they said, because 'it gave an account of the uprisings in 1991 and of the relationship between Saddam and the US'. One Friday, halfway along the street, I met Haidar Muhammad, a man in his mid-thirties with nervous, darting eyes, who had been the book's main seller. He was known in the street as Haidar Majala, meaning Haidar 'Magazine', because he pretended he was only interested in selling magazines. He said that he found life flat since the fall of Saddam, 'because in the old days, when I had to take a customer down an alleyway to secretly sell him a book and we both knew we could go to jail, life had a taste to it'. The first copy of *Out of the Ashes* he bought was an Arabic translation made in Beirut and smuggled into Iraq by a man called 'Fadhel', who other booksellers believed was later hanged. Haidar used a photocopier to make fifty copies and sold them to relatives and close friends for two dollars each. He then made another 200 copies and sold them quickly as well. He said: 'Once when a man who had bought the book was arrested in Kerbala I disappeared for three weeks, but he didn't give me away and told them that he'd bought it on the street from a man he didn't know.'

Haidar, who had been selling books in Baghdad and Najaf since 1994, was finally arrested in November 2000, when he was caught by Captain Khalid with a book by Saad al-Bazzaz, an Iraqi editor, once a Saddam loyalist, who had gone into exile and published an exposé of the regime. 'I pretended I was a little simple and did not know what the book was about,' Haidar said ruefully. 'The judge accepted that my story was true so he only gave me two years in prison, though this was extended to three years when they found out that I had deserted from the army.'

The booksellers in al-Mutanabi were relieved that, with the fall of Saddam, Major Askar and Captain Khalid had disappeared, but by the end of this first summer under occupation they were already wary of talking of the future. By now they were selling books by Shia clerics as well as big pictures of Hussein and Abbas, the Shia martyrs. When I asked a group of booksellers standing beside Haidar what they thought would happen, one said, without much confidence, that 'Saddam Hussein was difficult to overthrow, but the Americans will be easier to get rid of'. Iraqis were having difficulty adjusting to the sheer pace of events since the beginning of the year: the bombing of Baghdad, the end of Saddam, the looting, the broiling summer without electricity, the banditry and the first sporadic guerrilla attacks. New problems appeared almost daily. As I walked away from the book market a Kurd came up to us. He had just heard that the US had invited 10,000 Turkish troops into Iraq. 'I want to tell you that the Americans are going to betray us again just as they did in 1975 and 1991,' he said.

I visited al-Mutanabi market every few weeks during the summer and autumn. Works by Shia theologians still lay on the ground beside elderly volumes of Shakespeare and Dickens. Then one evening at the end of October I heard there had been a bomb explosion in the area. When I got there next morning I saw that several tall houses supported by white pillars on the corner of Mutanabi and Rashid Street had been burned out. Distraught booksellers, whose shops had been on the lower floors, were looking at the smouldering ruins. 'They are destroying our history,' shouted Dr Zaki Ghazi, waving his arms in anguish. 'I have lost everything,' said Munaf Fatah Mahmoud more quietly. 'I had two shops with books on Iraqi folklore and they were both burnt. I have sold books here for twenty years and how am I going to feed my children?' His voice was almost drowned by Dr Ghazi's lament over the damage: 'This area is at the heart of Iraqi history and the Iraqi people's struggles. First we lost the museums. Now they are letting Arabs into the country to do things like this.'

In fact, such was the level of violence in Baghdad that by now nobody knew the real cause of the explosion. The police said it was a time-bomb at first but changed their minds and thought it might have been an exploding gas cylinder. Local people were convinced it was a mortar bomb, though one resident suspected that, in one of the poor tenements in al-Rashid Street, somebody had been making a bomb, which had accidentally blown up. Bookselling continued in undamaged buildings, but al-Rashid Street was more and more under the control of violent criminal gangs. In the next few months it became too risky for me to visit al-Mutanabi.

VII

I N BERLIN IN 1945, six days before the fall of the city, the
Soviet army put a senior general in charge of getting essential
services going again. As fighting still raged in other parts of the city
he summoned to his headquarters the German officials already in
charge of, or capable of running, Berlin's electricity, water, sewers,
trams, underground railway, gas supply, factory owners and other
public figures. They were instructed to restore the civil life of the
German capital to normal as quickly as possible. Burgermeisters
were told to arrange work parties to clear the streets of rubble.
'They all received their appointments here in this office. Vice-
directors became directors, chiefs of regional enterprises became
magnates of national importance,' recorded Vasily Grossman, the
great Soviet war correspondent, who was impressed by the
military's speedy restoration of services.[11]

It was all very different when the US army entered Baghdad
fifty-eight years later. The scale of destruction in the Iraqi capital
was far less than in Berlin, ravaged as it was by bombing and street
fighting. There was no last stand by Saddam loyalists as had been
feared. But, as the weeks passed, Iraqis realized that the American
civil and military authorities were failing to restore essential
services or personal security. It was not what Iraqis expected.
In the 1991 war the US air attack had targeted electric power
stations, oil refineries, telecommunications centres and essential
bridges. In the following months Saddam Hussein's government

largely succeeded in getting them working again. In 2003, on the contrary, the US had deliberately avoided bombing the Iraqi infrastructure. But as the months passed after the war Iraqis found they were still getting less electricity, water and gas than under the old regime. They had assumed that under American occupation their living conditions would improve; instead they were worse. People in Baghdad soon began to vie with each other with bitter comments about the occupation. 'They can take our oil, but at least they should let us have electricity and water,' said Tha'ar Abdul Qader, a worker at the Central Teaching Hospital for Children, the main door of which I had only reached by walking gingerly through a fast-flowing stream of raw sewage. Astonishingly, three years later the performance of Iraq's oil, electricity, water and sewerage sectors was still below their pre-invasion levels by almost all measurements, US government witnesses told the US Senate Foreign Relations Committee.[12]

It was a failure of great political significance. Iraqis had refused to fight for Saddam because they wanted to live normal lives after enduring war and economic siege since 1980. By late 2003 they believed that there was no improvement in their living conditions because the Americans did not really care what happened to ordinary Iraqis. In late June 2004 Paul Bremer, the US viceroy, called a meeting of some sixty Iraqi political leaders, most of whom had formerly belonged to the opposition to Saddam Hussein. It was attended by, among others, Mahmoud Othman, the acerbic but well-informed Kurdish leader, who bluntly suggested that the American army pull out of Baghdad and other Iraqi cities to camps in the countryside. 'I told Bremer that Baghdad was a paralyzed city,' said Othman. 'He and his staff really don't know what it is like, because if they go out at all, it is in air-conditioned cars. But I've walked the streets, and I know what it is like. They are ill-informed and ill-advised.'

Cocooned in the Green Zone and frequently advised by Iraqi Americans who had often not been in Baghdad for decades, the CPA officials remained extraordinarily ignorant about what was happening on the other side of the heavily fortified gates. Only fifteen minutes' walk from Bremer's office on the other side of the Tigris in an alleyway off Rashid Street I met a poor shop-keeper called Shamsedin Mansour. He painted a frightening picture of how he and his neighbours lived. 'We have had no electricity for six days,' he said. 'Many of our people are suffering from heart problems because of the heat. We live with as many as forty-two people in a house and do not have the money to buy even a small generator. Without light at night it is easy for gangs of thieves with guns to take over the streets, and shooting keeps us awake. If we try to protect ourselves with guns, the Americans arrest us.' It was at about this time that I decided that it was not really worth spending time talking to people, however highly placed, living and working in the Green Zone. To visit them was time-consuming, given the number of checkpoints to be nego-tiated, possibly dangerous and often ended up with me telling them what was happening a few streets away. One day I had gone to visit a pleasant and previously well-informed non-American diplomat. He claimed that, going by figures he had just received, the gasoline shortage had at last been sorted out. I pointed out mildly that I was a little late for our appointment because there were enormous traffic jams throughout Baghdad caused by long lines of vehicles, sometimes several miles long, queuing for gasoline.

The failure to get the electricity power supply up to the inadequate level provided by Saddam Hussein became a symbol for Iraqis of the general failure of the occupation. Iraq in summer is one of the hottest places on earth. With the temperature regularly over a scorching 45°C (113°F) electricity is essential. Without it there can be no air-conditioning, no refrigerators to prevent food rotting and no light in a city terrified by looters. Houses turn into furnaces. Aside from the Kurdish mountains in the north Iraq is very flat and electricity is necessary to pump water and sewage. One day people in al-Thawra, the vast sprawling Shia slum in east Baghdad that is home to two million people, decided they could no longer endure the lack of electric power. They unearthed hidden rifles and threatened to kill the manager of the local electrical substation if he did not restore power supplies. He was a harassed-looking man called Bassim Arman who looked nervously up and down the street as he explained to me a few hours later what had happened. 'Some had guns and others threw stones at us, but I told them this was just a substation and we aren't receiving any electricity,' he said. 'Now I have to close down anyway, because employees are too frightened to come to work.'

Why were US civil and military officials incapable of restoring public services in Baghdad, as the Soviet Army had largely succeeded in doing in Berlin in 1945? One reason was that the US administrative apparatus was more incompetent, bureaucratic, corrupt and divided than most Iraqis imagined. Its inability to respond swiftly and effectively to a crisis was demonstrated in New Orleans in 2005 when the levees broke in the aftermath of Hurricane Katrina. The failure of Washington to identify problems and remedy them was as bad as in Baghdad two years earlier, but with far less excuse since this time the disaster was within the US. Iraqis did not see it that way. They had an exaggerated idea of the power of the US, which few of them had visited, based largely on movies seen on television or on videos. Iraqi friends would endlessly ask: 'If the Americans can get a man to the moon surely they can get some generators to Iraq.' Later the insurgents were to make concerted attacks on the electrical pylons, but at this stage the problem was that the CPA simply did not know what to do.

The US occupation authorities suffered from a further disadvantage. Washington had always understated the devastating damage to the Iraqi economy by UN sanctions after they were imposed in 1990. Some of the problems were starkly stated by Denis Halliday, the UN humanitarian coordinator for Iraq, before he resigned in despair in 1998. He stated that, even if the money was available, Iraq's electrical system was beyond repair: 'We have generators that are twenty years old. When we go to the manufacturers [we find] they don't make the spare parts anymore.' His office estimated that $10 billion was needed to restore Iraq's electrical supply system, though only $300 million was available at the time. At the time US policymakers, particularly those on the far right, contended that sanctions had hurt ordinary Iraqis because of the corrupt machinations of Saddam and his lieutenants. Committed to this view, Washington was badly positioned to explain that it had inherited in Iraq a barely floating economic wreck. Its own experts estimated that $70–$100 billion was needed for reconstruction over several years.[13]

The American officials arriving in Baghdad in the summer of 2003 knew little of this background. Ignorant of the growing hatred of the occupation and the beginning of armed resistance they did not see that they had no time to waste. Iraqi engineers had kept ageing equipment going by patching it up and cannibalizing other plant. The American advisers wanted to junk old plans drawn up under the old regime, draw up new ones and then buy entirely new plant, usually from American companies. This was very time-consuming. It also opened the door wide to corruption since the CPA had few financial controls and much more money could be made contracting for wholly new electric power units than patching up old ones.

During the First Gulf War in 1991 I had visited Dohra power station in south Baghdad several times. One of its four tall chimneys which dominate the skyline had been toppled by a bomb. A strange fibre dropped by US planes on to the electric cables had short-circuited them. Nevertheless the station was soon working again, the rebuilt chimney painted in the Iraqi colours. I tried to go back after the 2003 war. I had permission from the electricity ministry but was turned back by a polite American officer at the gate who said I must get a further permit from his commanding officer at a nearby base. I drove there but al-Dohra, a largely Sunni district, was an early centre of the insurgency. Waiting at the entrance to a US base seemed highly risky so I went instead to the home of an Iraqi electrical engineer who worked in the power station. He was not optimistic. He said the Americans were insisting on renegotiating all contracts with German and Italian companies which had supplied the original turbines. He himself had just invested in a small generator able to power the lights and television in his house but not air-conditioning or the fridge.

Baghdad was a city paralyzed by fear. I would ask people what they thought of Paul Bremer's claim that Saddam's supporters were being hunted down and life was returning to normal. Sitting outside his office in Saadoun Street in the centre of Baghdad – the electricity had failed and he said it was too hot to sit inside – Abdul Wahab al-Hashimi, a businessman, laughed contemptuously at Bremer's claim. He said: 'My company owns a lot of property in Baghdad but we haven't collected any rents because we have nowhere to put the money and we would be immediately robbed if we kept it in the office.' As looting ebbed away criminals in Baghdad discovered that they could make more money from kidnapping than theft. At first they did not target foreigners, fearing that this might lead to serious American retaliation. Since I was not threatened personally I was slow to realize the importance of this new form of crime. In time it was to drive much of the Iraqi middle class to flee abroad. 'In my college parents are mostly keeping their daughters at home because they are terrified of them being kidnapped,' said Adel Hameed Raheem, a teacher of English literature in Basra. As always in Iraq, as if reality was not bad enough, there were wild and terrifying rumours. Kuwaitis or gangs paid by Iraqis were rumoured to be searching for young girls to force them to work in brothels in Kuwait. Some forty of them were said to have been discovered by chance and set free in a house in the al-Mansur district, though nobody knew what street it was in. There was a school near the al-Hamra Hotel where I was living and I noticed that parents would become frantic, thinking their children had been kidnapped, if they could not immediately see them when they came to pick them up in the afternoon.

Nothing brought home the dire state of Iraq so much as the comical efforts by the American officials in Baghdad to prove to the world that life was returning to normal. One day they announced the reopening of the Iraqi National Museum, one of the five greatest museums in the world. On display was the fabulous 3,000-year-old golden treasure of Nimrud, grave goods from Assyrian royal tombs which it was believed had been lost or stolen. This was an effort by the CPA to counteract the bad publicity following the US military's failure to prevent the ransacking of the museum by looters after April 9. As propaganda stunts go it was not very successful. The treasure on display came from Nimrud, the ancient Assyrian capital outside Mosul, where it had been discovered by the Iraqi archaeologist Muzahim Mahmoud Hussein between 1988 and 1992. In the graves of the Assyrian queens and princes he found gold necklaces, bracelets, bowls and a magnificent gold head-dress. These treasures had then disappeared. Hussein was distraught at not knowing what had happened to them. There were rumours that Uday, Saddam's playboy elder son, had given them to his girlfriends or had sold them abroad. It turned out, after the invasion, that they were safe in the vaults of the Central Bank, and were found unharmed in a case, though they had been covered in sewage when pipes broke.

Two halls of the Iraqi National Museum were especially opened for the display. US soldiers had slept in the same room as the exhibits in case the looters might return to see if there was anything further for them to steal. I had last visited the museum in 1978 because soon afterwards it was closed because of wars or threat of wars. 'Now listen up folks,' shouted an American to the assembled media at the gate of the museum. 'Anyone caught wandering about the rest of the museum will be arrested, taken to the airport and shipped out.' At this point there was a six-minute-long burst of machine-gun fire from the other side of the museum. At first we thought this was looters, fighting over their booty at the nearby al-Alawi intersection, as had happened before. This turned out to be wrong. It was a measure of the chaos in Baghdad in the summer of 2003 that the shooting turned out to be the result of two quite separate incidents. The first was a funeral: as is normal in Iraq people were firing their guns into the air as a sign of grief. The American troops on the roof of the museum thought they were under attack and shot back. But most of the gunfire was in response to somebody firing a rocket-propelled grenade into an American Humvee in nearby Haifa Street, wounding several soldiers. The surviving soldiers then opened fire indiscriminately and killed a passing driver. As the Americans withdrew, the crowd, dancing in jubilation, set fire to the already-smouldering Humvee.

In the days after the capture of Baghdad the world was absorbed by the drama of Saddam Hussein's fall. The US and British governments trumpeted the ease of their victory. Critics of the war lamented the mass looting and destruction. Few noticed an unexpected event taking place in central and southern Iraq or foresaw its immense significance to the country over the next few years.

In late April vast numbers of Shia Arabs – between one and two million people by most estimates – were taking to the roads on foot or travelling in decrepit cars, pick-ups and buses to the holy city of Kerbala, sixty-five miles south-west of Baghdad. They waved green and black banners triumphantly as they went. Some beat drums or ceremonially lashed themselves with chains or flails. Those walking from Baghdad took about five days to reach Kerbala. The pilgrims were going there to take part in the mourning ceremonies of Arbain, forty days after the anniversary of the death of Imam Hussein, the grandson of the Prophet Muhammad, killed in the battle of Kerbala 1,400 years earlier. It was here in AD 680, betrayed and surrounded by their enemies, that Imam Hussein and his warrior brother Abbas made their last heroic stand. They were buried in two shrines, adorned with rich mosaics and golden domes, which became a place of pilgrimage. The events of this last battle, with its story of betrayal, suffering, endurance, martyrdom and redemption, play the same role in Shia religious belief as the Crucifixion in Christianity. Ashura, the day of the martyrdom of Hussein and Abbas and Arbain, forty days later, were the great Shia festivals of commemoration and lamentation. Saddam Hussein had banned most open displays of Shia piety up to 1998 when, in a brief attempt to reach out to Iraq's largest community, he allowed such festivals to be celebrated discreetly within Shia cities. But Arbain at the end of April 2003, only a few days after Saddam's overthrow, was the first time the celebrations could take place without fear of brutal retribution from the security services. The fact that over one million people took part showed that the Shia community's sense of identity had grown under Saddam and its religious leaders could mobilize immense numbers of the faithful. It took time for the US, Sunni Arabs and Kurds to take on board that a political earthquake was taking place in Iraq's largest community.

The Shia had played an important role both openly and covertly in the opposition to Saddam Hussein. Their religious leaders – particularly the clerical families of al-Sadr, al-Khoie and al-Hakim – had poured out their blood over the decades. No other religious faith in the world in the late twentieth century had provided so many martyrs to the torturer and the executioner as the Iraqi Shia. The myths of endurance, courage and martyrdom commemorated during Ashura and Arbain were given fresh substance by equally bloody persecution under Saddam Hussein. Muhammad Bakr al-Sadr, the spiritual leader of the Dawa party, was executed along with his sister and numerous Shia militants in 1980. Other Shia religious figures did not endorse armed opposition but Saddam Hussein knew that they fervently hoped for his fall. In the aftermath of the Shia uprising in 1991 Grand Ayatollah Abolqaem al-Khoie had been summoned to Baghdad and 102 of his students, including one of his sons, disappeared. Real or suspected insurgent fighters captured as the uprising was crushed were driven into the desert and slaughtered. Fifteen years later their skulls and bones were still being dug up in mass graves across southern Iraq. Grand Ayatollah al-Khoie, who always rejected an openly political role, was held under virtual house arrest in Kufa until he died in 1992.

Political power was not wholly divided along sectarian lines under Saddam Hussein, whose Baathist ideology was fiercely nationalistic. There were some Shia in the senior ranks of the Baath party and among the ruling elite. But under the Ottomans, the British and the post-independence regimes it was the Sunni who were in control. Not that the whole Sunni community benefited. After the military coup in 1963 when President Abd al-Karim Qassim was killed it was the provincial Sunni, strong in the army's officer corps, which took charge. Out of 500 Iraqi military generals in the late 1990s less than fifty were Shia.[14] In the coming years under Saddam secular Shia leaders like Iyad Allawi or Ahmed Chalabi were unable to build up an underground opposition in the face of savage persecution by the Iraqi security forces. It was the religious leaders who had the prestige and the following to take their place.

Friction between Shia and Sunni in Iraq had increased during the Iran–Iraq war. It was the Iranian revolution and the rise of Ayatollah Khomeini, for so long exiled in Najaf, which inspired long-established groups like Dawa or produced new ones such as the Supreme Council for Islamic Revolution in Iraq (SCIRI), founded in Tehran in 1982 under the leadership of Ayatollah Muhammad Baqr al-Hakim. He was the second son of Grand Ayatollah Muhsin al-Hakim, one of the most respected of the Shia clergy. In the 1990s, weakened by defeat in war and by sanctions, Saddam alternately persecuted or tried to co-opt members of the Shia clergy. After I met Grand Ayatollah al-Khoie in the wake of the uprising in 1991 I was constantly in touch with the al-Khoie Foundation in London, a charitable Shia institution which I thought was the best source of accurate information about what was happening in Iraq. In 1994, the head of the Foundation in Iraq, Muhammad Taqi al-Khoie, was killed near Najaf in a mysterious car accident which his relatives believed, probably rightly, was arranged by the regime. I became friends with his successor and younger brother Sayid Majid al-Khoie. Born in 1962, he had fled to London during the great Shia uprising in 1991 when, after driving through the desert in search of the advancing allied army, he had made the horrifying discovery that the US was going to allow the rebellion to be crushed. I found him a liberal, intelligent and modest man of great ability. The activities of the Foundation were cultural, educational and low-key, but it proved highly effective in animating opposition to Saddam.

Inside Iraq the regime was eager to co-opt or divide the Shia clergy. From 1998 they were allowed to carry out their religious ceremonies in Shia cities so long as these were kept within bounds. It gave some leeway to Ayatollah Muhammad Sadeq al-Sadr, the nephew of the Ayatollah executed in 1980. The aim was to try to drive a wedge between the Shia leaders in Iraq and those in exile. Saddam also wanted to emphasize the differences between clergy who were Iranian by birth like al-Khoie or Ali al-Sistani, al-Khoie's former student and effectively his successor, and those that were Iraqi Arabs like the al-Sadrs. The regime hoped Muhammad Sadeq al-Sadr would be a counterweight to the existing Shia religious establishment. He was free to criticize Iran, sanctions and even aspects of the current regime but not Saddam Hussein himself. From the point of view of the Iraqi leader this strategy was always playing with fire. Thousands of pious and enthusiastic followers attended al-Sadr's sermons. He wrapped himself in white martyr's robes as a man expecting death. It was a grim if sensible precaution. In February 1999 I got a telephone call from the al-Khoie Foundation. A voice said that Muhammad Sadeq al-Sadr and two of his sons had been killed. On a Friday evening the Ayatollah had left evening prayers in Najaf with his sons but as their car approached a nearby roundabout it was ambushed by gunmen. Caught in crossfire, all the men in the vehicle were killed. Few doubted that the assassins were Saddam's security forces. As news spread of his murder there were riots across southern Iraq and in Saddam City in Baghdad, all of which were ruthlessly suppressed.

Iraqi opponents of Saddam Hussein were inclined to under-estimate the extent to which their country was divided by deep sectarian or ethnic fault lines. They would point out that Iraqi tribes often included both Shia and Sunni. There was frequent intermarriage between Shia and Sunni. Communities were not monolithic, as in the case of Roman Catholics and Protestants in Northern Ireland or Christians and Muslims in Lebanon. But the secular intelligentsia which had fled abroad in the 1970s did not appreciate the degree to which the Iraq had changed since their departure. The secular middle class which stayed in Iraq, often employed by the government, had been progressively destroyed by the effect of war and sanctions. It was a lesson which Paul Bremer, the CPA and its successors took a long time to learn. The sort of educated middle class, yearning for an American or Western European standard and style of living, which was important in Moscow after the fall of Communism, scarcely existed in post-Saddam Baghdad.

There was a further compelling motive among the opposition in downplaying religious sectarianism in Iraq. The Shia leaders knew that a reason why the US-led coalition had not over-thrown Saddam Hussein in 1991 was the fear that he would be replaced by a Shia regime allied to Iran. American soldiers entering Iraq had been appalled to discover numerous posters of Ayatollah Khomeini pasted on to walls by the anti-Saddam rebels. In fact the posters were of Grand Ayatollah al-Khoie, but to US officers one elderly Shia clergyman with a white beard and a turban looked much like another. After the crushing of the uprising of 1991 opponents of Saddam by and large came to realize that the only certain way to get rid of the regime in Baghdad was for the US to launch a second war against it – and this time go all the way to Baghdad. The Americans were not likely to do so if they knew the main beneficiary of Saddam's overthrow was going to be the Shia allies of the Iranian regime. A number of arguments, none of them untrue but often over-stressed, were made to pacify Washington's fears. It was emphasized that the Shia clergy were theologically more quietist than in Iran and they opposed direct clerical rule. The Iraqi infantry which fought Iran to a stalemate in the 1980s was mainly Shia, though the officers were predominantly Sunni. This proved the Shia were not stooges of Iran. There was a traditional hostility between Najaf, for a thousand years the centre of Shia learning, and the Iranian holy city of Qom, which only became a theological rival to the Iraqi city in the 1920s. The result of such special pleading was that the US did not understand in 2003 the extent to which Iraq – and this was true of both Shia and Sunni – was a highly religious country. An Iraqi friend said to me: 'Iranians are a secular people with a religious leadership while Iraqis are a religious people with a secular leadership.' He exaggerated a little in order to produce a neat epigram, but he was largely correct. All the while Washington remained curiously under-informed about internal Iraqi politics. In the last years of the Clinton administration some of his senior Middle East advisers attended a meeting in Kuwait, the purpose of which was to ratchet up pressure on Saddam Hussein. 'What about taking advantage of the riots and disturbances following the assassination of Muhammad Sadeq al-Sadr,' asked one Kuwaiti. The Iraqi dissidents present were astonished when the Americans at the meeting looked surprised and admitted that they had never heard of al-Sadr or the popular unrest – the most significant in Iraq since the uprising in 1991 – following his death.

Exaggerating the influence of secular Iraqi leaders and under-estimating that of the religious leaders was to be a recurrent theme of the US occupation. When it supposedly handed over sovereignty in June 2004 Washington backed Iyad Allawi, the former Baathist and leader of the Iraqi National Accord, as interim prime minister. It was only after Allawi and Ahmed Chalabi did so badly in the election on December 15 2005 (Chalabi did not win a single seat) that the US seems to have appreciated the weakness of the secular anti-Saddam leadership which it had cultivated for so long.

It was not exactly traditional religion that triumphed in Iraq after the fall of Saddam Hussein, but religious nationalism. Muqtada al-Sadr, the son of the murdered Muhammad Sadiq al-Sadr, was able to build a powerful movement by combining religion, Iraqi nationalism and populism. The posters pasted on walls in cities, towns and villages where the Sadrists were in control showed him and his martyred relatives, all in their black clerical gowns, against an Iraqi flag in the background. Sunni guerrilla groups, shadowy though they were, similarly combined religion and nationalism. In Iraq Saddam had discredited secular nationalism through his disastrous rule. The failure of this set of beliefs was not unique to Iraq but had happened across the post-colonial world. Nationalist regimes which had replaced the imperial powers in the 1950s and 1960s had shown themselves to be incompetent and corrupt. Their governments, supported by brutal security services, were rackets rather than administrations. In the Arab world armies were unable to fight the Israelis or anybody else. In Palestine Yasser Arafat's Fatah, essentially a secular nationalist movement, was notoriously crooked and militarily inadequate. The only Arab group which proved capable of fighting the Israeli army was Hezbollah, its militants drawn from the Lebanese Shia community. Its success was interesting because its Islamic nationalist ideology and guerrilla tactics were very similar to those which were about to be used so effectively by the Sunni armed resistance against the American army now occupying Iraq.

I had heard when I was in Kurdistan during the war that Sayid Majid, as al-Khoie was usually called, had returned to Najaf as soon as the Iraqi army withdrew. I did not think much more about it except to reflect that he had been quick off the mark to return to Iraq. As he was the son of a revered Grand Ayatollah I assumed he was in no particular danger so long as Saddam's partisans had all fled. Then, on the evening of April 10, just after I had returned from Kirkuk following its storming by the Kurds, I was told that Sayid Majid was dead, shot and hacked to death by fellow Shia in a melee in Najaf. He had died within sight of the great shrine of Imam Ali, the son-in-law of the Prophet murdered in 661, whose golden dome rises above the closely packed streets. Al-Khoie was the first of many friends I was to see die in Iraq over the next three years.

I wondered how and why al-Khoie had been killed, and as soon as I left Iraq I started looking for those who were with him when he died and had escaped with their lives. I talked to three survivors in London in early May. There were still confused accounts of what had happened. It was reported that al-Khoie had not been the real target, but he had died because he was accompanying Haidar Rufaie al-Killidar, the hereditary custodian of the Imam Ali shrine, who was hated by many in Najaf as a collaborator with Saddam's regime. The men I interviewed had a different explanation. They believed that al-Khoie's death was a carefully planned assassination and suspected that Muqtada al-Sadr, fearing al-Khoie's influence in Najaf, had orchestrated the attack, a claim al-Sadr denied.

Al-Khoie had flown back to Iraq with a small group of supporters on a US plane on April 1, landing in Nasiriyah, a dusty city on the Euphrates recently devastated by heavy fighting. The road north to Najaf was deemed unsafe and al-Khoie was taken in a US helicopter, but on his arrival he refused further American protection. 'People in Najaf were amazed to see him,' said Ma'ad Fayad, an Iraqi journalist and friend of al-Khoie who was with him. 'Some abandoned their cars in the middle of the street so they could greet him.' But there was an undercurrent of tension. Fayad overheard people asking each other in low voices: 'Who is this coming from London?' Most

Iraqis regarded returning exiles with suspicion, convinced that they automatically wanted to be become leaders in Iraq after living in luxury hotels in exile, supported by foreign intelligence services. Abdul Mohsin al-Kafaji – a former colonel in the Iraqi army who joined the Shia uprising and later became a close aide to al-Khoie – admitted that at first people were nervous at seeing them, particularly as Baghdad had not yet fallen. 'They were frightened that Saddam might come back and said, "Maybe the same thing will happen as in 1991." But day by day the number of people coming to the shrine with us increased.' Al-Khoie told people not to resist the Americans and distributed $350,000 to the poor of Najaf.

On the morning of April 10, al-Khoie took a dangerous step as part of his campaign to reconcile different factions in Najaf. He went to the house of Haidar al-Rufaie al-Killidar and asked him to come with him to the shrine. Haidar was not popular in Najaf, where his family had for centuries been the hereditary custodians of the shrine of Imam Ali, the son-in-law of the Prophet Muhammad, murdered in 661 and venerated by Shias. To be custodian of the shrine was not an easy job. Radwan Hussein al-Rufaie, a cousin of Haidar, said: 'I turned it down because I was against the regime and my brother took over, but he disappeared in 1991, accused of plotting against the regime. Haidar on the other hand was seen as completely affiliated with the government. He appeared on television talking with Saddam Hussein and was a member of the Iraqi parliament.' Haidar had very sensibly not been to his office since the war began. But, looking nervous, he agreed to return there.

Al-Khoie and the group of clerics and supporters with him arrived at the shrine at about 8.45 a.m. A friendly crowd greeted them as they passed through the great gates of the shrine complex, walked across a stone-paved courtyard and prayed by the shrine itself. They then went to sit in al-Killidar's smart-looking office. The last photograph of al-Khoie still alive shows him sitting there. He is smiling gently but confidently at his companions.

Outside in the courtyard of the shrine an hour passed before there were the first signs of hostility. A crowd gathered and there were shouts of 'Long life to al-Sadr' and 'Give us Haidar or we will kill you.' At first al-Khoie tried to calm the crowd, which by now numbered about 400, but the microphone he was trying to use did not work. One man lunged at him with a knife as he stood at the door of the custodian's office and he jumped back. Al-Kafaji says the first shot was fired into the air by Maher al-Naseri, a cleric from Detroit, where there is a large Iraqi community, and a companion of al-Khoie who had travelled with him to Iraq. 'He became frightened and fired a shot. Many in the crowd ran away, but only to get their own guns.' There were two Kalashnikovs and two pistols in Haidar's office. Both sides began to shoot. In the exchange of fire al-Naseri was mortally wounded. Al-Khoie took off his turban and held it to his chest, shouting: 'Don't shoot! This young man is dying! He is a Shia! He is a Muslim!'

The shooting went on for ninety minutes. Ma'ad Fayan, who fired a pistol at somebody trying to get through the door, recalls: 'Somebody threw a grenade. I heard Sayid Majid [al-Khoie] call out: "I am hurt."' One of his fingers had been blown off and another was dangling by a piece of skin. Fayad tried to staunch the bleeding with a towel. The siege ended when al-Khoie's group ran out of ammunition and one man went outside with a white shirt and a Koran to surrender. Some of the crowd entered the office and tied the hands of those inside behind their backs. Shaikh Salah Bilal, one of those captured, says he was told by one of the men: 'We are taking you to Muqtada al-Sadr for him to pass sentence.' The prisoners were then taken out of the office. Ma'ad Fayan recalls: 'The first thing I saw was swords and knives flashing in the sun. I thought, "Oh my God, that's it."' Within minutes he saw Haidar al-Rufaie stabbed to death and al-Khoie repeatedly stabbed. Muqtada's house was a few hundred yards away from the shrine. Al-Khoie slumped by his door. 'Most of his body was bleeding and he lay down on one side,' says Shaikh

Salah. 'I put his head on my leg.' After some minutes, he says, a message came from al-Sadr: 'Don't let them sit in front of my door.' They took refuge in a shop which sold sewing machines where their hands were untied. The owner of the shop tried to save them by telling the crowd outside that al-Khoie was dead. It did not work; after some minutes he was dragged out of the shop and shot dead at the end of the street. According to one source al-Khoie's body was dragged behind a car before it was returned to his relatives for burial. The savagery of his own death matched al-Khoie's worst expectations about divisions between Iraqis. Saddam Hussein might fall, but the killings in the shadow of the Imam Ali shrine showed that hatreds between Iraqis were so deep that the bloodshed might only be beginning.

VIII

A SMEAR OF DARK blood on the dusty pavement marked the spot where an American soldier had been killed by a bullet in the neck and another wounded in the arm. Gunmen had shot the soldiers as they stood guard at Mahdia gas station not far from the al-Dohra power station with its four tall chimneys in south Baghdad. A crowd of a dozen Iraqi men, some of whom had seen the shooting, were peering at the rusty-brown bloodstains, already baked hard by the heat of the midsummer sun, and talking about what had happened. Without exception they all said they approved of the attack. 'We think they deserved it,' said a man called Muhammad Abbas with quiet earnestness. 'We admire the bravery of those who attacked them.' Another bystander, who refused to give his name, pointed to the American helicopters swooping and diving above our heads, commenting: 'Nobody cares when an Iraqi civilian is killed but as soon as an American dies there are lots of American helicopters flying about.' A third man added, to nods of approval from the rest of the crowd, that his family was very poor but 'We will celebrate by cooking a chicken. God willing there will be more actions like this.' Al-Dohra is a large, mostly Sunni Arab district in south Baghdad which was to become a centre for the insurgents over the next three years. It is easily accessible across thickly populated agricultural land to militant nationalist and Islamic fundamentalist or Salafi villages further to the south. By the end of June 2003, when the shooting at Mahdia gas station took place, we were still some way from the widespread guerrilla war which developed over the coming year. So far there had only been sporadic attacks by gunmen armed with automatic rifles and rocket-propelled grenade-launchers. Some forty US soldiers had been killed since President Bush had declared combat operations to be at an end on May 1 six weeks earlier. Other points should have been worrying to the White House and the Pentagon. The US was not in control of much of the country, though this might not have been obvious to US military commanders isolated in their headquarters at the airport or to the CPA in the old Republican Palace in the Green Zone. Tough Jordanian drivers, who had happily driven across the desert from Amman to Baghdad during the war, were now saying the road was too dangerous to travel. There were 55,000 American troops in and around Baghdad but they seemed curiously vulnerable and out of touch with the city. They largely stuck to their vehicles; there were few foot patrols. They established check-points and searched cars, but usually had no interpreters. 'Mou mushkila – no problem,' said one driver in front of me when asked to open the boot of his car. 'Don't contradict me,' a soldier yelled back.

US military vehicles were often stuck in enormous traffic jams (because of the electricity shortage the traffic lights were not working), making them an easy target for grenades. For a few weeks American soldiers could be seen eating in Iraqi restaurants. It did not last long. Soldiers discovered they could not relax even for a moment. Across the road from my hotel was Baghdad University. One day a soldier joined a queue there to buy a soft drink. An Iraqi man came up to him and said 'Hello mister', drew a pistol from his pocket and fired. There were shouts of 'Allahu Akbar' (God is Great) from a crowd of students as the badly injured soldier was driven away from the university campus. He died later in hospital. These were still pinprick attacks but whenever I talked to Iraqis standing near the scene of an incident they always said they approved of what had happened. I had spent enough time covering guerrilla wars in Northern Ireland, Lebanon and Chechnya to sense that, with this level of public approval and the vacuum of authority throughout Iraq, the anti-American armed resistance would find it easy to grow rapidly.

US counter-insurgency operations outside Baghdad in the villages and towns along the Tigris and Euphrates were visibly counter-productive. There was massive overuse of firepower. Military tactics had not changed since Vietnam, with success calculated by the number of supposed insurgents killed, weapons captured and suspects taken away with bags over their heads. One group of so-called guerrillas shot dead at night north of Baghdad turned out to be farmers who had run into their fields to extinguish fires caused by American flares. The operations themselves had macho names like 'Desert Scorpion' or 'Peninsula Strike'. The latter operation, the largest since the end of the war, took place in mid-June. Some 4,000 American troops moved in and occupied a string of prosperous fruit-growing villages along the Tigris near Balad, a town with a population of 20,000 people, sixty miles north of the capital. When I arrived from Baghdad people in the village of Dhuluaya were already mourning their dead. The prominent men in the village clustered round me to explain what had happened.

'I suppose it was a successful operation from the American point of view,' said Salah al-Jaburi bitterly as he pointed to two bloodstained quilts on which two men had died when American soldiers had tried to arrest them in the middle of the night. The quilts were on display beside a big tent, invariably erected in Iraq by a bereaved family so they can receive mourners, which was packed with angry villagers. Mawlud al-Jaburi, who was arrested along with 450 other people, said he was mystified why Dhuluaya had been singled out. 'We were pleased when Saddam fell,' he insisted. 'We have not fired a single bullet at the Americans.' He added that all the villagers were members of the Jubur tribe, one of the largest in Iraq, which was out of favour with Saddam

Hussein for the last twelve years because officers from the tribe had been involved in plots against him. 'Before I was afraid of Saddam,' said Muhammad, an elderly farmer too frightened to give his family name. 'Now I am afraid of the Americans.'

I believed some but not all of this. A US spokesman said that twenty-seven Iraqis had been killed. By the American account they had suddenly emerged from thickets of reeds on an isolated country road and fired rocket-propelled grenades at a tank. The Americans counter-attacked with Bradley Fighting Vehicles and Apache helicopters. No American soldiers were killed or wounded. Possibly local people, who like almost everybody else in Iraq were armed, had opened fire at the Americans invading their villages. The disparity in casualty figures suggested that the Iraqi attackers, if there were any, were angry local farmers and not guerrillas with military training. The latter, from an early stage, learned not to expose themselves to American firepower but to fight back with IEDs directed at supply columns, snipers shooting at sentries and sudden mortar barrages against bases.

There was no doubt in my mind that Operation Peninsula Strike was doing a lot more good to the insurgents than the Americans. One of the three men dead in Dhuluaya was Hashim Alawi, a fisherman who thought some men on a boat in the Tigris were thieves trying to steal his boat, moored by the side of the river. He fired his hunting rifle in their direction. In fact he was shooting at a boatload of American soldiers, who shot back and killed him. There was other evidence of indiscriminate use of force. Outside Dhuluaya a driver called Muhammad Rassim al-Jawari took us to a blue-painted Russian jeep in which the front seat was still covered with dried blood. His cousin had died when a soldier fired thirty bullets through the bonnet and windscreen of the vehicle. One explanation for the American aggression was that their commanders saw the possession of arms as a sign of hostility to the occupation. But in the wake of the mass looting Iraqis were even more likely to be carrying a weapon than previously. Mawlud al-Juburi said: 'They didn't find any heavy weapons. Most of what they took away was AK-47 machine guns, which we need to protect ourselves. I always carry one when I go into my fields at night.'

Why were the US operations so maladroit? Their military commanders seemed to take seriously the political line from Washington that the insurgents were a finite number of Saddam loyalists and foreign fighters. On June 22, a week after Operation Peninsula Strike ended, President Bush said in his weekly radio address, 'dangerous pockets of the old regime remain loyal to it and they, along with their terrorist allies, are behind the deadly attacks.' Four days earlier Donald Rumsfeld, the US Defence Secretary, had stated, 'In those regions where pockets of dead-enders are trying to constitute, General [Tommy] Franks [the commander in Iraq] and his team are rooting them out. In short, the coalition is making good progress.' If what Bush and Rumsfeld said was true then it would follow that once the remnants of the old regime, a finite number of fighters, were eliminated then Iraq would become peaceful. It was always an absurd thesis. The lack of resistance to the US invasion in March and April had demonstrated how few Iraqis, even among his closest allies, were loyal to Saddam Hussein and his regime. If they would not support him when he was in power surely they would not back him after his humiliating flight from Baghdad. The military incompetence of Saddam, who always had a touch of Gilbert and Sullivan about him when it came to making war, had been repeatedly demonstrated.

Paul Bremer did not win a reputation in Iraq for being a man who learned from his mistakes but it is nonetheless bizarre to find him still claiming in 2006 that a top-secret memo from the *mukhabarat*, dated January 2003, had established the armed resistance. Bremer writes excitedly in his memoir that the memo was the 'Rosetta Stone of the insurgency' because it recommends such obvious tactics as forming cells, sabotage, sniper attacks and ambushes.[15] In reality few insurgent groups ever called for the return of Saddam Hussein and some demanded he be put on trial.

There was never any evidence that he or his family played any role in organizing the insurgency. His sons Uday and Qusay had difficulty in even finding a hiding place for themselves in the months before they were betrayed and shot dead by US soldiers in Mosul on July 22. Bremer was to triumphantly announce the capture of Saddam Hussein on December 14 as if he believed it would be a body blow to the insurgency. But the capture or killing of Saddam and his senior lieutenants, the fifty-five former regime stalwarts pictured on the Pentagon's 'pack of cards', did no visible damage to the insurgents. It may, on the contrary, have strengthened them as, with Saddam out of the way, they could no longer be accused of seeking to restore the old regime. It had always been unpopular. A teacher in Basra, discounting the influence of Iraqis still supporting Saddam, put it succinctly, telling me, 'even at the height of his power only two million out of twenty-four million Iraqis ever supported him'. But over a year was to pass before the US military realized that they were not engaged in a mopping-up operation but were fighting a new war.

Even Iraqis who wanted to get along with the US occupation were having difficulties. The Americans for their part did not find it easy to understand the complex web of loyalties tugging at Iraqis. I visited al-Awja village in Tikrit province, notorious in Iraq as the birthplace of Saddam Hussein, which turned out to be a grim and menacing place just off the main road. There were few people around but I had a feeling of being continually watched. The roads were in better repair than in the rest of Iraq but the houses were not particularly luxurious. On the wall of the gatehouse to Saddam's local palace, its pretty blue mosaic and strange ceramic palm trees smashed by bombs, somebody had written: 'It is your house Saddam and it will always flourish and we will guard it forever.' Despite this the palace had been thoroughly ransacked.

But al-Awja was not a stronghold of pro-Saddam loyalists. Many of its 1,000 people drew no benefit from coming from the village where Saddam had been born in 1937. I went to the house of Sheikh Ahmad Ghazi, the leader of the Albu Nasir tribe to which Saddam belonged. He was a well-educated engineer speaking excellent English who at first said he did not want to talk to a journalist, but gradually thawed and spoke volubly about his troubles. He said it was not easy to explain to Americans or even to Iraqis that some of his tribe flourished but others were persecuted under Saddam. He said: 'He killed my own brother in 1995.' Nevertheless the first American soldiers to land in al-Awja on April 12 had assumed that the village would be filled with his supporters. Sheikh Ahmad took me to a long low house in an orchard below the hill on which al-Awja stands. Here his father and predecessor as leader of the Albu Nasir, Ghazi Ahmad al-Khatab, was shot dead as he opened the door to the soldiers in the middle of the night. There were blood marks on the floor where he fell. The Americans found a large sum of money in 100 dollar bills in the house. Sheikh Ahmad explained: 'The Americans regarded this as suspicious but Iraqis usually keep large sums of money at home, sometimes literally under the bed, because in 1991 Saddam closed the banks before the war. When they reopened their money was almost worthless.' He and his three brothers were arrested though later released with apologies.

Occasionally Sheikh Ahmad's gloomy eyes sparkled with brief amusement as he recalled his efforts to explain Iraqi politics and tribal life to a succession of local American commanders. 'They seem to get most of their ideas of the Arab world from Hollywood,' he lamented. 'We have also had three different commanders here in the last six weeks so I have to start all over again with each one. They don't seem to talk to each other. Since they don't pass anything on I've stopped talking to them.' Another reason for not talking to the Americans was that somebody, disapproving of Sheikh Ahmad's contacts with the occupiers, had thrown a grenade into the forecourt of his house. He was visibly shaken by the attack and his anxiety showed itself in the way he talked at high speed. I suspected the sheikh was reflecting, as were many Iraqis by this time, that he might have fatally miscalculated the risks of talking to the Americans in the first weeks of the occupation.

US officials in Washington and Baghdad paid little attention to the first signs that the ground was beginning to quake under their feet. They were oblivious to the simple fact that Iraqis objected to foreigners running their country. I had a friend in the CPA who would regale me, shaking his head in disbelief, with the latest lunatic schemes of his superiors. One day, early on in the occupation, he took part in a conference call with Donald Rumsfeld in which they discussed how to run the war-ravaged Iraqi capital. Rumsfeld came up with the novel suggestion that Rudy Giuliani, the stoic mayor of New York at the time of the destruction of the World Trade Center, be made the new mayor of Baghdad. The friend was aghast at the idea, pointing out that few Iraqis had ever heard of Giuliani and many of them had probably cheered when the Twin Towers went down. Even so it took forty-eight hours for the proposal to die. My friend told me wryly that 'Ever afterwards the neo-cons among the US officials in Baghdad regarded me with suspicion as a hostile element.'

American blindness to Iraqi nationalism, the hostility of the occupied to the occupier, was why the US was caught by surprise when a new guerrilla war started in June and July 2003. Its onset was not inevitable. Few people supported Saddam Hussein. Fewer still had fought for him. Opinion polls just after his overthrow showed that half of Iraqis thought they had been liberated. Two months later the majority of Iraqis outside Kurdistan had come to believe that the US had occupied their country to establish imperial rule, just as Britain had done in 1917 when General Sir Stanley Maude, the British commander, declared his only interest was to liberate Iraqis from the evil rule of the Turks. The disbandment of the Iraqi armed forces put a lot of angry and well-trained soldiers on the streets. It also showed that Washington envisaged in future a weak Iraqi state with a small army devoted to internal security. Whatever President Bush might say in public about wanting an independent and democratic Iraqi state, his actions suggested that in future Iraq would be a US protectorate. Ordinary Iraqis, cynical about the motives of all their rulers, foreign as well as domestic, were quick to see that the Americans were not going away. The only mistake made by Iraqis was to exaggerate the extent to which Washington had a coherent long-term policy.

All the ingredients leading to an insurrection against the US occupation were present in those first crucial months of the invasion. I had witnessed the palpable hatred of the US army in Baghdad and Sunni areas of central Iraq. Even so the guerrilla war developed at surprising speed. After the British captured Baghdad in 1917 it was still three years before the Shia tribes of the mid-Euphrates rose in rebellion. Iraq is a mosaic of communities with differing interests, but during the first disastrous year of the occupation the US showed a genius for offending everybody simultaneously. Even the Kurds, America's one reliable ally in the country, were outraged to discover that the Pentagon was hoping to bring in 10,000 Turkish troops to police western Iraq.

The successful US invasion was turning into a political catastrophe so swiftly because the occupation lacked legitimacy in the eyes of Iraqis and the world. Investigative teams failed to find the Weapons of Mass Destruction which had been America's and Britain's justification for going to war. The only way Washington could have overthrown Saddam Hussein and avoided a backlash against occupation would have been to hand over ultimate control of the country to the UN as quickly as possible. But this was never feasible because a purpose of the war, in the eyes of the American right, both nationalist and neo-conservative, was to show that the US was the sole superpower, and did not need the UN or any other allies. Writing in between the Boer War and the First World War in 1908, an astute senior official at the British Foreign Office called Sir Eyre Crowe wrote: 'Political and strategic preparations must go hand in hand. Failure of such harmony must lead either to military disaster or political retreat.'[16] But the Washington of President Bush saw no need for such harmony and was slow to perceive the necessity for a political retreat.

America's political position in the first crucial year of the occupation of Iraq was surprisingly fragile. Its military and political leaders only truly began to grasp the risks they were running during the twin Sunni and Shia uprisings of April 2004. Bush's ability to manoeuvre was limited and weakened by past boastfulness. He had notoriously told the world on May 1 2003 that the war was won. Over the next three years he could never quite explain why it was still going on. He had to give reasons to Americans why their soldiers were still dying. This made life easy for the guerrillas; they did not have to kill or wound that many US troops to do serious political damage to the administration.

It was the run-up to the 2004 presidential election. In its bid to convince American voters that all was well in Iraq the White House produced a picture of the country so distorted that it was close to fantasy. It heavily publicized a series of spurious 'turning points' in Iraq which were uncritically highlighted by a compliant American media as important steps forward. Though the post-9/11 hysteria had ebbed, US television and newspapers were still fearful of being accused of lack of patriotism.

Over the coming years the list of 'turning points' was to become ludicrously long. Saddam's sons Uday and Qusay were killed by US soldiers in Mosul in July 2003. Saddam himself was dragged from a hole in the ground on the other side of the Tigris from al-Awja in December. His chief lieutenants, shown on the famous pack of cards, were almost all in jail. Fallujah was lost in April 2004 and recaptured in a bloody assault by the Marines in November. There were regular reports by US military briefers of the capture or killing of senior aides of Abu Musab al-Zarqawi, later the head of al-Qaeda in Iraq, in 2004 and 2005. He had replaced Saddam in US demonology and all resistance to the occupation was attributed to him. Politically, Washington gave heavy publicity to shifts towards democracy while in private it only grudgingly ceded real power to Iraqis. A 25-member Iraqi Governing Council was established by the US on July 13 2003 but had little real influence. Sovereignty was handed over to an interim Iraqi government in June 2004; control of security, however, stayed in US hands. The parliamentary elections in January and December 2005 and the referendum in October were significant, but their importance was systematically over-played by Washington. For all its efforts the US never recovered from the mistakes it made in the first year of the occupation. Despite military victory it had too few friends inside and outside Iraq.

The rest of the world began to see the extent of the US failure long before it became conventional wisdom in Washington. A friend representing a French company in the US capital had gone with some trepidation to Paris in the autumn of 2003 bearing the unwelcome news that he had been told privately by the Pentagon that there was absolutely no chance of his employers getting a contract in Iraq. He was not looking forward to reporting total failure of his well-paid efforts, but to his relief the chairman of the company greeted his dire news with prolonged laughter, saying: 'Don't worry. Let's just wait a year or two and then it will be American companies that won't be able to do business with Iraqis.' In fact, the gloating Frenchman's prediction of a timeframe during which US businessmen could operate freely in Iraq turned out to be over-generous. In less than a year they were taking their lives in their hands if they moved outside the Green Zone.

As armed resistance to occupation escalated in central and northern Iraq in the coming years, the British forces in the south slyly implied that they were more skilled than the Amer-icans in guerrilla war. They claimed that they were able to avoid errors made by the US because of their hard-won experience fighting the IRA in Northern Ireland for a quarter of a century. There was something in this but not a lot. The British army was more careful in its use of firepower than the US. But like the Americans the British underestimated the hostility felt towards them by Shia as well as Sunni. Early on in the occupation, on June 24 2003, they had learned a bloody lesson about the limits of their authority when six Royal Military Policemen were hunted down and killed in a ramshackle town called al-Majar al-Kabir, eighteen miles from the city of al-Amara.

The place where this little battle took place is dangerous even by Iraqi standards. Al-Majar al-Kabir is on the edge of the Iraqi marshlands. Guerrillas had harried Saddam Hussein's army for decades from hideouts in and around the town and later, after their enemy drained the marshes, from holes dug in the ground. The marshlands were also the home of bandits preying on the traffic travelling on the main Basra–Baghdad highway. The Iranian border is close by and smuggling was a major local business. Some of the items smuggled were unique to the area. Pious Iranians who died in Iran often asked their relatives or arranged before their death to be buried in the great Shia cemetery in Najaf. For a fee people in al-Majar al-Kabir would secretly transport the bodies of the dead Iranians across the border and take them to the holy city for burial. All these illegal or semi-legal activities required people in the town to be heavily armed. It was not a good place for the British Army to start a search for weapons. 'Most people there [al-Majar al-Kabir] objected to the search operation because it's against the tribal principle of own-ing a gun,' explained Ali al-Atiyah, a guerrilla leader who had fought for years from a lair in the marches. 'They are used for tribal celebrations, funerals, fighting other tribes, protecting their cows and sheep and, most important, for fighting Saddam.'

We met al-Atiyah after driving the 210 miles from Baghdad to Amara on hearing the first reports that the Royal Military Policemen had been killed. I hoped to see the one man, Qarim Mahoud al-Muhammadawi, also known as Abu Hatem, whom I hoped would know how and why the British soldiers had died in al-Majar al-Kabir. A legendary guerrilla leader, also nicknamed

'the lord of the marshes', Abu Hatem, a former non-commis-
sioned officer in the Iraqi army, had fought government forces
from the marshlands for twenty years. He had even captured
Amara on April 7, the only Iraqi Arab city to be liberated by the
local resistance. He was immediately ordered out by the CIA in
Kuwait with the implied threat that if he did not retreat, his
forces would be bombed from the air. Abu Hatem had just gone
to Baghdad believing that he had defused friction between local
people and the British army, which had started patrolling the area
and searching for weapons. He had left Ali al-Atiyah and other
guerrilla commanders in his headquarters in a nondescript villa
on the bank of the Tigris. They explained how the agreement
had broken down.

Several days before the killings there had been confrontations
with British soldiers at a village near al-Majar al-Kabir called Abu
Alla. They were accused of bringing dogs into houses and
defiling places used for praying. They had entered the women's
quarters. But it was the hunt for weapons to which the local
leaders most objected. They did not see why, since they had
resisted Saddam Hussein for years, and had refused to give up
their arms, the British now had the right to take them away.
They could think of only one explanation. Al-Sayyid Kadum al-
Hashimi, a leader in al-Majar al-Kabir who I met later, said: 'It is
the belief of people here, and it is believed by all other Iraqis, that
the British want to disarm us so they can stay for a long time.'

If the British Army had really learned any lessons in Northern
Ireland about not provoking local communities they had been
forgotten somewhere between Belfast and Amara. The army,
aside from a breakdown in communications between its different
units, had also clearly underestimated the dangers surrounding
them. I was shown an agreement in Arabic and English according
to which military patrols were to cease and the British Army was
not to enter the town except in an emergency. Weapons such as
heavy machine guns, mortars, anti-aircraft guns, rocket-propelled grenade-launchers, grenades and weapons requiring more

than one person to use them were declared banned. Local leaders blithely confirmed that they had such a powerful arsenal in their possession, which appeared to them to be entirely normal. The agreement, at the bottom of which were scrawled the signatures of a British officer and tribal leaders, had a very short life. The day after it was signed a unit of British paratroopers arrived in the town. 'They wanted to make a foot patrol,' said al-Atiyah. They were told 'It is unsafe for you to walk in the city, it is against the agreement. Maybe many problems will follow.' The advice was unheeded. The patrol started down a street in the town. Soon children were throwing stones. The crucial moment came when a British soldier went into a firing position pointing his gun at a child. Atiyah said: 'A local man called Taissir Abdul Wahad thought the soldier was going to shoot and pointed his own gun and was shot dead by the soldiers. After the death of Taissir nobody could control their anger.'

After the first shots were fired local people ran to get their guns. But it was the unfortunate six Royal Military Policemen, visiting the local police station at the time and unaware of what was happening, who were the targets for their vengeance rather than the paratroopers. They were killed in the street or shot dead as they ran out of ammunition inside the station. Two dozen Iraqi policemen fled through a back window. It had been a grimy depressing-looking building to start with and after the fighting it was pock-marked with bullet holes and the floors covered with broken glass and blood. I visited it with one of Abu Hatem's men called Maythem al-Muhammadawi sitting in the car to vouch for us and act as a bodyguard. He was a sharp-faced fierce-looking man who cradled his sub-machine gun in his lap and spoke of his days as a guerrilla against Saddam. Even with his protection our stay at the gutted police station did not last long. It was still surrounded by a crowd, many of them carrying weapons. Maythem seemed more and more edgy and suddenly exclaimed: 'It looks dangerous. Let's get out of here. We can't control the situation because our people are very angry.' As we drove back to

Amara he became more confiding. He said he thought the real reason for the British and Americans to disarm the people was that they intended to remain in Iraq for a considerable time. 'We are just waiting for our religious leaders to issue a fatwa against the occupation and then we will fight the occupation. If we give up our weapons how can we fight them?'

Back in Amara Abu Hatem had just got back from Baghdad. He was a tall, impassive-looking 45-year-old in a brown camel-hair cloak and a white headdress. Unlike most Iraqi leaders he was self-confident enough not to travel with a large entourage of bodyguards though Amara, at this moment, was fully under his control. Unlike any other city in central or southern Iraq there was no curfew, people walked or drove cars on the streets at night and it was possible to eat kebabs sitting in an open-air restaurant on the bank of the Tigris. When I asked Abu Hatem if he had, as everybody in Amara believed, an army of 8,000 men he pointed to the Koran and biro on the table in front of him and said: 'I just have this book and this pen.' He explained how he had tried to broker an agreement between local leaders in al-Majar al-Kabir and the British army and when this was broken the killings had taken place. Told by the leaders that they feared a long foreign occupation, he said they should wait and see if the British and the Americans made good on their promises of democracy. He added that if there was, as they believed, a prolonged occupation, he would join them in fighting it. He asked for their support and they swore he would have it.

The bloody skirmish in al-Majar al-Kabir was important because it showed the weakness and vulnerability of the British position in southern Iraq. It was a tough and violent town but Iraq is full of such places. British officials tried to portray what had happened as an unfortunate and atypical incident in which both sides were at fault. But the real message was much grimmer. The Shia Arabs would not accept long-term occupation any more than the Sunni. They were cynical and suspicious of the motives of their American and British liberators, but for the moment their leaders had a temporary interest in not opposing the occupation so long as elections, which they were bound to win, took place. The British were more restrained in their patrolling and searches in southern Iraq after al-Majar al-Kabir. Over the coming years they tried to gain a measure of control over the militias, like Abu Hatem's men, by making them part of the local security forces. This was a short-term palliative. It meant that the British were permanently under threat from the very police they were trying to train.

Over the next two years the British military had ever-diminishing control in Basra and neighbouring provinces. By 2006 local governors and provincial councils had broken off relations with them after a video of British soldiers beating up rioters in Amara was shown on television. Iraqi policemen were even suspected of detonating the very mines that killed British soldiers. After clashes between the British and local security men the latter were often referred to in British media as 'rogue policemen' while in fact they were entirely typical. Local British commanders were very conscious of the thinness of the political ice on which they and their men were standing. When two British soldiers disguised as Iraqis were captured and imprisoned in a Basra police station in September 2005 their officers remembered what had happened in just such a police station in al-Majar al-Kabir more than two years earlier. They sent in armoured vehicles to smash down the station walls and rescue the soldiers. In the wake of the incident army press officers made comical and counter-productive efforts to prove to the British media that there were pro-British as well as hostile police stations in Basra. On one occasion journalists and accompanying British officers were ordered out of a police headquarters at gunpoint. On another a pro-British police commander agreed to meet the journalists in a deserted warehouse but he pleaded with them not to reveal to other police officers that he was meeting with the British.

IX

ENORMOUS CONCRETE BLOCKS like giant grey tombstones became the physical symbol of the new Iraq. Placed together to form long blast walls, they were designed primarily to stop suicide bombers or at least to limit the damage when they blew themselves up. Soon these ugly prefabricated walls were being erected everywhere in Iraq, protecting American checkpoints, police stations and government buildings. The concrete blocks came in different sizes, though all were gigantic, named by the manufacturers after American states such as Arkansas and Wisconsin. A Kurdish businessman running a factory outside Arbil told me that he had made 150,000 of them working from specifications given to him by the US military. I first saw them when they became part of the elaborate fortifications defending Saddam Hussein's old Republican Palace, where Bremer and the CPA lived and worked in the Green Zone. It was soon surrounded by serried ranks of these tombstones on which were written in red paint warnings to drivers forbidding them to stop beside the new walls. The few entrances to the zone were protected by tanks and rolls of razor wire. New notices went up on the banks of the Tigris saying it was forbidden to swim in the river outside the Palace, presumably for fear of underwater saboteurs. Saddam's security men had had the same paranoid thought and had also banned swimming before the invasion. The period during which Iraqis were allowed to swim in the Tigris after the occupation, if they were not deterred by the raw sewage dumped in it, had lasted just six months. Faced by the threat of being bombed, the British Embassy had abandoned its spacious enclave and fled, first inside the Rashid Hotel and later to modest but safe accommodation elsewhere in the Green Zone. At first I was contemptuous at the speed with which the British diplomats had retreated but the next months showed they had every reason to feel frightened.

The bombing campaign began in August 2003. There was an attack on the Jordanian embassy, which was followed by a horribly effective destruction of the UN headquarters on Canal Street in east Baghdad on August 19. I had gone there a few weeks earlier seeking information because the UN provided far more honest figures than the US about the amount of electricity and clean water available to Iraqis. Sergio de Mello, the UN special representative, died in the ruins, crushed to death by the concrete debris. On August 29 a suicide bomber in a vehicle detonated a powerful bomb outside the Imam Ali shrine in Najaf – on the other side of which my friend Sayid Majid al-Khoie had been murdered five months earlier – killing Muhammad Baqr al-Hakim, the head of SCIRI, and 125 of his followers as they left the building after attending prayers. It was the first sign that the suicide bombers were prepared to wage holy war with the same savagery against Shia Iraqis as they were willing to fight the Americans. The Shia were also much easier to kill since the victims were often unemployed young men queuing unprotected and in the open for jobs in the army or police, or simply waiting for work as day labourers.

It soon became clear that nobody, whether they were an Iraqi or a foreigner, was safe. At 8.30 a.m, on October 29, the first day of Ramadan, a stolen ambulance packed with explosives drove up to the Baghdad headquarters of the International Committee of the Red Cross, where the driver detonated a bomb killing at least ten people, two of them security guards, along with eight labourers in a passing truck. I was to witness the same devastation many times in the coming years. The gruesome scene was almost always the same. There would be a sinister crater in the road where the vehicle, in this case the stolen ambulance filled with old artillery and mortar shells, had exploded. In front of the ICRC the crater was half full of dirty water and workmen with a mechanical excavator were digging at the bottom of it trying to repair a smashed water main. The explosion had decapitated several palm trees, their trunks burned black by the heat of the blast. The ICRC building itself had survived because of the low wall of sandbags in front of it, but its interior was gutted and its white painted walls were scarred and cracked. This was the day on which the suicide bombers first showed that they could carry out several operations at the same time. Minutes after the ICRC attack the sound of more explosions had reverberated across Baghdad. Suicide bombers had attacked three police stations, killing at least thirty and injuring 220 people in the worst day of violence since the overthrow of Saddam Hussein. A fourth bomber failed to detonate his bomb outside a fourth police car and was dragged from his car screaming: 'Death to the Iraqi police! You're all collaborators!' He was later identified as a Syrian.

Who were the suicide bombers? The suicide bomb is hardly a new tactic in the Middle East. It is horribly effective because, unlike conventional guerrilla warfare, it does not require military experience or training to carry out. All that is needed is a volunteer willing to kill himself – and of these there was no shortage. I had seen the remains of the US Marine barracks in Beirut in 1983, reduced by a suicide bomber in a truck to a pulverized heap of concrete in which 242 Marines were entombed. Some months later I saw a patrol of Israeli soldiers in south Lebanon hurl themselves to the ground as an old man driving a donkey with a pack on its back, which they wrongly feared might contain explosives, trotted past them. When I lived in Jerusalem between 1995 and 1999 there were frequent suicide bombings by Palestinians with explosives and shrapnel strapped to their bodies who had boarded buses on the Jaffa Road just behind my apartment. But the suicide bombings in Iraq were on a different and ever more lethal scale. On some days in Baghdad in 2004 and 2005 there would be ten or more on a single day. The weight of explosives used was much greater than anything I had seen in Jerusalem. A legacy of Saddam Hussein's long wars is that Iraq is filled with old ordnance: military explosives and artillery shells can be easily obtained. The second of two suicide bombers who blew up the room in the Hamra Hotel where I was living in November 2005 – fortunately for me I was not there at the time – had an estimated 1,000 kilos of explosives in his vehicle.

The suicide bombers were usually non-Iraqis, with the majority coming from Saudi Arabia and others from Jordan, Syria or Egypt. They were motivated by Islamic fundamentalism and hatred of the occupation. It was the invasion of Iraq which radicalized them. An investigation into 300 young Saudis, caught and interrogated by Saudi intelligence on their way to Iraq to fight or blow themselves up, showed that very few had any contact with al-Qaeda or any radical organization prior to 2003. Some thirty-six Saudis who did blow themselves up did so for the same reasons, according to the same study commissioned by the Saudi government and carried out by a US-trained Saudi researcher, Nawaf Obaid, who was given permission to speak to Saudi intelligence officers. A separate Israeli study of 154 foreign fighters in Iraq, carried out by the Global Research in International Affairs Centre in Israel, also concluded that almost all had been radicalized by Iraq alone.

The suicide bombers were Salafi, intent on returning the Muslim world to the pure Islam of the seventh century AD, by means of a jihad against all the enemies of their narrow version of Islam. They took their vision of restoring this mythical past quite literally. Their propaganda videos showed 'insurgents in traditional Salafi dress code, particular pants known as Sarawil that had virtually disappeared in Iraq. Foreign jihadis most likely at first played an inspirational role among other insurgents, posing as early Muslim warriors, duplicating their garb and religious practice.'[17] These extreme Islamic groups, typified by that led by Abu Musab al-Zarqawi, until he was killed on 7 June 2006, saw themselves as fighting a world full of 'infidels', 'apostates' and 'crusaders' in which an Iraqi Shia or Christian was as deserving of death as a US soldier. When American troops allegedly damaged two mosques in Mosul in 2004, insurgents promptly blew up two Iraqi Christian churches in retaliation.

The importance of the foreign fighters was systematically exaggerated by the Americans to downplay the indigenous resistance. Iraqis themselves were often eager to believe that the men carrying out atrocities were all non-Iraqi Arabs from outside their community. In reality most of the Salafi, including those butchering helpless Shia workmen, were Iraqis. Despite their propaganda claims the US military confessed to holding very few foreign prisoners. Nor would foreign fighters, who unlike so many Iraqi men had no military training, have been much use in conventional warfare. The only role in which they could be truly effective was to die in suicide attacks. But even to do this they needed local help. The bomber himself might be from any country but the infrastructure he needed – the transport inside Iraq, safe-houses, intelligence, vehicles, explosives and detonators – could only be provided by Iraqis. Nor could a non-Iraqi Arab be anything except highly visible in a country in which a person from a neighbouring town is regarded with suspicion. The great bulk of members of the resistance were Iraqi, almost all Sunni Arabs, combining Salafism and patriotism, often belonging to different groups but united against the occupation.

The role of Abu Musab al-Zarqawi was elusive because both the Americans and his supporters portrayed him as being at the cutting edge of the resistance. The White House and the Pentagon pretended, and may even have believed, that armed resistance was largely inspired from abroad, and was only the

Iraqi branch office of al-Qaeda and international terrorism. This view conveniently enabled them to rebut the charge that by invading Iraq and overthrowing Saddam Hussein, who had no demonstrable links with al-Qaeda, the US administration had let Osama bin Laden off the hook. The primacy given to Zarqawi, a Jordanian, was self-fulfilling since many Iraqis and Arabs gravitated to anybody proclaimed as being at the heart of the anti-American resistance. Zarqawi himself was an obscure figure until Colin Powell, the Secretary of State, denounced him before the UN Security Council in his notorious justification of the coming war in February 2003. Ironically, parts of the Iraqi resistance may also have wanted to exaggerate Zarqawi's importance by ascribing to him attacks in which large numbers of civilians were slaughtered and for which they did not want to take responsibility. Zarqawi became part of the US military spokesmen's demonology after the Powell speech, but it was only after the capture of Saddam Hussein, removing another useful demon, that American officials promoted him to being their arch-enemy in Iraq.

I never got used to the suicide bombing. Everybody was vulnerable all of the time. I was edgy walking into the Green Zone to meet CPA officials or Iraqis who were members of the Governing Council and later the Interim Government. The suicide bombers were not the sole danger. There was also the very serious risk of being accidentally shot by a nervous American soldier, Iraqi policeman or some politician's bodyguards. One day when I was crossing the road to reach the entrance to the Green Zone an old man in a battered red car stopped near me. He looked confused and either he had lost his way or his engine had stalled. But the Iraqis on guard were not waiting to find out what he was doing and opened fire immediately, spraying bullets just over my head as I scampered for cover. The Hamra Hotel looked like a military strongpoint from World War Two, as more armed guards and blast walls were added to its defences. One guard who looked underneath cars searching for bombs with a mirror on a stick in one hand took to carrying a pistol in his other hand. He said that if he saw a bomb, he reckoned he had about one second to shoot the driver in the head before he detonated his bomb. In Baghdad people lived in permanent fear of sudden death. Any stranger seen loitering or taking photographs was suspected of preparing the ground for a suicide attack. In Saddoun Street in central Baghdad a newly arrived French camera crew was caught in a traffic jam caused by the massive concrete walls protecting the Baghdad Hotel. It was conventional wisdom among Iraqis, with what truth I never knew, that the hotel was a CIA headquarters. One of this French team idly picked up his camera and started taking still photographs to pass the time. Instantly Iraqi guards dashed forward, guns at the ready, and dragged the Frenchmen out of their car. It took two days for the French embassy to get them released from a prison in the Green Zone. Previously I had often taken photographs as I moved around Baghdad but on hearing the story I decided it would be best to leave my camera at home.

From the point of view of the men who dispatched the bombers on their missions of death the suicide bombing campaign was highly effective. It created an atmosphere of permanent crisis and terror in Baghdad. Iraqis might detest the insurgents for slaughtering ordinary people, but they also blamed the Americans and their Iraqi allies for failing to restore normal life. The US military became ever more isolated. Notices appeared on the back of their Humvees warning that anybody approaching within 100 metres risked being shot. They did not explain how anybody could stay at a safe distance in a city like Baghdad where fortifications and the increased number of cars had produced a permanent traffic jam. There was a lengthening list of Iraqis that I knew who had been shot by nervous or trigger-happy American soldiers. I had interviewed a police general who was the deputy head of the Serious Crime Squad about kidnapping. He was helpful and well-informed. The next I heard of the general he was in hospital with a serious bullet wound in the head, shot by an American soldier who deemed the movements of his car suspicious. It was not only Iraqis who died. One day there was fighting around Abu Ghraib prison. A brave and experienced Reuters cameraman called Mazen Dana, a Palestinian and an old friend of mine from Hebron on the West Bank, was shot dead by American soldiers who thought his camera was a gun.

Isolated inside their headquarters, American and British officials were unable to see how fast their position in Sunni Arab districts was unravelling. These were critical months for the occupation. 'The people have decided that the disasters they suffer under the Americans are worse than those suffered under Saddam Hussein,' a sheikh living in a house overlooking the Tigris near al-Awja told me. He pointed to a small pit in the concrete courtyard of his house where a grenade had exploded, thrown by somebody who thought him too close to the Americans. The area he lived in, the heartland of Sunni Muslim Iraq, was not typical of Iraq. It was from these Sunni towns and villages along the central Tigris and Euphrates that Saddam Hussein had recruited his security men. These people, who had not fought the Americans in March and April 2003, were staging guerrilla attacks by October.

The only way to find out what was happening across Iraq was to get in a car and go there. Dramatic and important events went unreported. One day I went to Baiji, an oil refinery town with a population of 60,000, some 145 miles north of Baghdad, where I was told there had been an uprising. I was sceptical, suspecting the account was exaggerated, but in the main street of the town a crowd of thousands was holding up pictures of Saddam Hussein and chanting: 'With our blood and our spirit we shall die for you Saddam.' The previous morning, the local Iraqi police had fired at demonstrators who were demanding the dismissal of the US-appointed police chief, wounding four of them. More protestors gathered and burned down the mayor's office. The police – 300 of them – fled to a nearby US base, where American officers told them to go back or be sacked. The police refused, saying they would be killed if they did so. The US military command had been trying to leave these confrontations with protestors to the Iraqi police to deal with, but finally their tanks moved gingerly back into Baiji, most areas of which remained in the hands of the protestors. Soon there were pinprick guerrilla attacks on US troops with home-made mortars, mines, bombs and Kalashnikovs.

The reasons behind the brief uprising in Baiji were common to all the Iraqi provinces immediately north of Baghdad. There was anger over the loss of jobs in the army, security forces and civil service. 'Half the teachers in the schools have been dismissed because they were Baathists and there is no one to teach our children,' one man complained. Prices had risen because cheap Iraqi kerosene and bottled gas were being smuggled into Iran and Turkey. Protestors had set fire to two Turkish road tankers in the main street. Above all there was day-to-day friction with the occupation forces. 'My nephew Qusai went on to the roof to fix the TV antenna and the US soldiers shot him dead,' Faidh Hamid told me. A US patrol had beaten an elderly man half to death with their rifle butts because they thought a mortar had been fired from the window of his house – a Swedish journalist embedded with the US patrol had watched in horror as the beating took place. A 75-year-old merchant was trying to recover $16,000 in Iraqi dinars and $4,500 in gold taken from his house in May during a US raid. He showed me an elaborate petition he had sent to Baghdad: an official had scribbled a curt note along the bottom saying the money was being permanently confiscated because a Fedayeen had been found in his house, something the merchant stoutly denied.

I did not take the pro-Saddam slogans too seriously, but there was no doubt about the simmering hatred for the occupiers. This was not just confined to Sunni villagers. Hussein Kubba, a Shia businessman in Baghdad, said to me acidly: 'They claimed that we are smart enough to build weapons of mass destruction capable of threatening the world, but they treat us like Red Indians on a reservation at the end of the nineteenth century.'

At times it seemed as if the American military was determined to provoke an uprising. One day I went back to Dhuluaya, the fruit-growing village fifty miles north of Baghdad that I had visited a few months earlier. After our car left the main highway we drove down a narrow road on the left of which we saw the remains of orchards, which looked as if they had been destroyed by a peculiarly destructive storm. The stumps of date palm, some of which going by their size must have been over seventy years old, protruded from the brown earth. Local women were busy bundling together the branches of the uprooted orange and lemon trees and carrying them back to their homes for firewood. We stopped to talk to a group of farmers standing disconsolately beside the road. They said that US soldiers driving bulldozers and with jazz blaring from loudspeakers had destroyed the orchards as part of a new policy of collective punishment of farmers who did not give information about guerrillas attacking US troops. When I looked more closely I could see where the bulldozer blades had scraped away the brown coloured topsoil. Nusayef Jassim, one of the farmers who saw their fruit trees destroyed, said: 'They told us that the resistance fighters hide on our farms, but this is not true. They didn't capture anything. They didn't find any weapons.'

Other farmers standing nearby said that the US troops had told them, over a loudspeaker in Arabic, that the fruit groves were being bulldozed to punish the farmers for not informing on the resistance. 'They made a sort of joke against us by playing jazz music while they were cutting down the trees,' said one man. Sheikh Hussein Ali Saleh al-Jabouri, a local leader, had gone as part of a delegation to the nearby American base to ask for compensation for the loss of the fruit trees. They got nothing. The delegation was told by an officer that trees and palms were being destroyed as 'punishment of local people because "you know who is in the resistance and you do not tell us".' What the Israelis had done by way of collective punishment of Palestinians was now happening in Iraq, concluded Sheikh Hussein. The farmers said that fifty families had lost their livelihoods, but a petition addressed to the coalition forces in Dhuluaya pleading in broken English for compensation had only thirty-two names on it. It read: 'Tens of poor families depend completely on earning their life on these orchards and now they become very poor and have nothing and waiting for hunger and death' (sic). The children of one woman who owned some trees lay down in front of a bulldozer but were dragged away. An American soldier was said to have broken down and cried during the operation. I tried to find independent confirmation about the destruction of the orchards. It turned out that it had been witnessed by a badly frightened local journalist working as a stringer for a small paper in Baghdad. He had attempted to take a photograph of the bulldozers at work but a soldier had grabbed his camera and tried to smash it. His paper quoted a Lieutenant-Colonel Springman, the US commander in the region, as saying: 'We asked the farmers several times to stop the attacks, or to tell us who was responsible, but the farmers didn't tell us.' Nor was it ever likely that they would. The farmers who had lost their fruit trees all belonged to the Khazraji tribe and were not going to inform about fellow tribesmen even if they were, in fact, attacking US troops. I asked Nusayef Jassim how he felt about the loss of his date palms and fruit trees and he replied in a voice of anguish: 'It is as if somebody cut off my hands and you asked me how much my hands were worth.'

There were growing signs that skilled guerrilla fighters with good intelligence were at work. Paul Wolfowitz, the US deputy defence secretary, visited US soldiers and Iraqis who had joined the defence forces in Tikrit. He praised the latter enthusiastically, saying 'These young Iraqis are stepping forward to fight for their country along with us. It is a wonderful success story.' Wolfowitz also met with local notables, treating them, to their total bemusement, so an informant later told me, to a talk in which he expounded on the merits of the nineteenth-century French political scientist Alexis de Tocqueville. The next morning Wolfowitz had a dramatic illustration of the limits of US success in Iraq. At 6.10 a.m. he was dressing in his room in the al-Rashid in Baghdad when the hotel was struck by a barrage of rockets which killed an American colonel and wounded fifteen others. Officials fled the hotel in pyjamas and underpants and Wolfowitz himself stumbled out of the building down a smoke-filled staircase. I was impressed by the technical expertise and accurate intelligence behind the attack. Twenty rockets, each three feet long, had been placed in a home-made launcher disguised as an electric generator on a trailer. At about 6 a.m. a Chevrolet towed the trailer to a side street 800 yards from the Rashid. Security guards were not alarmed as generators were a common sight in Iraq because of the blackouts. They were strolling towards it when the first rocket was fired automatically at the Rashid. Wolfowitz stoutly refused, even after his recent experience, to inject a note of realism into his vision of the opponents of the occupation, saying 'There are a minority who refuse to accept the reality of a new and free Iraq. We will be unrelenting in our pursuit of them.'

Unlike most Iraqi politicians, the veteran Kurdish leader Mahmoud Othman had the gift of thinking outside the confines of his own community. In late 2003 he told me: 'Day by day the Iraqi people are getting more hostile to the Americans. The majority don't like them.' He believed the main reasons for this were lack of security and lack of jobs. He also detected something dysfunctional about the occupation. They had not at this stage reopened the airport or set up a satellite television station. Iraqis got their news from Arab channels like al-Jazeera, which were wholly hostile to the US occupation, and about whose biased coverage the CPA continually complained. Othman was a member of the US-appointed Iraqi Governing Council but said it 'does not have much power and if you don't have real authority you lack credibility. We will be seen by the Iraqis as puppets.' The other person I often consulted about what was happening was Ghassan Atiyyah, a commentator long active in the opposition to Saddam Hussein. He saw that the occupation was in deep trouble. He believed that by disbanding the army the US had in effect turned the Sunni into second-class citizens, and they would never accept this lowly status. He believed 'the Sunni have the strength to destabilize the country, just as the Kurds were able to do for fifty years'.

During that first year after the fall of Saddam Hussein reporting in Iraq was not as dangerous as it later became. When nothing was happening in Baghdad I used to drive west along the highway to Fallujah, where I ate in a restaurant on the main street called the Haj Hussein because my driver said it served some of the best kebabs in Iraq. Local people were helpful. They said they saw journalists as neutral, or possible allies in their struggle against the occupation.

The war was getting more intense. I was in Fallujah in November 2003 when a man who owned a shop selling musical cassettes and who also worked as a freelance cameraman told me that a Chinook helicopter had been shot down nearby. We drove across an iron bridge over the Euphrates past fields filled with cattle and crops, asking farmers the way to the crash site. Within minutes I was nervously peering through the bushes at the still-smoking wreckage of the giant Chinook in which sixteen US soldiers had just died and twenty-one were wounded. 'I saw two helicopters pass overhead when two missiles were fired at them,' said Daoud Suleiman, a farmer working among the date palms. 'One missed and the other hit a helicopter at the rear-end and flames started coming out of it before it crashed into a field.' Above us half a dozen Black Hawks swooped and dived as if to avoid more missiles. The farmers passed around pieces of twisted metal they had taken from a helicopter. One of them waved a piece of metal derisively at the Black Hawks. The others shouted at him: 'Put it down! They might think it is a gun and fire at us.' 'I am not afraid!' he yelled and waved the piece of metal defiantly above his head again before other farmers wrestled it away from him.

I did not realize at the time that an important change was about to happen. It seemed to me that the absurd optimism of the US military briefings in Baghdad and statements from the White House were bound to be exposed by events. The US increasingly controlled only parcels of territory in Iraq in the months before the US presidential election in 2004. But President Bush's campaign was to receive an unexpected ally in the shape of Abu Musab al-Zarqawi, whose brand of religious militancy held that all foreigners including journalists were spies. I soon became the only non-Iraqi eating in the Haj Hussein. When I came into the dining room the other diners became more and more suspicious about who I was. The last time I visited the manager pointedly seated me in an empty room upstairs. A few months later a US plane bombed and destroyed the restaurant.

X

THE OCCASION HAD the air of a revivalist meeting at which penitents denounce their past sins. On a wet day in January 2004 hundreds of former officers in the Iraqi army rose to their feet in the hall of the police academy in the northern city of Mosul, raised their right hands and solemnly renounced the Baath party and all its works. General David Petraeus, the commander of the 101st Airborne Division based in Mosul and in charge of most of northern Iraq, was ecstatic at the turnout. 'It is beyond our wildest expectations,' he said enthusiastically outside the hall in the drizzle as a fresh batch of sinners filed past him. Long lines of former officers snaked down the hill in front of us and by evening 2,243 officers, including many generals, had taken the pledge. Each was given a piece of paper showing that he had done so. 'Whatever you do don't run out of Baath denunciation certificates,' General Petraeus, a lean, hyperactive man told the US commanders standing around him.

In a homily to the repentant officers the general warned them not to expect anything except a sense of personal closure. But when I spoke to them later it was clear that they all had very precise objectives standing in the rain for hours to take part in the somewhat humiliating proceedings. They hoped to be paid pensions which they believed they had earned and to no longer be blacklisted for jobs they desperately needed. Major Faiq Ahmed Abed, a grizzled veteran with twenty-six years' military service, had served in the Republican Guard until the previous April, when he stopped being paid. 'Since then I have been selling my furniture to feed my children,' he said. Abdul Wasit, formerly a captain in Saddam Hussein's much-feared Amn al-Amm security services, believed his experience should be put to use in restoring peace to Iraq. I asked about the unsavoury reputation of his former employers but the captain was not at all abashed. 'We security men are just like you journalists,' he said. 'Your newspaper asks you to write an article about something and you must obey the order.' I thought briefly but then dismissed the idea of suggesting that the actions of the *Independent* newspaper, for which I was writing, and those of the Iraqi secret police were not strictly comparable. But the scene at the Police Academy in Mosul touched on the central issue in Iraqi politics. General Petraeus was the only senior American I met who not only foresaw the danger if these ex-officers were shut out from power and employment, but did something about it. He had been quick to claim that the ceremony at the Police Academy was organized by a committee of retired Iraqi generals, but in practice it was an American-run affair, a first step towards including the old Sunni Arab elite in the new Iraq.

The 101st Airborne Division, its headquarters in a former Saddam Hussein palace (whose pillars and mosaics were more attractive than in most such buildings), was much more politically proactive than American military units in the rest of Iraq. It needed to be. Mosul, with a population of 1.7 million people, was by far the largest Sunni city in the country and the traditional centre for Arab nationalism in Iraq. A large part of the Iraqi officer corps came from the city, which sprawled along the Tigris river, and under Saddam Hussein the defence minister usually came from there.

Surprisingly, the city had quieted down since those first explosive days after its capture. The 101st Airborne, numbering about 20,000 men, had lost only sixty dead from both hostile fire and accidents over the previous ten months. Guerrilla war was not as intense as it had become further south around Baghdad. The insurgents did not use roadside bombs so frequently and there had been only one suicide bomb attack. A lot of this had to do with the sophisticated policies pursued by General Petraeus. He had tried to give the US presence some legitimacy. Lieutenant-Colonel D. J. Reyes, the senior divisional intelligence officer, said: 'We held elections and engaged with the local population within two weeks of arriving here.' This was the reverse of what was happening in Baghdad. In Mosul carpet-bagging exiles, eager for jobs and money, were politely received but kept on the margins. Petraeus tried not to drive the great number of Iraqis associated with the old regime into a corner. The renunciation of the Baath party I had witnessed was really an attempt to short circuit the de-Baathification campaign launched by Baghdad. Paul Bremer was later to write in bewilderment that he expected only 20,000 senior Baathists to be excluded from jobs. This showed how little he understood Iraq. In a country of mass unemployment the Shia, the Kurds and returning exiles would kick out as many Sunni from their jobs as they could possibly manage, so they could take them themselves. I went to the daily operational meeting between Petraeus and his commanders at which three quarters of the topics discussed were about the local administration and economy, and had nothing to do with the military situation. Statistics flashed up on a screen about the availability of fertilizer for local farmers and the state of truck traffic across the Turkish border.

For all Petraeus had achieved, the situation in Mosul had a fragile feel to it. Nothing was going to make local people like the occupation but they might live with it for a while. I had driven up to Mosul along the main highway from Baghdad. As I entered Nineveh province, of which Mosul was the centre, I passed through one of the enormous archways which Saddam had built to mark provincial boundaries across the country. It was also a police checkpoint. In pride of place high above my head on the archway, visible to all oncoming drivers, was a picture of the head and shoulders of a young man in police uniform. I asked the checkpoint police who he was. They replied sadly: 'He is one of our martyrs who was killed a month ago.' Was he killed by the insurgents, I enquired? 'Oh no,' they answered in surprise. 'He was killed by the Americans when they ran him over with a tank.'

After seeing General Petraeus I went to the police head-quarters in the centre of Mosul, where I saw their commander, a fast-talking man with an oleaginous manner called Muhammad Kaweri, whom I had met briefly at the Police Academy and who kissed me warmly on both cheeks. He expressed firm confidence in the future. The 8,000 policemen he had under his command were to be doubled in number. He admitted, however, that his job was not without its dangers. He rolled up his trouser leg to show where he had been hit by five bullets the previous July when two of his bodyguards were killed and eight wounded.

Probably Petraeus was only delaying the inevitable moment when the Sunni insurrection engulfed Mosul. For one thing, the 101st was leaving Mosul and was being replaced by the Stryker Brigade, which had only half its numbers. US military units seemed to make it almost a point of honour to pursue different policies from their predecessors. But, as Paul Bremer was later to point out and illustrate with many examples, what was done in Baghdad was on the orders of the White House and the civilians running the Pentagon. However successful the 101st had been in Mosul its approach was never going to become general American policy. The Sunni Arabs were always going to resist occupation. The crass decisions of the CPA and US army in and around Baghdad speeded up the pace at which we were approaching a rebellion, while in Mosul the 101st had slowed the process down. But the same ingredients for an uprising were present all over Sunni Iraq. Lieutenant-Colonel Reyes said the most dangerous development would be if the pro-Saddam supporters linked up with those who were anti-Saddam but also anti-occupation. In practice this meant well-trained army officers, such as those standing in line at the Police Academy, sharing their military expertise with religious zealots, once persecuted by Saddam, but now fighting the occupation.

Petraeus may have received excessive plaudits from the media while in Mosul, but was blamed unfairly when the city rose in rebellion later in the year. The Kurdish leaders, in particular, were furious at his conciliatory approach to the Sunni and former Baathists. But Petraeus was one of the few Americans with authority in Iraq who had an inkling of the nature of the political and ethnic minefield into which the US had blundered. I asked him what was his most important advice was to his successor. He said, after reflecting for some moments, that it was 'not to align too closely with one ethnic group, political party, tribe, religious group or social element'. This was sensible and perceptive but as a policy it could not work in the long term because strict neutrality in the maelstrom of Iraqi politics would leave the US without Iraqi allies.

In central Iraq US soldiers were much less confident than in Mosul about the kind of war they were fighting. The brief celebrations following the capture of Saddam Hussein on December 15 2003 died away. The US military command in Baghdad claimed that the number of attacks on its forces had gone down but soldiers in the field told me that to avoid bureaucratic hassle they often didn't report incidents when they came under fire. One day I decided to drive the seventy miles to Ramadi to see if the road was getting any safer. We never got there. On the outskirts of Baghdad we ran into a stalled convoy of tanks and armoured personnel carriers loaded on to enormous vehicle transporters. A soldier stopped us. He said, 'We discovered an IED [Improvised Explosive Device] on the road and we are trying to defuse it.' Along with other Iraqi cars and trucks, we turned off the road and drove along a track between a stagnant canal and a rubbish dump.

After half an hour we arrived in Abu Ghraib market, full of rickety stalls selling fruit and vegetables. I stepped out of the car to make a call to my office in London on a Thuraya satellite phone. As I was talking, a US patrol drove by in their Humvees. Suddenly the vehicles stopped. Half a dozen soldiers ran towards our car, pointing their guns at our chests. 'Get down on your knees and put your hands behind your head,' they screamed. We did both. One of them snatched my Thuraya. When Muhammad al-Khazraji, the driver, said something in Arabic, a soldier shouted: 'Shut the fuck up.' I said I was a British journalist. We waited on our knees until the soldiers decided this was true and got back in their vehicles. The incident, dangerous for just a few seconds, was exactly similar to many grim occasions when Iraqis who did not understand English had misunderstood the instructions being yelled at them and had been shot dead. As we drove out of Abu Ghraib we heard the voice of a preacher at a nearby mosque denouncing the occupation. 'The occupiers,' he said, 'now attack everybody and make life impossible.'

A few miles further down the road we reached the turn-off for the town of Fallujah, but it was blocked by US soldiers and members of the Iraqi Civil Defence Corps (ICDC), one of the paramilitary organizations then being rapidly expanded by the US military. Building up a pro-American Iraqi armed force was a perennial endeavour of the US, often with comically disastrous results. (In February 2006 American generals admitted that, after prolonged and vastly expensive effort, the number of Iraqi army battalions capable of fighting insurgents without US help stood at exactly nil out of ninety-eight.)[18] On this occasion in Fallujah the ICDC was represented by a plump and friendly Iraqi soldier who, resting his hands on a sub-machine gun which was slung around his neck, said: 'The Americans are carrying out a big operation and there is big battle with the *mujahidin* around a mosque in Fallujah.' He seemed to have little interest in these activities and pointed to a track that would allow us to enter Fallujah, avoiding the cordon round the town.

In the first months of 2004 the insurgents were getting more confident. A few days earlier a Black Hawk medical evacuation helicopter had been shot down by a heat-seeking missile near Fallujah; the nine soldiers on board were killed. Although the resistance was very fragmented it contained enough trained soldiers to home in on the vulnerabilities of the US army, such was its dependence on a constant flow of road-borne supplies. The resistance swiftly discovered that its most effective weapon against supply trucks or soft-skinned Humvees were roadside bombs, the notorious IEDs or 'convoy killers' which usually consisted of heavy artillery rounds, 155mm and 122mm shells with a detonator. Again and again these bombs tore vehicles apart, often killing two or three soldiers. The local insurgents in Fallujah were also getting more confident. In one attack in February they almost killed General John Abizaid, the US Middle East commander; in another they overran the police headquarters, killing some twenty men.

I visited a base near Fallujah called Volturno, hidden inside an old Baath Party recreation camp beside a lake, where a platoon of combat engineers from the 82nd Airborne, in charge of clearing the road of mines, ruefully explained that they hadn't expected to be fighting this sort of war. In a dark hut, Staff Sergeant Jeremy Anderson, leader of a squad of eight sappers, said he and his men were trained to deal with big conventional minefields such as those laid by the old Soviet army. Nobody thought they would be dealing with the sort of amateur but lethal devices planted by guerrillas around Fallujah.

Outside the hut, Sergeant Anderson showed off with proprietary pride an old green-painted 155mm South African-made shell, whose TNT was wrapped around with plastic explosives; it would produce razor-edged pieces of shrapnel eight to twelve inches long. The guerrillas buried several of these a few feet from the road with the nose of the shell removed and replaced with blasting caps. These were connected to a battery, usually taken from a motorcycle. The bomb would then be detonated by means of a command wire three or four hundred metres long. Alternatively, the bombers would send a signal to the battery remotely by using a car door opener, the control for a child's toy or some types of mobile phone – which explained why the soldiers who had stopped us when they saw me using a Thuraya were so edgy: they had been told that it could be used to detonate a bomb under their feet.

Anderson displayed a certain grudging respect for the versatility of the bomb-makers. One bomb was found attached to the underside of a bridge over a highway: that way it would explode downwards as a US convoy passed underneath. Another was wired to a solar panel which would detonate as soon as a US soldier brushed away the dirt shielding it from the sun. The sappers walked gingerly along the verges of the roads. Anderson explained: 'We look for wires – anything that seems out of place.' They gently prodded the sandy ground with short, silver-coloured wands. The wands, eighteen inches long and looking like a conductor's baton, were made of titanium and were non-magnetic. They were curiously delicate and old-fashioned and in a way symbolic of the type of war the US was now fighting in Iraq. Against intelligent guerrilla tactics, such as the mass use of the notorious IEDs, sophisticated equipment and massive firepower were useless.

Conventional mine detectors, intended to detect metal, did not work here because Iraqis use the side of the road as a rubbish dump. It is impossible to distinguish buried shells from discarded cans and other junk. The guerrillas had also started planting booby traps specifically designed to kill sappers. 'Somebody has watched us at work,' Anderson said. 'They saw that we always pick up rocks and turn them over to make sure nothing is underneath. So one day they tied a string to a rock rigged to an old water bottle with a power source inside attached to some old mortar rounds.'

As convoys came under attack the Americans relied more and more on helicopters, which were always roaring across the sky 100 feet over our heads in Baghdad. I went to a helicopter base at Habbaniyah, ten miles beyond Fallujah, where there was a detachment equipped with light Kiowa Warrior helicopters (US helicopters are all named after Indian tribes) beside an old Iraqi air force hangar gutted by fire. There had been a steady trickle of losses. A few days before I arrived, one of the pilots had been killed when the medical evacuation helicopter taking him to Baghdad was shot down. His death was widely publicized, mainly because twelve years before, as a ground soldier, he had taken part in the failed attempt to rescue US helicopter crews in Mogadishu during the disastrous American intervention in Somalia.

The helicopter pilots discussed the chances of being shot down. They were not worried by being shot at with AK-47 sub-machine guns. Except at night, when they could see the tracer, they seldom knew when they were under fire. One pilot suggested that for an Iraqi farmer on the ground 'it must be difficult to resist the temptation to shoot at us, like duck hunting'. A few minutes later, evidently thinking that his remarks might be considered flippant, he asked urgently that they not be attributed to him.

These days the helicopters flew fast and low to avoid missiles. The gunner in one of the Kiowas said: 'The helicopter flies at 100 feet, so by the time anyone on the ground can react it's gone.' Less comfortingly, he said the device on the roof for confusing heat-seeking missiles 'works 85 per cent of the time'. He didn't add that the missiles, by forcing the helicopters to fly at such high speed at low altitude, made it very difficult for them to see anything on the ground.

I asked Major Thomas Von Eschenbach, the commander of the squadron, who he thought was shooting at him. He repeated the official line. 'One group are former regime loyalists, with tribal loyalties to Saddam Hussein, and a second are foreign fighters who may be coming in from Syria.' The pilots themselves admitted that they saw few Iraqis and then only from the air. A troop commander said: 'The men are mostly 5'6' to 5'10' and are between 150 to 180 pounds. The hardest part is picking out the bad guys. About half of the Iraqis seem to drive white pick-ups.' Von Eschenbach said that anybody could shoot at a helicopter with a rocket-propelled grenade-launcher – it required only ten minutes' training – but a surface-to-air missile was more complicated. He suspected foreign fighters were at work, though I pointed out that 350,000 former members of the Iraqi army might be involved. As for the proficiency of the guerrillas who were shooting down helicopters, Von Eschenbach said: 'It's just like the Afghans did with the Russians . . . They find out our weaknesses.' Helicopters fly in pairs and the guerrillas always attacked the second or 'trail' helicopter so there was nobody to see what was happening in the seconds before the missile struck.

There was nothing very new in what the resistance was doing. In South Armagh in Northern Ireland the IRA's use of roadside bombs had stopped the British Army using vehicles. In almost twenty years in south Lebanon the Israeli army had found no answer to Hezbollah's use of bombs, mortars and snipers. US commanders would say that their casualties were not high given the number of troops involved, but this missed the point. There are two types of guerrilla war. The first builds up guerrilla resistance step by step until a regular army is formed: the classic example is Mao Zedong in China. The second type involves sporadic attacks by a limited number of guerrillas, with the aim of putting irresistible political pressure on the enemy. This was the type of campaign waged by the IRA in Ireland in 1919–21, the Irgun in Palestine in the 1940s, EOKA under Grivas in Cyprus in the 1950s and the IRA again in the 1970s and 1980s in Ireland. It was this second type of war the US army was facing. The guerrillas did not have to do very much to have a serious political impact in the US, where support for the war was waning by the month. No WMD had been found and the capture of Saddam Hussein seemed to make no difference. Though President Bush had long before declared victory, more American soldiers were dying every day.

The speed with which US plans for Iraq fell apart was astonishing, but the reason was plain: the US military and Paul Bremer provoked simultaneous confrontations with Iraq's two main communities, the Shia and Sunni Arabs, who together make up 80 per cent of the population. At the end of March 2004, Bremer decided to squeeze Muqtada al-Sadr by arresting his chief lieutenant in Najaf, and shutting down his small circulation newsapaper, *al-Hawza*. 'Close down this rag,' Bremer had exclaimed on seeing an offensive article, so a contact in the CPA told me. Many Shia at this time thought Sadr a violent maverick: Bremer made him a martyr. Religion and nationalism came together. Bremer's plan to marginalize Sadr blew up in his face, and the black-clad gunmen of Sadr's Mehdi Army seized large parts of southern Iraq, including Najaf and Kut, the impoverished city on the Tigris where the British army had been forced to surrender by the Turks in World War One.

A few days later the US army provoked another crisis, this time with the Sunni community. In revenge for the killing and dismemberment of four US security men in Fallujah on March 31, three battalions of Marines surrounded the city and began to bombard it. To Iraqis this looked like collective punishment. Within a few days the Marines had managed to turn the Fallujans, previously regarded by most other Iraqis as dangerous hillbillies, into symbols of reborn Iraqi nationalism. Far from confining the insurrection to Fallujah, the siege of the city encouraged further uprisings in Sunni towns and villages along the Euphrates.

As US control over large parts of Iraq began to weaken, civilian and military officials responded by refusing to believe what was happening. Only occasionally were there visible signs of panic. The CPA website was normally full of upbeat information about reconstruction projects and improvements in the electricity supply. It also had news about security, the chief preoccupation of the foreign businessmen who made up most of its readership. As the crisis grew worse the CPA decided that the information was too alarming to report. A brief message on its website read, unpretentiously: 'For security reasons there are no security reports.'

American soldiers were being killed because their commanders couldn't believe that the rebellion was spreading. The army was still sending convoys of petrol tankers down the highway from Baghdad to Fallujah after guerrillas had taken control of the road. Five days into the rebellion, as I tried to get into or at least close to Fallujah, I was caught in an ambush at Abu Ghraib, a district of scattered houses, abandoned factories and date palms which offered plenty of cover to guerrillas. We knew that the war had moved closer to Baghdad only when we saw four American tanks, their barrels pointing towards us, closing the road that runs behind Baghdad airport. This meant the uprising was spreading from Fallujah towards the capital. Everywhere in Abu Ghraib there were freshly painted anti-American slogans on the walls. One read: 'We shall knock on the gates of heaven with American skulls.' Another: 'Sunni+Shia=Jihad against occupation.'

In the distance we could see three columns of black smoke rising into the sky: local people told us that an American convoy had been attacked a few hours earlier. We decided to follow an aid convoy bound for Fallujah; young men were waving Iraqi flags from the backs of trucks. The main road was closed, so we drove down narrow tracks through shabby brown villages where people clapped as we passed. Aiding Fallujah was obviously popular. We had been weaving around the countryside for what seemed a very long time until we suddenly found ourselves close to the highway again. Just as we reached it, another convoy of gasoline tankers accompanied by US soldiers on Humvees drove past. It was immediately attacked. When we heard the bark of machine guns and the whoosh of rocket-propelled grenades overhead, we drove off the road on to a piece of wasteland and lay on the ground with our faces pressed into the sand; other Iraqi drivers took cover near us. Bassil al-Kaissi, our driver, shouted at them: 'Take off your *keffiyehs* [headdresses] or the Americans will think you are *mujahidin* and kill you.'

There was a pause in the firing, and we got back into the car and drove off down a narrow road away from the fighting. We moved slowly: I had told Bassil not to raise dust and attract attention. We had reached a small bridge over an irrigation canal when several *mujahidin* ran towards us carrying a heavy machine gun on a tripod and rocket-propelled grenade launchers. They had stopped on the bridge and were listening to the shooting, which had started up again, seeming not to know where it came from. One of them shouted: 'What is happening?' Bassil, not wanting to arouse their suspicion by driving away too quickly, stopped the car. 'We were trying to bring help to Fallujah,' he told them, 'but those pigs opened fire on us.'

The convoy we had seen attacked was, I think, the fourth to be ambushed on this stretch of road over a period of twenty-four hours. Several US soldiers had been killed in the earlier fighting. For two or three days US generals, still believing they were facing a finite number of former regime loyalists and foreign fighters, would not accept that spontaneous uprisings were taking place in towns all the way to the Syrian border. There was other grim news for the US commanders. One battalion of the new Iraqi army refused to go to Fallujah; the soldiers said they were not prepared to fight fellow Iraqis. The 36th Battalion of the 40,000-strong Iraqi Civil Defence Corps, a special unit recruited among militiamen from the anti-Saddam opposition parties, at first fought hard. The parties claimed that this was evidence that only their men had the political commitment to form the core of the new Iraqi security force. But after eleven days in the front line this battalion also mutinied, with only Kurds prepared to go in fighting.

The mutinies and desertions should not have come as a great surprise. The US-trained soldiers were at this stage paid only $60 a month, half the money made by garbage collectors in Baghdad. Early on in the crisis I met five pilgrims walking to the Shia holy city of Kerbala as part of the Arbain festival. Dressed in black, they were carrying a green banner with a religious slogan on it. They expressed routine anti-American sentiments: the surprise came when they told me that they were all soldiers in the Iraqi Civil Defence Corps. 'The Americans are just as bad as Saddam Hussein,' said Hamid al-Ugily from Baghdad's Sadr City, who was proudly carrying a green flag. 'We think they will attack Muqtada in Najaf. We will defend our religious leaders.'

A week after the ambush on the road to Fallujah I decided to drive to where al-Sadr and his Mehdi Army were besieged by 2,500 American soldiers. The black-clad militiamen loyal to al-Sadr were not well trained but had become increasingly visible. All went well until we were stopped at a militia checkpoint at a crossroads near Kufa, a few miles from Najaf. I was sitting in the back of the car and wearing a red-and-white *keffiyeh* to hide my brown hair and pale skin. I hoped that this would prevent anybody spotting me as a foreigner unless they got close. The disguise turned out to be a bad idea. The Mehdi army militiaman peered into the car and recognized me as an obvious Westerner. The fact that I was partly dressed as an Arab made them even more suspicious. They examined my satellite phone, mobile and camera as if they were proof that I was a spy. Nobody seemed to be in charge of the checkpoint. Two of the angriest militiamen tried to bundle me into another car and I resisted. Finally three gunmen, clutching their Kalashnikovs and their chests covered with ammunition pouches, clambered into our car. We followed a second car, also filled with heavily armed militiamen, to their headquarters in the green-domed Imam Ali mosque in the centre of Kufa.

The militiamen gradually became less aggressive. They offered me cigarettes and, though I had given up smoking some time before, this did not seem to me to be a good moment to refuse the offer. They were poor young men, mostly from Sadr City. They minutely examined a copy of the *New Yorker* they found in the back seat, one of them muttering 'haram' – forbidden – at a cartoon of a woman with a low-cut blouse. My belongings were gradually returned apart from the satellite phone. I saw a black-clad gunman stuff it into his ammunition belt but it would have been unwise to protest. At this moment a firefight broke out with US troops on the other side of the Euphrates. We saw machine-gun bullets strike the wall of the mosque above our heads, sending up little puffs of dust. In the face of the attack our captors became much friendlier and took us to their headquarters beside the shrine in Najaf, where we were freed.

After a month of besieging Fallujah and Najaf it became clear that the US did not have the political strength to assault and capture either city. Any attempt to do so risked alienating the Sunni and Shia communities at the same time. The last thing the White House wanted six months before the presidential election in November 2004 was high US casualty figures and pictures on US television of bloody house-to-house fighting across Iraq. The course of the twin rebellions showed the residual strength of Iraqi nationalism, but also deepening sectarianism. I visited the main blood bank in Baghdad where Shi'ite executives from the oil ministry wearing suits and ties were giving blood for Fallujah alongside Sunni farmers who had driven into the capital in ancient battered buses from country villages. But national solidarity between Sunni and Shia was very temporary. The Shia sent a convoy of trucks piled with food to support Fallujah only for seven of the Shia drivers to be executed by the very insurgents they had come to help. Many of the Sunni fighters, Salafi and Jihadi, were as hostile to Shia Iraqis as they were to the Americans. Neither had a place in the pure Islamic state these ferocious and bigoted men were fighting for.

XI

WHEN I FIRST saw the cheerful colours it reminded me of a beach umbrella but many Iraqis saw it as a final and humiliating insult. Overnight the Iraqi Governing Council (IGC), the 25-member unelected body appointed by the US, abolished the old red-white-and-black Iraqi flag with its three green stars, and chose a new and unwelcome replacement. It was white and had two parallel blue stripes along the top and bottom, symbolizing the Tigris and the Euphrates rivers, a yellow band representing the Kurds and a blue crescent for Islam. It bore, many enraged people in Baghdad claimed, a sinister resemblance to the Israeli flag. The episode showed the insensitivity of the IGC to the continued potency of Iraqi nationalism, even if the Sunni and Shia had their own increasingly different versions of Iraqi identity. During his long rule Saddam Hussein left the flag unchanged aside from adding the words 'Allah-u-Akbar', God is Great, during the First Gulf War to burnish his Islamic credentials. Hundreds of thousands of young Iraqi men had fought and died under the flag in the Iran–Iraq war. I had often seen it used as a shroud to cover their cheap wooden coffins. Muqtada al-Sadr, with an acute political sense of what appealed to the Iraqi street, always had the Iraqi flag as a backdrop in posters showing himself and his martyred relatives. Now the IGC, many of whose members never left the Green Zone, chose a moment when half of Iraq had risen in rebellion to abolish it.

'What gives these people the right to throw away our flag, to change the symbol of Iraq?' asked Salah, a building contractor of normally placid political views whom I knew slightly. 'It makes me very angry because these people were appointed by the Americans. I will not regard the new flag as representing me but only traitors and collaborators.' Even at this tumultuous moment, at the end of April 2004, people in Baghdad sounded more infuriated by the unexpected abolition of their old flag than by the fact that Iraqis were now being killed in unprecedented numbers across the country every day. It was also telling that an ever-decreasing number of people would not give me their full names when I talked to them. Jassim, standing behind the counter in his grocery shop, said: 'The flag is not Saddam's flag. It was there before Saddam and it represents Iraq as a country. The whole world knows Iraq by its flag.' The new flag was seldom flown, though crude copies were made in Fallujah and promptly burned in the streets. Dhurgham, a 23–year-old student, said: 'We cheered Iraqi footballers under the flag for a long time. I feel it represents me as an Iraqi. I don't like this new flag. It does not look Iraqi. It is more like the Turkish or Israeli flags. The main reason I don't like it is that it comes from the Americans.' Other critics wondered why only the Kurds should have a stripe of their own on the flag. Was it because they were the only Iraqi community supporting the occupation?

I was intrigued by the whole flag incident, to which nobody in the Green Zone paid much attention, but which was the talk of Baghdad outside its guard posts and concrete walls. On one level one could see the changing the of flag as convincing evidence, if any were needed, of the crass stupidity of America's allies in Iraq and their lack of contact with ordinary Iraqis. It was also an example of the nepotism for which the IGC and subsequent Iraqi governments were notorious. Investigation revealed that the new flag was the work of an Iraqi artist long resident in London called Rifat al-Chaderchi. He happened to be the brother of Nassir al-Chaderchi, member of a prominent Iraqi family and the chairman of the IGC committee in charge of choosing a new flag for Iraq. 'My brother just called me and asked me to design a flag on behalf of the IGC,' explained Rifat, who was bemused by the controversy. But the row over the flag reflected something more important than the tendency of America's Iraqi allies to shoot themselves in the foot whenever the opportunity offered itself. The fierceness of the dispute illustrated the genuine hatreds dividing Iraqis, people who were supposed to be members of one nation. The most powerful objector to the old red-white-and-black flag was Massoud Barzani, the Kurdish leader, who refused to allow its use in western Kurdistan where he ruled. For Kurds the old flag was the one that had been carried by the Iraqi army units which had destroyed their villages and massacred their people. For the Kurds it had the same appeal as a popular emblem as the Swastika in post-war Poland or the Soviet Union. Nevertheless it was all too obviously a bad moment to raise the issue, and showed a certain detachment from the problems of Iraq on the part of the Council members who were seeking to rule it. This did not pass unnoticed by ordinary Iraqis. 'I don't care about the flag,' said Adnan, a retired army officer in his forties. 'I care about the Iraqi people. The Council does nothing for them but spends its time worrying about such issues as what flag we should have.'

The Iraqi Governing Council was openly despised by many Iraqis at the time and was covertly criticized by the Americans who had created it. Paul Bremer is contemptuous of its members in his memoirs, which are fascinating because he unconsciously paints such a revealing picture of his own failings and those of the administration in Washington. He repeatedly chides the Iraqis on the Council for being lazy, divided and incapable of action. But he also makes clear how little power he was prepared to cede to Iraqis of any description. He even suggested soon after the IGC was set up that it might like to demand, in order to give Iraqis the false impression that it wielded real authority, the immediate implementation of measures that the CPA had already decided to carry out. American officials working in the CPA told me they believed Bremer had what they called 'a MacArthur complex', the US viceroy believing he could be as all-powerful in Baghdad as his predecessor in Tokyo half a century earlier. But even at the height of the British Raj in India few imperial officials would have treated prominent Indians with the rudeness and arrogance that Bremer thought in no way abnormal. He records himself, in full MacArthur mode, as telling members of the Council: 'Look, you can't very well hope to run a country of twenty-five million without working hard. The Governing Council works fewer hours a week than the CPA works every day.' The obvious thought did not occur to him that Council members were unlikely to attend meetings simply to rubber-stamp decisions he had already made.

Bremer believed that, given time, a host of well-qualified and pro-American Iraqis would emerge from the maelstrom of post-Saddam Iraq. He wanted to postpone elections until this happened. He persistently underestimated the influence of Grand Ayatollah Ali al-Sistani who from the first days of the occupation demanded that elections take place and insisted that a constitution should only be written by elected Iraqis. Sistani refused to meet Bremer and once sent a message to him saying: 'You are an American and I am an Iranian. Why don't we let the Iraqi people decide?' It was something that Bremer was averse to doing, but in the end he had no choice. The political ground began to crumble under his feet. The US army was facing an escalating rebellion by five million Sunni Arabs and could not afford a second uprising by the fifteen to sixteen million Shia Iraqis as well. The sort of pro-Western secular Iraqis whom Bremer hoped to nurture were thin on the ground outside the Green Zone, as the two elections for the National Assembly in 2005 were to prove.

In reality the much-despised opposition leaders I met at their meeting in the Metropole Hotel in London in December 2002 and two months later in Salahudin in Kurdistan were by and large the same men – aside from several who had been assassinated in the meantime – who won most of the votes in the two 2005 elections. Hoshyar Zebari, the highly effective Foreign Minister of the IGC and later governments, used to tell me laughingly: 'Patrick, they [the Americans] may believe there are other leaders out there for them but, believe me, they really don't exist.'

Iraqis were always telling me that for all the talk of Governing Councils and interim governments it was the Americans who remained in control behind the scenes. They were not entirely wrong. In the last days of the IGC, I was once briefly trapped in the Green Zone because I had taken too seriously the idea that Iraqis were running the government. I had gone to see Ali Allawi, the extremely able and intelligent Trade Minister, who had just taken over the Defence Ministry. It was housed in a villa in the Green Zone. I left my car outside, walked through the so-called Assassin's Gate and was picked up by one of Allawi's aides and taken to the villa. I had a useful interview with the minister, who was full of innovative ideas. The meeting was truncated a little because Allawi had to leave early in order to attend a meeting elsewhere in the zone. It was now that my problems began. After Allawi had gone I asked his efficient secretary if she could find a driver or aide to drive me back to the entrance to the Green Zone. She shook her head and said that unfortunately the minister's staff was small and all of them had left with him. It suddenly became very clear to me that if the Iraqi Defence Ministry headquarters employed only a dozen people then American plans to delegate real military power were indeed cosmetic. After half an hour I located a kindly American contractor decorating a house who drove me back to the Assassin's Gate.

The US, like so many imperial powers in the past, wanted to have it both ways. It hoped to find Iraqis who carried weight in their own country to take part in running it. But at the same time America wanted these same highly representative Iraqis to be wholly compliant with its wishes. This made it impossible for the US to cultivate an Iraqi Charles de Gaulle, somebody who would cooperate with them but could also disagree and did not act like a pawn.

In 2004 the White House wanted an Iraqi leader who would endorse whatever it said about Iraq in the run-up to the presidential election. Bush himself made no bones about this in discussing the choice of an interim prime minister. The President told an NSC meeting: 'It's important to have someone who's willing to stand up and thank the American people for their actions for their sacrifice in liberating Iraq. I don't expect us to pick a yes man. But at least I want someone who will be grateful.'[19]

There was a further reason, which cannot be blamed on the Americans, why no Iraqi leader of real authority emerged after the invasion. The country reminded me of Lebanon, where communal differences ensured weak and ineffective governments. Divisions between communities in Iraq were always deeper than most Iraqis would admit. Communities were also internally divided. After all, the Kurds had no sooner got rid of Saddam Hussein after the First Gulf War in 1991 than they started a bloody civil war pitting Barzani against Talabani, in which thousands of Kurds were killed. Sayid Majid al-Khoie had apparently died at the hands of supporters of Muqtada al-Sadr. This divisiveness encouraged the appointment of prime ministers who, at least at the moment of their appointment, were the politicians with the least enemies. This factor helped Iyad Allawi become prime minister in 2004 and Ibrahim Jaafari to get the job a year later. None of the political parties wanted an authoritative government to emerge. Ministries were allocated on a sort of quota system and, once appointed after prolonged negotiations, a new minister could not be sacked by a prime minister. The new minister would also treat his new ministry as a fiefdom of his party, a deep well of patronage, money and power from which members of his party alone could draw. The Health Ministry was run by Dawa, the Transport Ministry by the Sadrists and the

Ministry of the Interior by the Supreme Council for Islamic Revolution in Iraq. The democratic process which was supposed to bring Iraqis together was in fact bringing the country closer to disintegration. Iraqi friends looked unhappy at the comparison with Lebanon, with its history of weak governments and prolonged civil war, but admitted that the analogy was all too real.

In the years after the invasion I was impatient at having to describe the formation of governments and the holding of elections, as if these were really determining the distribution of power in Iraq. People go to the polls to elect a government which is capable of doing something to improve their lives. In reality nobody after the destruction of the Iraqi state in April 2003 was truly able to put this Humpty-Dumpty together again. Iraqi governments, constructed after prolonged and rancorous negotiations, seldom did very much when they were in office. During the Iyad Allawi administration in 2004–5 a Baghdad newspaper claimed that at one moment all government ministers were out of the country. After the twin uprisings in April 2004 the US saw real authority slipping out of its hands. Its army controlled only parts of Iraq. One year after Bush declared major combat in Iraq over, insurgents had their own capital in Fallujah. By early June 2004 the road to the airport, the main US military base in Baghdad, was no longer safe. Four security men who had been staying two floors above me in the Hamra Hotel were killed as they drove to the airport by guerrillas armed with machine guns and grenade-launchers. I had often travelled with Dan Williams of the *Washington Post*, who was almost killed when his car was attacked on the road between Fallujah and Abu Ghraib. Gunmen in another vehicle fired AK-47 rounds into his car at point blank range. He was saved only because his car was armoured, had bulletproof glass windows and his driver kept going even after the two back tyres were shot out. Suicide bombers, car bombs and rocket attacks paralyzed Baghdad; US bases were defended by increasingly elaborate fortifications. The

14 July Bridge over the Tigris, which led to the Green Zone, was blocked by sandbags and razor wire. A notice hanging from the wire read: 'Do not enter or you will be shot.'

Twenty years earlier I used to go to open-air restaurants that lined Baghdad's Abu Nawas Street to eat *mazgouf*, fish from the Tigris cooked over a wood fire, and drink arak, a spirit made from dates and flavoured with aniseed. The restaurants had been badly affected when Saddam, to bolster his Islamic credentials, banned the public consumption of alcohol. After his overthrow, the owners hoped their customers would return. But by the end of 2004 Abu Nawas was deserted even in the middle of the day and used mainly by military vehicles. The street could be entered only from one end while at the other there was a US checkpoint intended to protect the Palestine and Sheraton Hotels, both of them full of foreigners, who knew that Abu Nawas was too dangerous for them.

I talked to Shahab al-Obeidi, the manager of the Shatt al-Arab restaurant on the east bank of the Tigris in the centre of Baghdad. Dark fish swam in a pool with blue tiles (the river was so polluted that they had to come from fish farms). Shahab said that business wasn't too good: three-quarters of his customers used to come in the evening but now he shut at 6 p.m. Once he stayed open because he had a large table of customers who seemed to be enjoying themselves and were surprisingly unworried about staying out after nightfall. 'When I gave them the bill,' he said, 'they laughed and took out their pistols and fired them into the ceiling and through the windows.' He pointed disconsolately at numerous bullet holes in the corrugated iron ceiling.

Iraqis were desperate for the return of some form of security. They were preoccupied with day-to-day survival. There was something absurd and offensive about the pride the US and Britain took in publicizing new constitutional arrangements or plans to hold elections when it was becoming lethally dangerous to walk down Saadoun Street in the heart of Baghdad. Among the better-off there was a pervasive fear of kidnapping. This was one of the few local industries showing signs of growth. It became so common that new words had been added to Iraqi thieves' slang: for example, a kidnap victim was called *al-tali*, or 'the sheep'. I visited Qasim Sabty, a painter and sculptor who owned a gallery and a café frequented by intellectuals, to ask him about an exhibition he'd held of work depicting torture at Abu Ghraib, but the first thing he spoke about was kidnapping. 'So many of my friends have been kidnapped,' he said. 'I fear I am going to be next.' He mentioned another gallery owner who had just paid $100,000 for the return of her son. A businessman friend of mine living in Jordan had just paid $100,000 to have his brother-in-law released. Doctors were a favourite target. Operations were postponed because surgeons had fled the country. The owner of the dilapidated Shatt al-Arab restaurant disappeared to Syria after his son was kidnapped. I asked Lieutenant-Colonel Farouk Mahmoud, the deputy head of the police kidnap squad, the best way to avoid being kidnapped. 'Go abroad!' he said brightly, to laughter from his officers.

It wasn't only the better-off who felt threatened. Gangs of thieves hopped on and off buses in Rashid Street in the city centre and robbed passengers at gun- and knife-point. Ali Abdul Jabber, a bus driver, had been robbed three times. 'On the last occasion,' he said, 'the thieves jumped on board because the doors have to be open in this hot weather. Two of them stood guard at the back while two others walked down the bus looking in people's handbags and stealing money and jewellery.' Jabber didn't dare turn round: he thought that if the thieves suspected he could identify them they would kill him. Nobody went to the police. 'The passengers didn't even discuss it among themselves because this sort of thing is so much part of daily life in Baghdad.' He believed most of them suspected that he was in league with the gang.

The drumbeat of violence never ceased in the years after the US had removed Saddam in April 2003. It discredited Iraqi governments both elected and unelected. The profound lawlessness ensured that nobody had any trust in the Iraqi police or army. There were so many killings that it was difficult to make out changes in the pattern of attacks or identify precisely who was carrying them out. American soldiers were always being blown up by roadside bombs. No less than 768 soldiers were killed by these lethal devices between May 2003 and February 2006. Suicide bombers were always targeting Iraqi police and army recruits, though ordinary Shia labourers or people buying and selling in the market were increasingly attacked. Iraqi governments and the US and British embassies hid in the Green Zone, where they were regularly mortared. But many killings were mysterious. Assassins were easy to hire. In Baghdad's al-Jadida market a group of killers put up a poster advertising their services with a price tag of $300 to $400 a murder. Even in Baghdad people found this hard to take.

In Washington and London, journalists were often accused of ignoring good news and neglecting to report on those parts of Iraq which were free of violence. I found on the contrary that, when trying to find out about one tragedy, I would almost automatically learn of another as bad if not worse. Early in September 2004 somebody had shot and badly wounded Professor Khalid al-Judi, the dean of al-Nahrain University (once called Saddam University, it had the reputation of having the best-qualified teachers in Iraq). He was being driven to a degree ceremony in the al-Khadamiyah district of Baghdad when a man opened fire from another vehicle. Professor al-Judi was hit by a bullet in the abdomen and critically wounded. I went to the al-Khadamiyah Teaching Hospital, where he had been taken after the shooting. An elderly man with a pointed beard, al-Judi was too sick to see me. I talked to his bodyguard, Muhammad Abdul Hamid, who had been in a second car just behind al-Judi, and saw the attack. 'We were driving on the highway near the Umm al-Qura mosque,' he said, 'when a big modern GMC four-wheel drive coloured grey and with the windows open overtook us. I could see the men inside were wearing flak jackets and carrying American rifles. We got stuck in a traffic jam. When they got close to Professor al-Judi's car one of the men in the GMC opened fire.' It did not sound unlikely. A GMC with the windows down so the men inside could shoot quickly usually indicated former soldiers working for a foreign security company. They were as likely to be British as American. Perhaps the professor's car had got too close and the security men had shot at what they suspected was a suicide bomber.

Squatting on the floor of the hospital corridor with his back against the wall while the bodyguard talked to me about the assassination was a depressed-looking middle-aged man. His name, he said, was Jamal Gafuri. The previous day his son Khalid had been in Haifa Street, a tough Sunni neighbourhood and bastion of the resistance, where he was a street cleaner. At about 7 a.m. a suicide bomber had blown up an American Bradley Fighting Vehicle. Cheering crowds swarmed over it. Somebody stuck an improvised black flag of Tawhid and Jihad, Abu Musab al-Zarqawi's group, in its gun barrel. Then they set fire to it. An hour later, two US helicopters, claiming they had been shot at, fired seven rockets into the crowd. It was more likely they were provoked by the black flag. Killed along with twelve other people was the correspondent of al-Arabiya, the Arabic satellite channel, who died on air. His blood was on the lens of the television camera which recorded his last moments. Jamal Gafuri said: 'My son Khalid was cleaning the street at the time and he was hit in the head by shrapnel. He is still unconscious.' He showed me a piece of paper written by a doctor itemizing his son's many wounds.

I went to al-Nahrain University to see if they knew anything more about the shooting of their dean. Saadoun Isa, a neat-looking man with quick nervous movements who was acting dean, said he got a phone call on his mobile from Professor al-Judi just after he was hit. 'I've been attacked by the Americans,' said the professor, adding that the man who shot him was black. I asked Dr Isa, who taught physical chemistry, if other academics had been attacked. He said: 'Myself for a start.' In May he had been in England when he got a phone call from his wife in Baghdad. His son Muhammad, a 22–year-old student, had been kidnapped and his house stripped. 'They wanted $40,000 but I was able to reduce it to $7,000.' When Muhammad was returned, Dr Isa found he had been tortured and kept alone in a room for three days without food or water. As he was being freed by the gang one of them had said to him: 'Tell your father to leave the country.' Dr Isa was wondering if he should take this advice and join the great exodus of educated Iraqis who were fleeing Iraq.

XII

'I RAQ IS BEING destroyed by the occupation, terrorism and corruption – and all are doing equal damage,' Dr Mahmoud Othman used to tell me wearily during the first three years of the US occupation. Soured by his decades of experience of Iraqi politics he never sounded as if he expected anybody to do anything about it. I liked talking to him because his acerbic realism was so different from the vague optimism of other former members of the Iraqi opposition living isolated in the Green Zone. Unlike many returned exiles he understood the pervasive hostility of most Iraqi Arabs to the occupation. In their eyes US and British support tainted and delegitimized the Iraqi governments they supported. In theory, of course, the occupation had ended on June 28 2004 with the highly publicized transfer of sovereignty to Iyad Allawi as interim prime minister. His government was to hold power until a new one was chosen reflecting the results of the election for an interim National Assembly on January 30 2005.

I was disappointed in the choice for several reasons. My relations with Allawi and his Iraqi National Accord party were frosty. In our book *Out of the Ashes* my brother Andrew and I described his close links to MI6 and the CIA. Intelligence officers from both organizations had for years shown touching faith in Allawi's abilities as a leader, belief wholly at odds with his record. We had given the first full account of his disastrous attempt to mount a military coup against Saddam Hussein in 1996. The Iraqi security services had crushed it savagely even before it got off the ground. The military officers implicated in the plot were arrested, tortured and killed. Abdul-Karim al-Kabariti, the Jordanian prime minister at the time, had a close-up view of what was happening since Allawi had moved to Amman to mastermind the coup attempt. He told us later that the Accord's networks 'were all penetrated by the Iraqi security service. The reason I think they were manipulated by Iraqi intelligence is that nothing succeeded, nothing worked.'

Most Iraqis I spoke to were cynically convinced that the occupation would continue in all but name after the supposed handover of power. Allawi had a very narrow political base. As an ex-Baathist he sought to appeal to secular Iraqi nationalists but, as parliamentary elections in January and December 2005 were to prove, these were small in number. In any case, how could Allawi present himself as the new strongman of Iraq when he was so compliant in carrying out Washington's wishes? He had no other military force to rely on aside from 138,000 American troops. George W. Bush had told Bremer that he wanted an Iraqi leader who would 'stand up and thank the American people'. He also, though he did not say this, wanted one in place who was willing to carry out this humiliating duty before the US presidential election in November. Bush got what he wanted. In September Allawi stood before the US Congress and claimed that fourteen or fifteen out of eighteen Iraqi provinces 'are completely safe'. This was entirely untrue but impossible to disprove because if I or any other journalist had gone on a grand tour of Iraq to prove how dangerous the country was we would have been kidnapped or killed. To get an idea of what was happening in Iraqi provinces I dared not visit I went to truck depots in Baghdad to ask drivers, who had to travel the country to feed their families, what they thought of Allawi's claim. 'The truth is exactly the reverse,' said a driver called Abu Akil as he queued for diesel. 'There are fifteen provinces which are dangerous and only the three Kurdish provinces in the north which are OK. This speech was designed to be heard by Americans not Iraqis.'

The lorry drivers painted a picture of a country with a degree of insecurity not seen in Western Europe since early medieval times. The only economic activity in some villages on the main roads around Basra was the systematic robbery of travellers. There were bandits in a village west of Baghdad who routinely chopped off the heads of drivers and stole their trucks. In one hamlet in the south a single sheikh was known to handle all negotiations on ransoms for kidnapped drivers and travellers. The insurgents, in control of the road from Jordan, were often tipped off by sympathetic customs officials on the border about loads they might be interested in. It was fatal for a driver to carry prefabricated housing on his truck because the insurgents believed this must be destined for US military bases. Irrigation equipment was allowed through because it had no military application and was of use to the people. 'The speech was ridiculous,' said Maithan Maki, a driver I asked about what the prime minister had said. 'When Allawi became prime minister I was in favour of him but things have got worse and worse.' The drivers all had a lot to be afraid of. Several of them were caught carrying sugar for the Ministry of Trade – to be distributed as part of the food rations – and were promptly executed by one particularly bloodthirsty band of insurgents south of Baghdad which deemed them to be working for the government. Their bodies bloated in the sun for several days because nobody dared remove them.

I did not think anybody living permanently in Baghdad could take seriously the line pumped out in Washington and London that the dangers of Iraq were being exaggerated by the media. It seemed obvious that such nonsense was aimed solely at a non-Iraqi audience. How could anybody miss the signs of disintegration? Oily columns of black smoke billowed up from the airport road where US patrols were regularly hit by suicide bombers or roadside bombs between Baghdad and Camp Victory, the gigantic US headquarters on the edge of the airport. A family living on the airport road showed me the shattered stock of an American machine gun, its barrel twisted sideways, hurled on to the roof of their house by the bomb which had destroyed a Humvee outside.

It was astonishing to discover that, despite this obvious mayhem, some foreigners were behaving as if they believed what Bush and Blair said about much of Iraq being safe was true. I went one morning in September 2004 to look at an undefended and nondescript villa in a quiet street in the al-Mansur district where three middle-aged men, a Briton and two Americans, had just been kidnapped. Soon after dawn ten masked men in a mini-van had driven up to the house. Inside were Kenneth Bigley, Eugene Armstrong and Jack Hensley, all building contractors employed at an American base. 'I heard screaming from inside the house early in the morning at about 6 a.m.,' said Bahir Salim, a neighbour. The three men had not made any effort to conceal their presence.

I could see two four-wheel-drive cars parked in the road advertising the presence of foreigners. Some reports of the abduction said the men lived in the affluent al-Mansur district, though their house was not in a wealthy part of it. I knew the place a little because I used to eat in a nearby kebab restaurant called the Zarzur al-Fallujah. The owner was from Fallujah, where he had another restaurant, and so were many of his customers. When Fallujah had come under the control of insurgents in April it seemed foolish to go on eating in their favourite Baghdad restaurant. Bigley, Armstrong and Hensley, unarmed and without even a nightwatchman, must have seemed easy pickings. Going by the accounts of neighbours the kidnappers behaved confidently. When an old man on his way to a green-domed mosque a few hundred yards away had walked past them while the abduction was going on one of the masked men said to him: 'Haji, go on your way and don't look back.' A woman who started to shout was politely told to keep quiet and go into her house. After the usual grotesque videos of the kidnapped men they were all murdered.

It was tempting to see the US handover of power to the Allawi government as a fake, but this would not have been entirely true. He started off with some goodwill. Iraqis might be cynical about the real independence of the interim government, but thought that nothing could be much worse than direct rule by Paul Bremer. They were also desperate for peace. There was a brief moment when Iyad Allawi tried to put some real distance between himself and the Americans. He produced a plan which would have allowed Iraqi guerrillas who, thinking they were doing their patriotic duty, had killed US soldiers, to be amnestied. The idea was to split the Sunni Muslim resistance, or at least show that the interim government was not entirely a pawn. It was too much for Washington to stomach. The plan was watered down and soon forgotten.

The interim government put thousands more blue-shirted police on the streets of Baghdad, and briefly there was a fall in ordinary street crime (significant if you live in the city since even petty thieves carry a gun). But the police often acted as one more militia hungry for perks. Their arrival did not necessarily mean a reduction in violence. A few hundred yards from the al-Hamra Hotel where I was living was a compound with seventeen luxury houses shaded by green bushes and trees, once occupied by guards and relatives of Saddam Hussein. When he was overthrown, fifty-four poor families moved in. They lived there until one morning the police turned up firing into the air and announced that the compound was going to be their new headquarters. 'We complained to an American patrol but the police said we were members of the Mehdi Army,' said Khadir Abbas Jassim, standing beside a heap of broken furniture and brightly coloured toys which the police had tossed into the street. We went round the back of the building to talk to Hussein

Abdullah, the police general in charge of the operation. He was dismissive of the squatters' complaints. 'We are a legal state and we are just applying the law,' he said. All the while there was a man standing behind the general jumping up and down trying to attract my attention. We moved out into the street but half a dozen police came with us. The man, who was called Ahmed Hussein, unwisely told a complicated story about how the police had looted his house six months previously. The policemen thought he had just accused them of stealing and reached for their pistols. Ahmed looked terrified. 'The police are going to kill me,' he said, 'unless you take me with you in your car.' I spent an irritating hour persuading the police to let me drive him to safety.

The insurgents did not have it all their own way. National solidarity with the besieged insurgents in Fallujah soon dissipated after April 2004. Shia in Baghdad, perhaps 70 per cent of the capital's population, saw Fallujah as the launching pad for the suicide bombers who blew themselves up every day. Again and again these attacks butchered the young men who waited for days outside police stations and army recruitment centres looking for jobs. Even on days when the police told them they were not interviewing recruits, or even that a bomb was suspected, the job applicants would refuse to go away. They suspected it was a trick by the police to get them out of the way so they could give the jobs to their relatives or men who had paid them bribes.

Allawi was determined to show that he was a force to be reckoned with but he could only do so by using the American army. In August he chose to confront Muqtada al-Sadr and his Mehdi Army militiamen in Najaf. The city endured its second siege inside six months. After three weeks much of it was in ruins, 400 people had been killed and 2,500 wounded, but Allawi still had not eliminated Sadr or his men. But Allawi and the Americans did not dare assault the shrine of Imam Ali which Sadr had made his headquarters. It was Grand Ayatollah Ali al-Sistani, returning from medical treatment in London, who once again showed his immense influence by negotiating an end to the fighting. I wondered if the Mehdi Army militiamen who had given me a nasty moment when they detained me outside Kufa six months earlier had survived the battle.

It was evident that the US Marines were going to storm Fallujah as soon as the US presidential election was over. Political circumstances were easier than in April. The Shia in Baghdad now saw the city as a threat. It had become the redoubt of the most extreme Salafi and Jihadi fighters. It was they who decided to make a stand while the more nationalist guerrillas left the city before the attack on November 7. It was the sort of set-piece battle at which the American military excelled, in the sense that their victory was guaranteed because of their vastly superior firepower. Success on the ground was accompanied by the usual excessive use of force, which destroyed most of the city. 'During preparatory operations in the November 2004 Fallujah clearance operation, on one night over forty 155mm artillery rounds were fired into a small sector of the city,' recalled Brigadier Aylwin-Foster, the perceptive British commander serving with the US forces in Baghdad. 'Most armies would consider this bombardment a significant event. Yet it did not feature on the next morning's update to the 4-Star Force Commander: the local commander considered it to be a minor application of combat power.'[20] Fallujah became a city of ruins. Some Sunni may have been intimidated but the guerrillas simply drew the tactical lesson that they must not try to hold cities or towns they had captured.

The assault on Fallujah was also a turning point for media coverage of Iraq. The fighting in Najaf in August had been covered from both sides. There were journalists with the Mehdi Army within the shrine and with the US troops outside. But in Fallujah ten weeks later there were almost no journalists reporting from inside the city. The insurgents said they would kill any they found. A few brave photographers who took the risk of staying there were ordered to leave. Iraqi journalists were viewed by the resistance fighters with almost the same suspicion as foreigners. As a result the battle was heavily covered by the media but only from the US side. Correspondents and television crews were embedded with the Marines and reflected their perceptions.

As fighting raged in Fallujah the US and the Iraqi government suffered a serious defeat further north that went unnoticed by the outside world because there were almost no foreign reporters present. American military spokesmen in Baghdad and Washington had every reason to keep quiet about what had happened. On November 11 the insurgents had captured Mosul, the third largest city in Iraq, with a population of 1.7 million compared to 350,000 in Fallujah. General David Petraeus, whom I had met at the start of the year, had long departed and his attempt to conciliate the Sunni Arab establishment in Mosul had been abandoned. The insurgent takeover of the city was obviously planned to coincide with the assault on Fallujah when US attention and troops were elsewhere. The police and Iraqi army soldiers abandoned their barracks – some thirty of them were still empty six months later – and the police commander disappeared, seeking refuge with the Kurds. The resistance seized $40 million worth of arms and equipment, including 11,000 assault rifles.

General Petraeus had tried to avoid relying on Kurdish military forces, but as Mosul's defences crumbled they were the only reliable military units able to intervene. The commander of the entirely Kurdish 3rd Brigade of the Iraqi army was an ebullient ex-*peshmerga* commander called General Muthafar Deirky, based in Dohuk forty minutes' drive north of Mosul. 'There were over 10,000 police in Mosul but they never fired a shot,' he told me later with disgust. 'Even the coalition [US] forces left the city centre and went to their bases.' General Deirky received a telephone call from General Babaker Zebari, the chief of staff of the Iraqi army, telling him: 'Mosul is under the control of terrorists and the coalition has asked for support from our forces.' General Deirky gathered together 700 well-equipped *peshmerga* and headed for Mosul. He arrived just in time to fight a skirmish with insurgents who were about to capture the television station.

Loudspeakers on the minarets of the mosques were calling for a jihad and general uprising. The general made the alarming discovery, when he reached the main Iraqi army base, that out of 1,800 soldiers in the brigade stationed there all except thirty Kurds had deserted. 'The commander of the brigade was in a panic and it was only when he saw me that the colour came back into his face. He was so happy he couldn't even shake hands.' Iraqi army soldiers had a reason to run. Weeks later the corpses of those captured and shot by the insurgents were still turning up in Mosul. Over the next few days General Deirky's Kurds and the US took back the city as the resistance faded away, having decided, unlike Fallujah, not to stand and fight.

It was not only in Mosul that the war was difficult and dangerous to report. The insurgents made no effort to cultivate the media. When they appeared to be willing to talk it was often a trap to set up a foreign journalist as a kidnap victim. In Baghdad, not far from the Hamra Hotel in the grounds of al-Nahrain university beside the Tigris, there was a mosque with a pretty light-blue dome like an upturned bowl surrounded by tents, in which refugees from Fallujah were living. Some months after the battle for Fallujah I went to talk to them. But I sent my translator Haidar, in whose ability to anticipate danger I had great confidence, to talk to them first while I waited a hundred yards away. I became bored and irritated by the length of time I had to wait by the car. When he finally returned he said he did not like the look of the young men hanging around the mosque. Haidar had spoken to the Imam of the mosque who had at first seemed friendly but later volunteered that the murdered Irish aid worker Margaret Hassan, whom I had got to know before she was kidnapped, had been 'a spy in Iraq for thirty years'. We jumped into the car and escaped. In February 2005 an Italian journalist called Giuliana Sgrena working for *Il Manifesto* went to the same mosque. She was asked to wait for three hours so a sheikh could come from Fallujah to talk to her. It turned out that somebody among the refugees had other plans in mind and when she did leave, two carloads of gunmen were waiting to kidnap her. When she was finally freed, after a ransom was paid, the car taking her to the airport was fired on by an American checkpoint and the Italian security man who had arranged her release was shot dead.

In 2005 the war became increasingly sectarian with ever more attacks by Sunni suicide bombers on Shia civilians. The war against the US forces continued at about the same level of intensity as the previous year. In 2004 the American forces in Iraq lost 848 dead and 7,989 wounded and in 2005 a further 846 dead and 5,944 wounded. These were small losses compared to World Wars One and Two, but politically unsustainable because President Bush and Tony Blair had gone to war with such shallow political support at home. In early 2006 there was only a slight fall in American casualties as Iraq slid towards a low-intensity civil war between Sunni and Shia in and around Baghdad. There was another important figure which did not change much in three years of guerrilla war. Most of the five-million-strong Sunni community supported the insurgents. A poll of 1,150 Iraqis carried out by WorldPublicOpinion.org in January 2006 showed that 88 per cent of Sunni Arabs approved of attacks on US-led forces. Of these 77 per cent said they strongly approved of attacks and 11 per cent said they somewhat approved (ominously for the US, approval among Shia for attacks was 41 per cent, though only 16 per cent among Kurds). This level of support was strong enough to keep the insurgency in business for as long as its leaders wanted.

The heightened sectarianism came about as the Shia began to take over important parts of the new Iraqi government under Ibrahim al-Jaafari from May 2005. The Shia had been under attack from Sunni suicide bombers for eighteen months but were restrained from retaliating by Grand Ayatollah Ali al-Sistani. It was only now that revenge killings, orchestrated by the Shia-controlled Ministry of the Interior, became common.

The main signs of this double war – Sunni against Americans and Sunni against Shia – in Baghdad were suicide bombs directed at soft targets, assassinations and infrequent but well-organized large-scale attacks. The bombings were very similar and describing them became a gruesome ritual. Usually I would hear the boom of the bombs exploding between 7.30 and 10 a.m. in the morning. These were so notoriously the most dangerous hours that some officials deliberately waited until after 10 a.m. to go to their offices. When the first suicide bombers blew themselves up at the end of 2003 I would try to reach the site of the explosion. This became increasingly difficult to do over the next two years because one invariable result of a suicide attack was a traffic jam in the streets around where the bomb went off. Given that traffic in Baghdad was at the best of times close to gridlock it became immensely time-consuming to drive anywhere in central Baghdad after an explosion. If I did reach the bomb site the scene was always the same: the crater in the road, the shattered glass underfoot, the plastic shoes and torn bloody clothes of the victims. I stopped going directly to where bombs had detonated, often outside army and police recruiting stations, and headed directly for hospitals where I could talk in person to the victims and their relatives. A further reason for not going to where the bombs had gone off was that suicide bombers began to operate in pairs or even in larger numbers. In the attack on the Palestine and Sheraton hotels on October 25 2005 at least three bombers had worked together. One had let off a diversionary blast, a second blew open the protective concrete barrier so a third man driving a tractor packed with explosives could break through. Fear of a secondary or tertiary attack meant that Iraqi police and soldiers, trigger-happy at the best of times, were apt to open fire at anything suspicious after the first bomb had gone off.

The ferocity of the attacks induced terror thoughout Baghdad. It is worth describing in some detail the aftermath of one suicide bombing, no different from many others and which caused limited carnage, to convey the sense of fear in the capital at this time. It happened at 8.30 a.m. on January 24 2005, a week before the parliamentary election, when a suicide bomber driving a Toyota tried to enter the heavily guarded Zaidoun Street which housed many government offices on the edge of the Green Zone. These included the headquarters of the Iraqi National Accord, the party of Iyad Allawi, the interim prime minister. The bomber did not get very far. He was stopped by heavily armed police commandos at a concrete barrier and blew himself up. 'Going by the remains of the face that we found later, we think he was a non-Iraqi Arab, maybe a Sudanese or from the Gulf,' a detective investigating the case told me in the Yarmouk hospital in west Baghdad to which the injured commandos had been taken. Compared to other suicide bombs the casualties were light – only nine security men and one civilian were injured. But as the wounded were carried into the Yarmouk they showed how frightened they were. Even those with severe burns or broken bones were less concerned by their injuries than fearful that the doctors treating them would remove the black ski-masks hiding their faces. 'You mustn't take any photographs,' screamed a masked policeman, his assault rifle at the ready, as he blocked the path of two Iraqi press photographers trying to enter the emergency ward. Later an insurgent website claimed the attack, saying that 'one of the young lions in the suicide regiment' had carried it out against the offices of Iyad Allawi, 'the agent of the Jews and the Christians'.

The slaughter inflicted by the suicide bombers was so blatant that it was easy to forget that they were only a part of the insurgency. They seldom attacked US troops or heavily fortified American military outposts. The political and psychological impact of the bombings was out of proportion to the numbers involved in organizing the bombers and sending them on their deadly missions. The insurgents who carried out the highly effective roadside bomb attacks on US convoys and patrols were far less visible. So too were the men who assassinated or ambushed senior officials. A few hundred yards from my hotel was the headquarters of the Interior Ministry, housed in an old bomb shelter dating from the Iran–Iraq war. In February 2005, a few months before the Ministry was taken over and purged by the Shia Supreme Council for Islamic Revolution in Iraq (SCIRI), I met a badly wounded officer at the entrance. He was called General Mudher, a burly middle-aged man who had created the police commandos, whose black ski-masks and camouflage uniforms had recently become a common sight in Baghdad. A veteran soldier, he was famous in Iraq for bringing his tank safely from Kuwait to Baghdad during the 1991 Gulf War. He explained that he had been very careful about his own security and was always changing his address. It did not do him much good. Somebody in the resistance decided he posed a real threat. Two months before I met him gunmen attacked his car and he was shot twice in the back, the bullets just missing his heart. He was lucky to be alive since he counted 150 bullet holes in the remains of his vehicle. Largely recovered from his wounds, the general still winced with pain when he walked.

It was not difficult to work out where the insurgents' intelligence about the movements of men like General Mudher came from. Old Iraqi army and intelligence officers, some still serving, were mostly sympathetic to the resistance. The American recipe for making army and security forces more effective was to embed US training officers in Iraqi units. 'They keep saying they don't need better training but better weapons,' said Sabah Khadim, a senior adviser in the Interior Ministry, of the Iraqi soldiers and police. There was outrage among some Iraqi military units when they discovered that some long-promised tanks were outdated Soviet-made T-55s. 'The one thing the Americans seem determined about is to retain control of the Iraqi army,' a foreign diplomat told me. For all the talk from George Bush about building up the Iraqi security forces, the US forces on the ground feared that one day weapons they handed over would be used against them by Iraqis or sold to the resistance.

General Mudher explained he was worried about his personal survival for another reason. The United Iraqi Alliance, the coalition of Shia parties, had just triumphed in the January election. The general was wondering what would happen to old Iraqi army veterans like himself when such parties, some of which had supported Iran in the Iran–Iraq war, started to take over the security ministries. At best he would be deprived of his bodyguards and left to be hunted down by the insurgents; at worst the triumphant Shia paramilitaries would kill him themselves.

The purpose of the assassins and suicide bombers was to prevent the American government establishing control of the country. In this they were wholly successful. In late 2005, when Ibrahim al-Jaafari, the prime minister living in the Green Zone, wanted to visit President Jalal Talabani who had his own heavily defended enclave half a mile away in Baghdad, his security men explained that the short journey was too dangerous. They asked Jaafari to wait twenty-four hours so they could secure his route. Whenever there was any sense that normal life might be returning suicide bombers struck immediately. People in Baghdad and the cities of central Iraq were paralyzed by fear. One Friday in July, there were twelve attacks in a single day. A bomber with explosives strapped to his chest blew himself up beside a petrol tanker in the truck-stop town of Musayyib south of Baghdad. The explosion incinerated people walking in the market and visiting a Shia mosque. After their bodies were taken away there was the usual debris of charred shoes, broken bicycles and pools of dried blood. The local hospital estimated that ninety-eight people had died and 156 were injured. The studied cruelty of the bombers got worse by the day. During the same period a man driving a car packed with explosives blew himself up beside a US army Humvee in a Shia district of Baghdad and killed at least eighteen children playing in the street. A distraught man called Qais who was mourning for his children said to us: 'I have to move from my home because I cannot bear to look at the place where my two sons – Ali was five and Abbas was six – were playing before they died.'

XIII

IN THE SUMMER of 2005 a government-owned news-paper in Baghdad ran a laudatory article about reconstruction in the capital. The text highlighted new achievements and spoke hopefully of others planned. But the paper faced a delicate problem when it came to illustrating the piece. Despite billions of dollars supposedly spent on reconstructing the capital over the previous two-and-a-half years there were no cranes visible on the skyline. This was despite 'the biggest rebuilding project since the post-war rebuilding of Europe in 1945'. When I took the lift to the flat roof of the Hamra Hotel to see where bombs had exploded I never saw any signs of old buildings being repaired or new ones under construction. The paper's editors proved equal to the challenge. When the article appeared it included a striking photograph of a large crane beside a half-completed building. My translator Haidar looked mystified when he first saw it and then, after examining it carefully, began to laugh. He pointed out to me, between guffaws, that the picture was indeed of a crane in Baghdad but one which had been standing abandoned since 2003 beside a giant mosque which Saddam Hussein had under construction when he was overthrown.

Dr Mahmoud Othman had told me that 'corruption' was destroying Iraq just as surely as the occupation and terrorism. It was not as obvious a point as it might appear to somebody living outside Iraq. He was not speaking of corruption in the sense that bribes were being paid or crooked officials were taking a percentage of the contract price, although this was happening. The corruption which became pervasive under the CPA, the Iyad Allawi interim government and now under Ibrahim al-Jaafari was far more extensive and destructive. There were no cranes to be seen in Baghdad because all the money was being stolen and nothing was being done in return. My friend Ali Allawi, the Finance Minister in the Jaafari government, lamented that Iraq 'is becoming like Nigeria in the past when all the oil revenues were stolen'. There was always money to steal because, however bad the state of Iraq, there were oil revenues even when insurgents were blowing up pipelines. Crude exports might be down but the price of oil was up so revenues were still running at over $2 billion a month in the summer of 2005. But the mass theft of money meant that the Iraqi state withered. It did not do people any good. When I stopped people in the street in Baghdad and asked them what they thought of the government they would often ask in reply: 'What government? It does nothing for us.'

The corruption had started early. Stuart Bowen, special investigator for Iraqi reconstruction, revealed that under Paul Bremer's CPA $8.8 billion was unaccounted for because oversight was practically non-existent.[21] Frank Willis, the number two man in the transport ministry when it was run by the US-led coalition in 2004–5 related how not only was there no accounting for money spent, but that funds were kept in cash. 'Fresh, new, crisp, unspent, just-printed $100 bills,' Willis recalled. 'It was the Wild West.'[22] Baghdad was filled with stories of money misspent or stolen. An American soldier was put in charge of helping the Iraqi boxing team to re-establish itself but gambled away the money given to him to assist them. The cash was certainly gone but nobody knew if he had lost $60,000 or $20,000 because no record was kept of how much money he had received in the first place.[23]

Word had spread at the start of the occupation that there was easy money to be made in Iraq if you were brazen enough and had the right contacts. I suddenly began to see the insignia of a company called Custer Battles at the airport. Frank Willis said it was formed by former army ranger Scott Custer and a failed congressional candidate, Mike Battles, who claimed to be active in the Republican Party and knew people in the White House. He added: 'They came in with a can-do attitude, whether they could or not. They were not experienced. They didn't know what they were doing.' Despite this they won a $16.8 million contract to secure Baghdad International Airport. Colonel Richard Ballard, the inspector general of the army in Iraq at the time, said Custer Battles, later under federal investigation, were paid up front for X-ray equipment which they failed to acquire. They did provide a bomb-sniffer dog that was meant to detect explosives in cars and trucks through its acute sense of smell but Ballard said the dog resolutely refused 'to sniff the vehicles'. Ballard suspected that the bomb-detecting dog and his handler were simply 'a guy and his pet'. In a memo obtained by CBS's '60 Minutes', the airport's director of security wrote intemperately to the coalition that 'Custer Battles have shown themselves to be unresponsive, uncooperative, incompetent, deceitful, manipulative and war profiteers. Other than that, they are swell fellows.'[24]

There were many other swell fellows around in post-Saddam Iraq. The shortage of American troops, the lack of trustworthy local allies, the free-market principles of the Bush administration and simple greed meant that Iraq became the hunting ground for the world's shadier characters. In some cases the deceptions were touchingly simple. A British security man formerly in the British army related that once in the Green Zone he saw a group of western security men clustering around an Iraqi politician getting into a car. He did not think they were protecting their charge very effectively and drew nearer to see who they were. He suddenly recognized one of the guards, went up to him and said: 'Hello, Fred.' The man looked aghast at being addressed by name. He was, in fact, the assistant barman in a pub near an army base in England. While pulling pints for soldiers he had overheard enough military patter to pass himself off as one of them and, citing his British Army background, had subsequently persuaded a US security company to pay him a substantial salary so it could put his expertise to work on their behalf.

Many of the foreign security men in Iraq were veteran troops. Armies in Europe, west and east, had downsized in the wake of the Cold War and there were plenty of expert soldiers looking for jobs. From the American point of view there were several advantages in employing them. It cut down on the number of regular troops, already in short supply, needed for guard duties. They were also, quite literally, cannon fodder since nobody in their home countries either knew or cared if they were killed. Between March 2003 and October 2005 some 412 contractors were killed, or one for every five dead American soldiers. Rising US and British military casualties were central to deflating popular support for the war in the US and UK but nobody paid attention to how many military contractors, usually portrayed as bloodthirsty mercenaries, were being killed or injured.

This was politically convenient for the US and British governments but the use of private security companies had serious disadvantages. It was very expensive. Security costs made up a quarter of all spending on US-funded reconstruction, instead of a budgeted figure of 9 per cent, which meant that many such projects were never completed or even started (the chronic lack of security also made fraud easier because nobody could check on the progress of a contract). Some security men found that it was unwise, and possibly unhealthy, to take their duties so seriously that they impinged on the rackets run by those more influential than themselves. One Australian was put in charge of protecting Basra oil refinery. The Supreme Council for Islamic Revolution had an office there. By the Australian's account the main activity of this office was siphoning off fuel and selling it for a sizeable profit. He closed down their activities. SCIRI then made

representations to the British authorities threatening withdrawal
of cooperation in Basra unless the over-enthusiastic security man
was sacked which, in due course, he was.

Overall the use of private security companies increased the
sense of lawlessness in Iraq. Like US soldiers they had immunity if
they killed Iraqis. Nobody was sure of the identity or background
of many of the men who turned up on guard duty. The entrance
to the Convention Center, where press conferences took place,
had been defended by affable Nepalese, many of them former
Gurkhas. They were suddenly replaced, presumably because
they were relatively less well paid, by disconsolate Peruvians
who seemed terminally homesick and occasionally showed me
postcards of the Inca ruins at Machu Picchu. The US Defence
Department's privatization of a variety of military jobs may have
seemed sensible in peacetime America but not in war-ravaged
Iraq. My friend Adrien Jaulmes, the intrepid correspondent of
the French daily *Le Figaro*, made a discovery at the large US camp
near Fallujah which showed the difficulties inherent in employing civilians to do jobs previously carried out by the military
themselves. In one part of the camp Adrien discovered a large
number of portable lavatories, only a few of which were in use. It
turned out that latrine duty, the job of emptying the lavatories
when they were full of shit and urine, had been privatized and
given to an American company. Unfortunately its employees
refused to go anywhere near Fallujah because it was too dangerous. Consequently the lavatories had to be abandoned when full
up with their evil-smelling contents and new ones erected by the
army. I wondered if, when the US army came to leave its camp,
the rows of abandoned toilets would remain as a monument to
their presence.

Corruption came in all sizes after the invasion. Not surprisingly
many Iraqis saw government as simply a way of extorting money
from the people. This view was not necessarily an exaggeration.
A friend who wanted to get a new number plate for his car sat in

a queue of vehicles for five hours without moving. Then he went home, made a telephone call to the government office involved, agreed to pay $100 and the new plates were delivered to his office the next day. At the Transport Ministry a newly appointed minister who took up his duties in 2005 said that so far as he could see everything had been stolen from the ministry except the name. There were fewer buses on the streets because they were sold off by officials and cannibalized for spare parts. Their hulks, stripped of anything worth selling, turned up at rubbish dumps all over Baghdad. Saddam Hussein's government had been corrupt enough, but also intermittently effective. People in Baghdad recalled that it took him six months to restore electricity supplies after power stations were hit by bombs and missiles in the First Gulf War. Thirty months after the Second Gulf War, Baghdad was getting two hours of electricity for every four hours of blackout. Iraqis in the street had no doubt about what was happening. 'The government claims that they have projects to increase the supply of electricity, but in fact the money ends up in their pockets,' said Haider Ali, a student. In Najaf during the January 2005 election it was impossible to buy petrol legally since the supply was diverted into the black market controlled by the local police. 'You can't get the smallest contract from the government without bribery at every level,' a businessman told me.

Corruption was so destructive because it weakened those functions of a state supposedly fighting a brutal war in which its very existence was at stake. When Iyad Allawi became interim prime minister in June 2004 a prime aim of his administration and of its American backers was to build up the Iraqi armed forces. These had melted away during the April uprisings in Fallujah and in the Shia cities of the south. In November the army and police had either deserted or joined the insurgents in the struggle for Mosul. It was vital that the new troops and policemen receive modern weapons, vehicles and other equipment. But in 2005 and 2006 it was still common to see Iraqi troops riding around Baghdad in elderly white pick-ups or trucks which looked as if they were designed to carry cauliflowers or cabbages to market. Sometimes metal plates were roughly screwed or welded on to the sides of the pick-ups to give their occupants some protection. It was not enough. Soldiers and police were routinely butchered by better-armed insurgents or their vehicles torn apart by roadside bombs.

There was a reason why the new Iraqi army, so critical for the survival of the Iraqi government and the success of the US in Iraq, had so few modern weapons. It was not just that the Americans thought they would be sold or used against US troops. No less than $1.3 billion was allocated for arms procurement under Iyad Allawi, but it had been siphoned abroad in cash and had disappeared. 'It is possibly one of the largest thefts in history,' Ali Allawi, the Finance Minister in the succeeding government, told me. 'Huge amounts of money have disappeared. In return we got nothing but scraps of metal.' The fraud had taken place between June 28 2004 and February 28 2005 during the Iyad Allawi administration, though details did not emerge until later in the same year. The carefully planned theft had so weakened the army that senior Iraqi officials admitted that it could not hold Baghdad against insurgent attack, making it difficult for the US to withdraw its 135,000-strong army from Iraq, as Washington claimed it wanted to do.

Most of the money was supposedly spent buying arms from Poland and Pakistan. The contracts were peculiar in four ways. According to Ali Allawi, they were awarded without bidding, and were signed with a Baghdad-based company, and not directly with the foreign supplier. The money was paid up front and, surprisingly for Iraq, it was paid at great speed out of the ministry's account with the Central Bank. Military equipment purchased from Poland included 28-year-old Soviet-made helicopters. The manufacturers said they should have been scrapped after twenty-five years of service. Armoured cars purchased by

Iraq turned out to be so poorly made that even a bullet from an elderly AK-47 assault rifle could penetrate their armour. A shipment of the latest MP5 American machine guns, at a cost of $3,500 each, consisted in reality of Egyptian copies worth only $200 a gun. Other armoured cars leaked so much oil that they had to be abandoned. A deal was struck to buy 7.62mm machine-gun bullets for 16 cents each, although they should have cost between 4 and 6 cents.

Given that building an Iraqi army to replace American and British troops was a priority for Washington and London, the failure to notice that so much money was disappearing argues at the very least a high degree of negligence on the part of US officials and officers in Baghdad who oversaw the defence ministry. The report of the Board of Supreme Audit on the Defence Ministry contracts was presented to the office of Ibrahim al-Jaafari in May 2005. But the extent of the losses only gradually became apparent. The sum missing was first reported as $300 million and then $500 million, but in fact it was at least twice as large. 'If you compare the amount that was allegedly stolen of about $1 billion compared with the budget of the Ministry of Defence, it is nearly 100 per cent of the ministry's [procurement] budget that has gone AWOL,' said Ali Allawi.

The money missing from all ministries under the interim government of Iyad Allawi was probably about $2 billion. Of a military procurement budget of $1.3 billion, some $200 million may have been spent on useable equipment, though this was a charitable view according to officials. As a result the Iraqi army had had to rely on cast-offs from the US army, though even these had been slow in coming. Ali Allawi said a further $500 million to $600 million had allegedly disappeared from the electricity, transport, interior and other ministries. This helped explain why the supply of electricity remained so poor. The money had disappeared while Hazem al-Shalaan, previously a small business-man in London, had been Defence Minister. Charged with public corruption, he moved to the UK. The other figure at the centre of the affair was Ziyad Cattan, the defence procurement chief, who had run a pizza parlour in Germany in the 1990s. Of joint Iraqi-Polish nationality, he spent twenty-seven years in Europe before returning to Iraq where he became close to Paul Bremer, who said that Cattan 'embodied the dedication so many Iraqis felt for their nation'.[25]

So many Iraqi parties and political leaders were involved or affected by the disappearance of the defence procurement budget that knowledgeable Iraqi officials doubted if the investigation would ever be completed. For eight months the Defence Ministry had spent without restraint and without any visible return for its money. Everybody, Iraqi and American, claimed to have noticed nothing amiss. Contracts worth more than $5 million should have been reviewed by a cabinet committee, but Shalaan had asked for and received an exemption for the defence ministry. Contracts for large sums were short scribbles on a single piece of paper. So sparse was documentation that auditors even had difficulty working out who Iraq had a contract with in Pakistan. The only certainty was that a large sum of money had been paid up front and pieces of military equipment of doubtful usefulness were intermittently arriving in Iraq.

In the midst of this savage war and disintegration of the state Iraqis did not enjoy many jokes. But a long-running source of merriment in Baghdad was the amount of time government ministers spent out of the country. A magazine claimed to have discovered that at one moment all ministers were abroad on essential missions. Once safe in hotels from New York to London and Dubai, ministers were happy to give speeches and interviews bidding defiance to the insurgents. Once I went to the Iraqi Airways office on the ground floor of the Palestine Hotel in Baghdad to get a ticket to fly to Amman. I had to wait a few minutes because the manager had a phone in each hand and was alternately talking into each. When he had finished speaking he apologized and explained that once again his morning had been spent arbitrating between two ministries whose ministers and entourage were vehemently demanding they be given the limited number of first-class seats on the same plane. 'Perhaps we should have a separate aircraft just for government officials leaving the country,' he said resignedly.

XIV

O N THE DAY of the election, January 30 2005, the streets of Baghdad were clear of traffic. Families, mainly Shia, drifted down the main road in the Jadriyah district to the polling stations near the al-Hamra Hotel, where I was living. The thump-thump of mortars in the distance did not affect the festive mood. The odd bicycle rattled past. Civilian vehicles had been banned from the streets. For the first time for over a year there was no danger of suicide car bombs. A blue-and-white police vehicle hooted at a small child kicking a ball. Children often played in an alleyway behind the hotel – their favourite game, played with plastic Kalashnikovs, was Americans vs. the resistance – but it had been a long time since I had seen any of them on the main road.

By midday the Western television correspondents who had poured into Baghdad the previous week were exclaiming enthusiastically at the massive turnout of voters in Shia and Kurdish districts of the country. This shouldn't have come as a surprise. It was, after all, the Shia leaders who had demanded an election after the fall of Saddam Hussein in April 2003. They wanted the polls to show that Shias, who made up 60 per cent of the Iraqi population, had the right to hold political power. Eighteen months earlier the US had recoiled at the idea of an election in the belief that, with the help of a few tame Iraqi exiles, it could rule Iraq itself. Excuses were made. US officials said there had to be a census first to identify potential voters. The attraction of the census for Washington was the length of time it would take (although American and British generals in command in northern and southern Iraq assured me that an election in late 2003 or early 2004 was both feasible and necessary). Instead of an election the US toyed with the idea of appointing caucuses of local elites to draw up a constitution. Only when guerrilla attacks escalated in Sunni districts did the US realize that it could not afford to alienate the Shia as well as the Sunni. It was also faced by a *fatwa* from Grand Ayatollah Ali al-Sistani in June 2003, which stated that those who drew up the constitution must first be elected. He issued a further statement in November 2003 demanding that a transitional National Assembly also be chosen by ballot. Imperial direct rule was already in deep trouble. Suddenly the holding of elections turned out to have been the centrepiece of American policy all along.

Iraqis were desperate for peace. I also felt I was being ground down by the permanent anxiety – the need always to be on the alert for any sign of danger – that was the daily experience of anybody living in Baghdad. It had, for instance, been a long time since I had walked down Jadriyah Street. It was safer than many roads in the capital – not that this was saying a great deal: gunmen and kidnappers could watch potential victims coming and going from the hotel. To be as inconspicuous as possible I travelled in an elderly car, caked with dust, more likely to belong to an Iraqi than a Westerner. We peered nervously out of the rear window to see if we were being followed. If anything looked suspicious the driver immediately turned off the main road into smaller streets, until he was sure nobody was following us. Another simple gambit was to drive through a police checkpoint near the Hamra where the police knew us and waved us through but would stop and question anybody behind us.

Jadriyah, a middle-class neighbourhood built on a large loop in the Tigris, was considered by people in Baghdad to be one of the least dangerous areas in the city. It was one of the few places where, when it was warm enough to sit outside in the evenings, families ate kebabs and drank tea in makeshift restaurants beside the main road. But even here things were changing and for the worse. The previous month a suicide bomber had blown himself up beside a large half-finished office block that served as a guard post for Australian soldiers who protected their embassy nearby. The building, on the main road, was turned into a concrete sandwich by the blast, as one floor collapsed on top of another. 'He must have been one of the stupidest bombers in the world,' said Nabil, a businessman who was sitting on a chair in the street watching voters go by. 'He killed two people, both Iraqis. One of them was a mentally ill man everybody liked who'd never recovered from his son being killed in the Iran–Iraq war.' A few hundred yards further down the road was a battered white kiosk where a middle-aged man was selling cigarettes. On the inside wall was a picture of him and his fourteen-year-old son. The boy was called Ali Abbas. He used to sell me cigarettes until I gave up smoking in December 2003. When another suicide bomber blew himself up in Jadriyah Street – his target was never clear – I had forgotten that the explosion was close to Ali's kiosk; I didn't know that it had killed him.

The election was the first of three polls in 2005 which were supposed to create a new democratic Iraqi state. The first, that January, was a nationwide vote for a transitional National Assembly which would draw up a constitution. The second poll was a referendum on this constitution to be held on October 15. The third election was for a permanent Iraqi parliament, the Council of Representatives, serving a four-year term, which would take place two months later on December 15. Perhaps in the White House or 10 Downing Street this looked like steady progress – and certainly it could be presented as such. But the closer one got to Iraq the more this progress seemed to be a mirage. The three polls were more likely to crystallize rather than eliminate differences between the three main communities: the Shia, Kurds and Sunni. In the January election only the Kurds and Shia took part: the Sunni boycotted it. Any Shia–Kurdish government formed after the election would deepen the sense among the Sunni that they were being marginalized. Any constitution agreed, given the agenda of those negotiating it, would certainly weaken the central government and create powerful Shia and Kurdish cantons. The Sunni, with only seventeen members in the National Assembly, would continue to rely on armed resistance to make sure that the US and other Iraqi communities knew that there could be no peace without their participation. After the interim National Assembly was elected they had every incentive go on fighting the US with the same intensity as before, and to escalate their attacks on Iraqi government forces and Shia civilians.

It was always a weakness of the US in Iraq after overthrowing Saddam Hussein that its policies and actions were determined by American domestic politics rather than Iraqi reality. I was reminded of the Austro-Hungarian commander in World War One who prematurely attacked and captured Belgrade in November 1914. He then suffered a catastrophic defeat, as his fellow-generals had warned him he would, when the Serbian army briskly counter-attacked. It emerged later that he had undertaken his risky and subsequently disastrous advance because he wanted to seize Belgrade in time for the Emperor Franz Josef's birthday celebrations. He thought this would do his reputation a lot of good back in Vienna. In Iraq almost a century later Washington was likewise hamstrung by the priority it gave to producing synthetic political and military victories for home consumption. Holding the elections and a referendum were not wrong in themselves but they were not going to bring peace to Iraq.

Few elections have been regarded with such trepidation by potential voters as that for the transitional National Assembly on January 30. Iraqis had not had a free election for half a century. 'Baghdad will surely burn during the election days,' said one voter. 'I think more about my own survival than I do about the election campaign.' Many who could afford it left the country for Jordan, Syria and Dubai. Others abroad on business or the *haj* pilgrimage delayed their return. Students stayed away from the universities. It was not difficult to see why. On a website associated with Abu Musab al-Zarqawi candidates were denounced as 'demi-idols' and voters as 'infidels'. He said: 'We have declared a fierce war on this evil principle of democracy and those who follow this wrong ideology.' Nobody took such threats lightly. I fell into conversation with three young Shia men lolling by the door to the Yarmouk hospital. They said they wanted to vote – 'it is our religious duty' – but went on to explain that 'we live in al-Dohra, a very dangerous district, and maybe we will not dare go to the polls'.

In fact most Shia and Kurds did go to the polls and voted enthusiastically, though at least thirty-five people were killed by nine suicide bombers in Baghdad on election day. The poll was well-organized. US troops kept in the background. In Baghdad most of the police and army units were Shia who thoroughly approved of the election. But the approval of the Shia was accompanied by wariness, a suspicion that whatever the election's outcome the US would never allow the Shia to rule Iraq. I wandered around my district interviewing people on the street (the safest way to do this before the election was to approach people queuing in their cars for petrol, whom I could talk to by rolling the window down without leaving the safety of my own car). Many of the voters were more concerned by day-to-day survival than the election. 'We are suffering from many crises: lack of food, electricity and fuel,' said a Mr Anwar. 'It was bad enough under Saddam but now it is ten times worse. I graduated from college but now I have to work as a taxi driver and I do not have enough money even to buy shoes.' Several of those I talked to said they saw the election as a movie directed by the Americans to impress the outside world. 'It is like a film,' said Abu Draid, an unemployed carpenter. 'It will be the Americans who will control the next government whatever happens.' Not everybody agreed. I saw a group of young men, all of whom turned out to be Shia, unloading bottles of gas, which Iraqis use for cooking, from a battered pick-up. Their mood was bitter. They pointed out that the bottles, which once sold for the equivalent of 16p, now cost £3 each. Even so several said they did not think the election was a waste of time and they would vote for the Shia slate of candidates, the United Iraqi Alliance, put together under the auspices of Grand Ayatollah Ali al-Sistani.

The results of the election were announced after a long delay. When they did come through I heard the voice of a friend say jubilantly down the phone 'it's a Sistani tsunami'. So it was. Iraqis had voted almost wholly along ethnic or sectarian lines. The United Iraqi Alliance, containing all the main Shia parties, had won 140 out of 275 seats, followed by the Kurdish bloc with seventy-five seats. Iyad Allawi, the prime minister and the hope of secular nationalists and the US, came a disappointing third with only forty seats. The Sunni boycott had been almost total. In Anbar province, the Sunni heartland to the west of Baghdad, less than 2 per cent of people had voted.

'The Shia had the right strategy,' said a friend. 'They put all their energy into mobilizing their vote and getting people to the polls.' The Hawza, the Shia religious establishment, showed its immense influence within its community. The new prime minister was going to be a Shia, either Ibrahim al-Jaafari, the leader of the Dawa party, or Adel Abdel Mehdi of the Supreme Council for Islamic Revolution in Iraq. The Shia success was also a jolt for the US, as one of the few consistent themes in US policy since the fall of Saddam Hussein had been to prevent the complete takeover of Arab Iraq by the Shia majority. Washington sometimes toyed with the idea of the so-called '20 per cent solution' to its problems in Iraq. This meant relying on the Shia and Kurdish communities, together comprising 80 per cent of the population, and ignoring the 20 per cent who were Sunni. It was never a feasible strategy. The Sunni Arabs had already shown that they could mount a revolt which could destabilize Iraq for as long as they wanted. The Shia had no wish in the long run to share power with an American occupation. The US administration was also sensitive to the allegation that the real strategic winner from the overthrow of Saddam Hussein was Iran, the third member of George Bush's axis of evil. Everywhere Iranian influence was on the rise in Iraq. 'Of course, the Iranians pay all the pro-Iranian parties,' said a Shia friend dolefully after a tour of southern Iraq. 'And they pay all the anti-Iranian parties as well.'

Journalists are notoriously prone to exaggerate the beneficial impact of elections and to ignore more complex developments. Television in particular likes these set-piece events, which can be portrayed as historic turning points. It was true that the new elected Iraqi government would have more legitimacy than the old, but this did not change the balance of power on the ground. Communities were becoming more not less fearful of each other. If a member of one strayed into the territory of another he or she could easily be killed. Ten days after the election some Kurdish officials from Kirkuk, unfamiliar with the sectarian geography of Baghdad, took what somebody described to me as 'the mother of all wrong turns'. They mistakenly drove into Haifa Street which, though less than a mile from the Green Zone, was largely under the control of resistance fighters. A gun battle quickly erupted as insurgents, delighted at finding such easy targets, opened fire. Soon, black smoke was rising from burning vehicles. By the time the fighting was over three officials from the Patriotic Union of Kurdistan, who had only come to Baghdad to discuss their election victory, had been shot dead.

Sectarian killings escalated. Insurgent gunmen and bombers were now killing Shia workers without any connection to the army or police. Soon after the election, for instance, two carloads of gunmen shouting 'Allahu Akbar' burst into a bakery filled with Shia workers in the New Baghdad district of the capital. They sprayed the bakers with machine-gun fire, killing nine of them, their blood spattering posters of Shia clerics on the walls.

Bakeries were a favourite target for Sunni death squads in Baghdad because the workers were almost always Shia. As sectarian violence worsened in the spring of 2006 no less than seventy workers in bakeries were killed in a six-week period. Soon the bakers were all armed, their guns propped against the ovens or ready to hand as they kneaded the dough.

The bloodiest single atrocity against the Shia since the fall of Saddam Hussein came a month later. Aside from an enormous casualty list it was typical of such attacks. A suicide car bomber blew himself up, killing 115 young men and wounding 132 as they queued outside a medical centre in the mostly Shia city of Hilla south of Baghdad. They were waiting to receive certificates that would enable them to apply to join the army or police. Even after their burnt and blackened bodies were removed, the street was still littered with the limbs of those torn apart by the blast. 'How can anybody do this to human beings?' asked one onlooker as these grisly remains were loaded on to wooden carts and into the backs of pick-up trucks.

The January election was misleadingly presented in the US and Britain as a rebuff to the insurgents. It was never this but it did presage revolutionary changes in the distribution of power in Iraq in which the Sunni and Americans would be the losers and the Shia and Kurds the winners. I was in Kurdistan when Jalal Talabani was chosen as President of Iraq in April 2005. As the news spread tens of thousands of Kurds sang and danced in triumph. Even somebody as tough and unsentimental as Sa'adi Pira, a Patriotic Union of Kurdistan leader, gazing at a sea of frantically waving Kurdish flags at a celebratory rally, told me: 'I feel for the first time we will be treated as human beings in Iraq.'

We were attending a giant rally outside the town of Altun Kupre on the fast-flowing Lesser Zaab river between Arbil and Kirkuk. All morning cars, buses and trucks had poured along the narrow road to the site of the demonstration. Children hung out of car windows waving the red, white and green Kurdish flag with a golden sunburst in the middle. The avuncular face of

Talabani peered from posters plastered on the windscreens of cars, making it hard for drivers to see. Throngs of Kurds, many wearing their tunics with baggy pants and turbans, crowded the sides of the roads. One man was dancing vigorously on the roof of a car despite the fact that it was travelling at twenty miles an hour. I knew this road well because before the war in 2003 it led through the front line dividing the Kurds from the Iraqi army. Most of the villages on either side of the road had been levelled and their fields sown with mines by Saddam or his predecessors in Baghdad. The danger of mines still meant there was no ploughing and yellow wildflowers carpeted the uncultivated ground. Another sign of the past presence of the Iraqi army was an enormous and menacing concrete fortress, built like a medieval castle with towers and arrow slits, overlooking the fields around Altun Kupre.

Not that peace had returned. As we drove out of Arbil we passed the old PUK headquarters where in February 2004 a bomber with explosives strapped to his chest killed forty-eight people. 'I lost five relatives, including my brother and my nephew, in the explosion,' said Sa'adi Pira, gesturing towards the ruins. But even amid these euphoric celebrations there were signs that the Kurds had limited loyalty towards the country of which they were now part-rulers. They were careful to emphasize that they wanted autonomy and not independence. Their leaders spoke of creating a 'federal and democratic Iraq', but out of the thousands of flags being waved in Altun Kupre I saw only one which was the official flag of Iraq.

The three months of negotiations it took to form a government after the election showed the depth of distrust between its future components. It never seemed likely to prove very effective. When in early May the cabinet led by Ibrahim al-Jaafari was finally sworn in, there were still no permanent ministers for oil, defence, electricity, industry or human rights. Even when finally appointed, ministers, as in the previous government, treated their ministries as the fiefdoms and sole preserve of their party, faction, ethnic or religious community. Most important, the Interior Ministry, commanding more armed men than the Defence Ministry, was to be led by Bayan Jabr, formerly the head of the Badr Organization, the military wing of the Supreme Council for Islamic Revolution in Iraq. He was to turn the ministry into the cutting edge of the Shia drive to acquire power.

The Shia leaders were intent on transmuting their election victory into real authority and were highly suspicious of US attempts to thwart them. They were very conscious that the CIA paid for and retained overall control of the *mukhabarat*, the main security agency. This was headed by Muhammad Abdullah Shahwani, whose three sons were executed after a failed coup organized by Iyad Allawi in 1996. His deputy in charge of daily operations was a Kurd, and only 12 per cent of *mukhabarat* officers were reportedly Shia. The Interior Ministry and Defence Ministry's intelligence agencies were also headed by Kurds – the one Iraqi community fully supporting the occupation. There were numerous covert signs of US lack of faith in the new Iraqi administration. It refused to allow the *mukhabarat*'s intelligence files to be handed over to the new government and had removed them to the US embassy in Baghdad. (A friend, formerly a member of Dawa, working for the Jaafari government who did see the files was astonished by how little important information they contained. 'We had better sources in Dawa in the 1980s,' he said contemptuously. Possibly he did not see them all.) The US justified not handing over these sensitive files to the new government by claiming that it feared Iran, the mentor of SCIRI, would find out from them how much the US knew about its operations in Iraq. The Shia parties' own explanation was more cynical. They suspected that the US did not want them to learn about the extent to which they had been prime targets of surveillance. Hadi al-Ameri, a member of the National Assembly and commander of the Badr Organization, was quoted as contemptuously denigrating the *mukhabarat*: 'I prefer to call it the American Intelligence of Iraq, not the Iraqi Intelligence

Service.' He added: 'It is not working for the Iraqi government – it's working for the CIA.'

The new Jaafari government inherited the problems of the old. Its control over large parts of the country was tenuous or non-existent. When I attended the Kurdish victory rally in Altun Kupre, a town which on the map was three hours' drive north of Baghdad, it was far too dangerous for me to go there directly by road. Instead I had set out to spend two-and-a-half days travelling: first to Turkey by road, then by plane to Amman and Baghdad. Back in the capital it was clear that the guerrillas were as lethally effective as ever. One morning soon after my return, I heard from a friend who had been driving by at the time that there had been an attack in the al-Shebab quarter. I drove there with some trepidation. It was a dreary looking lower middle-class neighbourhood where many people had clerical jobs working for the government. It was not known for its militancy and had a mixed Shia–Sunni population, but it was easy to reach from hardcore insurgent towns such as Mahmoudiya and Latafiyah on the southern outskirts of Baghdad.

Here, close to the al-Darwish roundabout at about 6 a.m., the insurgents had shot dead nine policemen and wounded two others in a bloody skirmish of a kind that was going on all over Iraq, though little of it was reported by the Iraqi or foreign media. In the first four months of the year the police had already lost 616 men killed. I talked to local people, none of whom wanted to be named, who had witnessed the gun battle. There were bloodstains and a few copper cartridges from a Kalashnikov on the concrete pavement in front of a shop dealing in real estate. The owner was stoically sweeping up broken glass. He pointed to a dozen holes where bullets had punctured the metal door of his shop, dug chunks out of the wall and ripped through the green sofa where his clients normally sat. By one account the insurgents had used a heavy machine gun mounted on a truck. Outgunned and caught by surprise, the lightly armed police never stood a chance. 'We were all very frightened when we heard the shooting,' said a man in a long brown robe. 'I came out as soon as it was over and found one policeman dead in the street. There was another one hit in the side and I tried to help him.' He had watched the insurgents pour fuel over a bullet-riddled blue-and-white police car before setting it ablaze along with its dead or badly wounded driver who was slumped over the steering wheel.

The government of Ibrahim al-Jaafari did not differ much from its predecessor when it came to expressing breezy optimism about the future of Iraq. Soon after his government was at last complete Jaafari stood beside Tony Blair in London and com-mented: 'I think two years will be enough and more than enough to establish security.'

Baghdad was such an extraordinarily violent city at all times that it was difficult to know if the rate of killing was going up or down. As the war entered its third year a diplomat told me that the level of violence was about the same but that 'the real change in the situation is the increased sectarian hatred between the Shia and Sunni in recent weeks'. This was undoubtedly true. The Shia had at last begun to retaliate. A senior official in the new government said to me: 'I was told in Najaf by senior leaders that they have killed upwards of a thousand Sunnis.' Many of these retaliatory attacks on Sunni by Shia were the work of the 12,000-strong police commandos controlled by the Ministry of Interior. Unlike the South American death squads of the 1970s and 1980s, to whom they were instantly compared, these units made no effort to conceal their identity. The openness of their murderous activities may have been quite intentional, a delib-erate warning to the Sunni that the Shia were now in charge and would hit back in future. Dressed in their garish green and yellow uniforms, the commandos would arrive at the houses of former Sunni officials and carry out arrests. A few days later the bodies of those detained – sometimes savagely tortured, with eyes gouged out and legs broken – would turn up in the morgue. One day in

west Baghdad in July 2005 the commandos took away a former
general in Saddam Hussein's army called Akram Ahmed Rasul
al-Bayati, and his two sons, Ali, a policeman, and Omar were
arrested by police commandos. Omar was eventually freed and
one of his uncles paid $7,000 for the release of the other two
men. But when he went to pick them up he saw them taken out
of a car and shot dead in front of him.

Such killings created terror in Sunni neighbourhoods, particularly among the hundreds of thousands who had served under
the old regime. The Badr Organization, which fought on the
Iranian side in the Iran–Iraq war of 1980–88, was seen by the
Sunni as an arm of Iranian intelligence seeking revenge and
determined to settle old scores. Sunni air force pilots believed
they were being singled out for assassination because they were
suspected of having bombed Iranian cities twenty years earlier.
Many of them tried to conceal their old profession or fled the
country. Fear of the death squads was pushing the Sunni community as a whole towards sympathy with the insurgents, who
were viewed as armed fellow Sunnis who might protect them.

Contrary to Jaafari's claim in London the resistance was
becoming stronger. At 5 a.m. one day in mid-June 2005
resistance fighters walked into Dohra, the large, mostly Sunni
district in south Baghdad, and took it over: the local police
disappeared. The insurgents retreated only when US helicopters
arrived overhead. One evening my driver was queuing for fuel at
a petrol station in a Sunni district in west Baghdad. Much to his
irritation it closed at 8 p.m. sharp, just as he got to the head of the
line. He complained to the manager of the petrol station that
curfew did not start until 11 p.m. 'That's true,' replied the
manager, 'but we need police here to protect us and they go
home at 8 p.m. because that is the time the resistance take over
and if they stayed longer they would be killed.'

Iraqis living in Baghdad and the centre of the country were
becoming more frightened by the day. Thirty months after the

US and British invasion Iraq appeared to be heading towards a civil war. Sectarian cleansing of Shia by Sunni assassins had started in south and west Baghdad. Interior Ministry death squads spread terror among the Sunni. Insurgents controlled large parts of the capital at night. They lobbed mortar bombs at will into the heavily fortified American, British and Iraqi government head-quarters in the Green Zone.

But, absurdly, it was in these circumstances that the Iraqi political parties were supposed to agree a new constitution – the rules of the game by which Iraq was to be governed – and the Iraqi people were to vote on it in a referendum on October 15. Whatever else it was, the document was not a recipe for peace. The International Crisis Group, the highly regarded research group, warned that the Sunni Arabs saw the constitution as legitimizing the break-up of the country, so a referendum approving it would ensure that 'Iraq will slide towards full-scale civil war and dissolution'.

The US wanted a constitution to be rushed through because this would show that there was political progress in Iraq. The Kurds were intent on creating a federal Iraq in which they would enjoy political and economic quasi-independence. They were also understandably intent on reversing the ethnic cleansing of which they had been victims in the past. They wanted to give legal sanction to the gains they had already made on the ground by holding a referendum to determine the future of Kirkuk and the other Kurdish regions from which they had been expelled. The constitution itself began with a fine flourish, recalling that Iraq was 'the land of the Prophets, resting place of the holy imams, the leaders of civilization, the creators of the alphabet, the cradle of arithmetic'. But the constitution envisaged a state that would be wholly decentralized, one in which 'any single pro-vince, or group of provinces, is entitled to request that it be recognized as a region'. The document was vague about ex-ploitation of oil resources but could be read as allocating future oil discoveries to the regions.

The Shia parties, notably Abdul Aziz al-Hakim's Supreme Council for Islamic Revolution in Iraq, were willing to go along with the Kurdish vision of the future of Iraq and create a Shia super-region out of nine provinces in which they were the majority in southern Iraq. This entity would also sit on top of some of the world's largest oil reserves. One minister remarked: 'The Iraqi government could end up as a few buildings in the Green Zone.'

The Shia and Kurds voted for the constitution and the Sunni voted largely and vainly against it. I was beginning to enjoy polling days in Baghdad because of the respite from traffic problems. The election in December, this time for a four-year parliament, turned out to be a re-run of the election at the start of the year. This time the Sunni community did go to the polls, but this was unlikely to do them as much good as they hoped: they were still heavily outnumbered by the Shia and Kurds. Once again Iraqis voted along ethnic and sectarian lines. The United Iraqi Alliance, the Shia coalition, won 128 seats, the Kurds fifty-three seats, the Sunni parties fifty-five seats and Iyad Allawi's party only twenty-five seats. The main change in the Shia Alliance was the success of Muqtada al-Sadr, the failure of Allawi and the departure from the coalition of Ahmed Chalabi, whose list did not win a single seat. 'Iraq is getting more like Bosnia every day,' lamented Ghassan Attiyah. 'The centre is becoming very weak. Officially they will keep the facade of a unitary state but in practice there is no effective government.' Sectarian identity had become all-important. 'It is getting so bad,' Attiyah concluded, 'that if a ministry appoints a Shia doorman, the Kurds and the Sunni will demand that doormen from their communities stand beside him.'

XV

A SENSE OF UTTER lawlessness permeated everyday life in Baghdad as the war approached its fourth year. In his *Memoirs of an Egotist* Stendhal describes how, when he visited a city or town, he tried to identify the ten prettiest girls, the ten richest men and the ten people who could have him executed; he would have had his work cut out in Baghdad. Veils increasingly concealed girls' faces, the rich had fled the country – and almost anybody could have you killed. To give a picture of Baghdad, surely the most dangerous city in the world at this time, it is worth explaining in greater detail just why a modern-day Stendhal would be in trouble if he tried to identify any of the three categories he mentions.

Iraqi women used to enjoy more freedom than almost anywhere else in the Muslim world apart from Turkey. Iraq was a secular state after the overthrow of the monarchy in 1958. Women had equal rights in theory and this was also largely true in practice. These were eroded in the final years of Saddam Hussein as Iraqi society became increasingly Islamic. But under the constitution negotiated with the participation of the American and British ambassadors and ratified by the referendum on October 15 2005, women legally became second-class citizens in much of Iraq. About three quarters of the girls leaving their schools at lunchtime in central Baghdad now wore headscarves. The reason was generally self-protection. Those girls who were truly religious concealed all their hair, and these were in a minority. The others left a quiff of hair showing which usually meant that they wore headscarves solely because they were frightened of religious zealots. There was also a belief that kidnappers, the terror of every Iraqi parent, would be less likely to abduct a girl wearing a headscarf because they would suppose she came from a traditional family. This is not because of any religious scruples on the part of kidnappers but because they thought that old-fashioned families were likely to belong to a strong tribe. Such a tribe will seek vengeance if one of its members is abducted – a much more frightening prospect for kidnappers than any action by the police.

The life of women had already become more restricted because of the violence in Baghdad. Waiting outside the College of Sciences in Baghdad one day was a twenty-year-old biology student called Mariam Ahmed Yassin, who belonged to a well-off family. She was expecting a private car, driven by somebody she trusted, to take her home. Her fear was kidnapping. She said: 'I promised my mother to go nowhere after college except home and never to sit in a restaurant.' Her father, a businessman, had already moved to Germany. She volunteered: 'I admire Saddam very much and I consider him a great leader because he could control security.'

Mariam's father was part of the great exodus of business and professional people from Iraq. A friend suffering from a painful toothache spent hours one day ringing up dentists only to be told again and again that they had left the country. If Stendhal was looking for the ten richest Iraqis he would have had to begin his search in Jordan, Syria or Egypt. The richer districts of the capital had become ghost towns inhabited by trigger-happy security guards. In some parts of Baghdad property prices had dropped by half. Well-off people wanted to keep it a secret if they sold a house because kidnappers and robbers would know they had money. 'Some 5,000 people were kidnapped between the fall of Saddam Hussein and May 2005,' said the former human rights minister Bakhtiar Amin. The real figure was in fact far higher since most people did not report kidnappings to the police. This was partly because they knew there was not much the police could do about it, partly because they feared retaliation by the criminals and had a shrewd suspicion that the police and the kidnap gangs were in league. One businessman I met said that somehow the police had learned that his brother-in-law had been kidnapped. They rang him up to ask if he wanted their help. He turned them down and said he would handle the matter himself. 'Half an hour later my telephone rang,' he said. 'It was one of the kidnappers. He asked for a large sum of money and added, "You were quite right to refuse the police offer of help." '

Iraq was all too clearly oversupplied with executioners, the last category on Stendhal's list. Even during a quiet day as many as forty bodies might turn up at Baghdad's morgue, dead at the hands of US soldiers, insurgents, Iraqi army and police, bandits, kidnappers, robbers or simply neighbours who settled a dispute with a gun. It was some indication of the level of killings that when fifty bodies, all of people who had been murdered, washed up on the banks of the Tigris south of Baghdad in the spring of 2005 nobody quite knew who they were or why they had been killed. Local doctors, inured to the high death toll after several years of war, said they were surprised by the fuss and pointed out that as the waters of the Tigris River warmed under the summer sun the bodies of those killed during the winter were rising to the surface.

High rank was no defence against violence. The Iraqi police general in charge of the serious crimes squad was shot through the head by an American soldier who mistook him for a suicide bomber. President Jalal Talabani's head of protocol was not with him when he visited Washington to see President Bush. Instead he was in a Baghdad hospital with a broken arm and leg after a US Humvee rammed his vehicle on the airport road.

So many people were being killed in Iraq every day for so many reasons that the outside world had come to ignore the slaughter and Iraqis themselves were almost used to it. The death of a thousand people in a stampede during a Shia religious festival in September 2005 was only a one-day wonder abroad. It is worth looking at just three acts of violence in a small part of Baghdad to show how casual killings and kidnappings impacted on the people of the city. They took place within a few days of each other in September 2005 in or close to al-Kudat, a previously prosperous district in the south-west of the city where many doctors and lawyers once lived. It was by no means the most dangerous part of Baghdad and the days when the following events occurred were quieter than those that followed.

The first killing was at the hands of the Americans. Early one morning a surgeon called Basil Abbas Hassan decided to leave his house in al-Kudat for his hospital in the centre of Baghdad at 7.15 a.m. in order to beat the morning rush hour. Dr Hassan, a specialist in head surgery, was the kind of man who should have been one of the building blocks of the new Iraq. He drove his car out of a side street on to the airport road without noticing that an American convoy was approaching from behind him. A US soldier thought the car might be driven by a suicide bomber and shot Dr Hassan dead. Not many of his friends attended his funeral because so many of them had already left Iraq.

Mobile phone theft is common all over the world, but in Baghdad people will kill for a handset. This is not because they are more expensive than elsewhere in the world – in fact they are cheaper because nobody pays any tariffs on them – but because murder is so easy. No criminal expects to be caught. A few days after Dr Hassan was killed by the Americans a sixteen-year-old, Muhammad Ahmed, was making a call on his mobile as he walked down the street. A car drew up beside him and a man pointed a pistol. He said: 'Give me your phone.' Muhammad refused or hesitated to hand it over for a few seconds too long and the gunman killed him with a bullet in the neck.

The third story has a happier ending, though at one moment it seemed likely to end in tragedy. It happened in another street in al-Kudat. The mother of a friend called Ismail told him that there was a strange car parked outside the house. She wanted him to find out to whom it belonged. It did not seem likely that anybody would leave a car bomb in a residential street because US or Iraqi patrols never used it. But anything out of the ordinary in Baghdad may be dangerous and is routinely checked out. Ismail spoke to two neighbours who denied any knowledge of the mysterious car. A third neighbour admitted that he knew about it and went on to give the dramatic reason why it was there. He said there was a meeting of his extended family taking place in his house because a few hours earlier his fourteen-year-old grandson Akhil Hussein had been kidnapped as he returned from school. The kidnappers called, demanding $60,000 for his release and threatening to kill him. The panic-stricken family had gathered their relatives together to try to raise some money. They were asked to park their cars far away from the house in case the kidnappers were watching and got an exaggerated idea of the family's wealth. This explained what a strange car was doing outside Ismail's house.

The problem was that the kidnappers had taken the wrong boy. His family was the only poor one in the street. They had moved into a large house to look after a well-off relative who was dying of cancer. They could not afford anything like $60,000. When the kidnappers called again the grandfather said: 'We are a poor family. Come and look at our house. When our generator caught fire a month ago it burnt part of the house and we did not have the money to rebuild it.' The kidnappers said they did not believe this, but a few hours later called again to say they had looked at the house and realized their mistake. A voice on the phone said: 'We are sorry. We kidnapped the wrong boy. We meant to kidnap the son of a rich man living next to you. Even so you must pay us the cost of our mistake which is one million dinars [$800].' The grandfather of Akhil – the father was in a state of shock – immediately went to his rich neighbour, a Kurd. He told him: 'Be careful: they want to kidnap your son.'

The neighbour bundled his family into several cars and fled. For once, the kidnappers kept their word and the grandson was released unharmed. He knew nothing because he had been tied up and his eyes taped from the moment he was seized. Akhil was lucky. Many kidnap victims are found tortured and dead even when the money is paid.

Stendhal would have been unwise to pursue his investigation into killers and kidnappers too energetically. I suffered from the same difficulty. I was interested in finding out how the criminal gangs operated but they were far too dangerous to approach directly and almost no cases ever came to court. One day in London, however, I was contacted by the family of a doctor who had survived his kidnapping unharmed because the men who had just seized him accidentally ran into a police checkpoint and he had escaped during the gun battle. Several of his captors were arrested and had made full confessions.

Dr Thamir Muhammad Ali Hasafa al-Kaisey, sixty, a senior consultant, had been kidnapped by a gang of eleven armed men in three cars as he drove home from his clinic in Baghdad at 6.30 p.m. on December 23 2004. 'I was fifty metres from my house when men with guns in a Cherokee jeep stopped me and beat me with their fists,' Dr Hasafa later told the police. 'They put me in their car with my face on the floor and tied me up with my own jacket.' The kidnappers may have been overconfident because they normally operated with impunity in Baghdad. Whatever the reason they ran into a police checkpoint and during the shoot-out which followed Dr Hasafa, even though his leg had been broken in the beating, was able to crawl out of the back of the car and shout to the police: 'I am a doctor and I was kidnapped.'

The case was a rare success for the police, though public cynicism about them was confirmed by the discovery that one of the captured kidnappers was himself a police lieutenant. His name was Muhammad Najim Abdullah al-Dhouri and his fellow kidnapper was Adnan Ashur Ali al-Jabouri, both members of powerful tribes from which Saddam Hussein drew many of his security men and army officers. But the motive of the gang was purely political. Adnan Ashur told the investigating judge that the leaders of the gang were Eyhab, nicknamed Abu Fahad, who ran a mobile phone shop, and his brother Hisham. Eyhab, he said, was a criminal sentenced to forty years in jail by the old regime. He had apparently been freed during the general amnesty by Saddam Hussein at the end of 2002.

Muhammad Najim, who was based in Sadr City in east Baghdad, lived in special police housing. He said: 'I was involved with Hisham prior to the fall of Saddam. Later he approached me about kidnapping prominent men. My task was to provide security for the gang.' All the gang members were armed with pistols. They had safe houses in which to keep kidnap victims. Both suspects said they had taken part in numerous other kidnappings in the previous few months, with their victims paying up to $60,000 each. Ironically, the informant who told them that Dr Hasafa was worth kidnapping was a guard hired by householders to protect the street where he lived.

The Iraqi police were jubilant that they finally had detailed information on how a kidnap gang operated. The two captured men were willing to provide the names and addresses of other gang members and the success was lauded by Iraqi television and the local press. To the consternation of the police, however, a convoy of US military police suddenly arrived at al-Khansa police station, where Muhammad Majim and Adnan Ashur were being held. The Iraqi police officer at the station recorded: 'They have requested the custody of the two assailants.' The men were handed over to an American police lieutenant for transfer to the US-run Camp Cuervo and later released. An American military spokesman said several months afterwards that there was no record of the two prisoners in the army database. An Iraqi government official told me that they were almost certainly freed after they agreed to inform on the insurgents. 'The

Americans are allowing the breakdown of Iraqi society because they are only interested in fighting the insurgency,' added a senior Iraqi police officer.

Dr Hasafa, meanwhile, received two visits from the families of the former prisoners. The first was from the father of Muhammad Najim, who offered money if the kidnap charges were withdrawn. He said he had been an officer in the Republican Guard and added menacingly: 'You know what we are capable of doing.' During the second meeting Dr Hasafa learned that his kidnappers had been freed. He refused to withdraw charges, despite death threats to his family, but in January 2005 he fled to Jordan and then to Egypt. At every stage of the case he had been betrayed by those – the street guard, the Iraqi police lieutenant in Sadr City and the US military police – who were meant to protect him.

By the end of 2005 it was difficult to find many optimists in Baghdad. The three polls had driven people further apart. 'If the constitution passes then the Sunnis will not accept it and if it fails the Kurds and Shia will be very angry,' said Nabil, whom I talked to as he queued at a petrol station near my hotel. There was no sign of reconciliation between the old regime and the new. Hatred was deeper than ever. I went to a meeting of nearly a thousand former Iraqi army officers and tribal leaders in a large, heavily guarded hall on the banks of the Tigris. It was called by General Wafiq al-Sammarai, a head of Iraqi military intelligence under Saddam Hussein who fled Baghdad in 1994 to join the opposition. He was now military advisor to President Talabani.

As reconciliation meetings go it was not a great success. General al-Sammarai called for support for the government and the elimination of foreign terrorists. No sooner had he finished than General Salam Hussein Ali, sitting in the audience, rose to his feet; there was 'no security, no electricity, no clean water and no government,' he thundered. He wanted the old Iraqi army back in its old uniforms. Other officers, making it clear that they sympathized with the resistance, denounced the way Iraq was being run. 'They were fools to break up our great army and form an army of thieves and criminals,' one of them said. 'They are traitors,' muttered another. Claims that Iraq had become a democracy were brushed aside: 'The government inside the Green Zone had no idea of the real condition of the country and ignored the grievances of the people.'

General al-Sammarai looked aghast as things seemed to be getting out of hand. At one moment he said, 'This is chaos,' though he later apologized and said it was democracy. A tribal poet who had unwisely tried to chant a poem in praise of the general was howled down. Most of the officers were probably Sunni but several were Shia. All were deeply hostile to the occupation. General al-Sammarai promised there would be no attacks on the Sunni cities of central Iraq but the audience looked dubious. One officer demanded that he stop using the American word 'general' and use the Arabic word *lewa'a* instead. Everybody was keen to say that Sunnis, Shias and Kurds were all Iraqis, with no differences between them. But Sunnis, who claimed to be non-sectarian, then went on to say they considered the Shias who controlled the Interior Ministry to be Iranians rather than Iraqis. Sheikh Ahmed al-Sammari, the imam of the Sunni mosque of the Umm al-Qura, the headquarters of the influential Muslim Scholars Association, called for Sunni and Shia solidarity. But he saw no contradiction in adding that Sunnis were being persecuted by Shias all over Iraq. He had just identified the dead body of his own bodyguard. He had also spoken to a Sunni from Fallujah who was arrested by the police and tortured. The imam claimed that the police had said: 'For every Shia killed in Fallujah or Ramadi, a Sunni will be killed in Baghdad.'

XVI

I RAQ WAS SPLITTING into three separate parts. The fault lines dividing Sunni, Shia and Kurd became wider by the day. Remembering my experiences in Lebanon at the start of the civil war in 1975 I suspected, as the atmosphere became more poisonous in Iraq, that a single atrocity or the assassination of a Shia religious leader might be enough to ignite a sectarian civil war. In fact the target selected by Sunni fundamentalists was a building and not a person. Rising above the rooftops of the city of Samarra north of Baghdad was the golden dome of the al-Askari mosque containing the tombs of the 10th and 11th of the Shia Imams, Ali al-Hadi who died in AD 868 and his son Hassan Ali al-Askari who died in AD 874. One of the most revered of Shia shrines, it has long been a place of pilgrimage. It was also poorly guarded. Samarra is a mostly Sunni city. When I visited al-Askari mosque a couple of years earlier I had been searched by the guards at the outer gates of the shrine, but they obviously could not hold off a serious assault by an armed and determined group.

At 6.55 a.m. on February 22 2006 a number of men in police uniforms entered the shrine, tied up the guards and planted explosives. When they were detonated a few moments later the blast brought down the golden dome and Shia patience in the face of Salafi atrocities finally snapped. It was as if 400 years ago, during the religious wars in Europe, militant Protestants had blown up St Peter's in Rome. Grand Ayatollah Ali al-Sistani and the Hawza could no longer restrain their people. The Shia were in a much stronger position to retaliate than they would have been a year earlier because they now controlled the Interior Ministry and most of the police and police commando units in central and southern Iraq. There were black-clad Mehdi Army militiamen in every Shia district. The Badr Organization, where they were not in police uniforms, patrolled Baghdad unimpeded by the official security forces.

In the days following the Samarra bombing some 1,300 bodies, mostly Sunni, were found in and around Baghdad. The Interior Ministry asked the Health Ministry, also Shia-controlled, to release a lower figure. Some fifty Sunni mosques were either burnt, blown up or taken over in Baghdad alone. In Basra Sunni prisoners were dragged from a jail and lynched by gunmen. A friend of mine, a normally pacific man living in a middle-class Sunni district in west Baghdad, rang me. 'I am not leaving my home,' he said in a nervous voice. 'The police commandos arrested fifteen people from here last night including the local baker. I am sitting here in my house with a Kalashnikov and sixty bullets and if they come for me I am going to open fire.'

It was strange to hear George Bush and the British Foreign Secretary Jack Straw deny that civil war was going on, given that so many bodies – all people strangled, shot or hanged solely because of their religious identity – were being discovered every day. The tit-for-tat killings did not die away. Early in March car bombs exploded in the markets of the great Shia slum of Sadr City. Several days later a group of children playing football in a field noticed a powerful stench. Police opened up a pit which contained the bodies of twenty-seven men, probably all Sunni, stripped to their underpants; they had all been tortured and then shot in the head. In another district people were worried by a bus abandoned on the road which they suspected might contain a bomb. In fact its grisly cargo turned out to be the bodies of eighteen Sunni, all of whom had been tortured before they were killed.

The conflict in Iraq had reached a new and bloodier phase. 'It is unfortunate that we are in a civil war,' said Iyad Allawi, the former prime minister. 'We are losing each day, as an average, fifty to sixty people throughout the country if not more. If this is not civil war God knows what is.' As so often in the past Allawi was over-susceptible to pressure from the US and British embassies and later retracted his perfectly sensible words. Once again the White House and Downing Street did not want to admit the extent to which the situation in Iraq was getting worse, not better. Over the coming weeks American and British officials repeatedly decried the use of the phrase 'civil war'. Possibly they feared that the admission that something like a civil war had begun at least in parts of Iraq could prove self-fulfilling. But a self-serving motive was also at work. For almost three years President Bush and Tony Blair had portrayed Iraq as on its way towards peace and a better life. They argued that whatever the rights and wrongs of the original invasion Iraqis were now better off than under Saddam Hussein. American and British voters had largely accepted this picture of Iraq since the two leaders had won re-election in 2004 and 2005 respectively. But if Iraq was now plunged into civil war this final justification for their Iraq venture would be fatally undermined.

Sectarian hatred was escalating rapidly. Until a few months before the bomb in Samarra, Iraqi friends used to say to me that Iraq was not like Lebanon. Now they were silent or asked what the Lebanese civil war had been like. Districts where Sunni and Shia had lived together peacefully for decades, if not centuries, were being torn apart in a few days. In the al-Amel neighbourhood in west Baghdad, mixed but with a Shia majority, Sunni householders found envelopes pushed under their doors with a Kalashnikov bullet inside and a letter telling them to leave immediately or be killed. It added that they must take all their goods which they could carry and only return later to sell their houses. The reaction to the letter, which could have been the work of one person, was immediate. The Sunni in al-Amel started barricading their streets. Several Shia families, believed to belong to the Supreme Council for Islamic Revolution in Iraq, were murdered the same day as the threatening letters were received. 'The local Sunni suspected those Shia of being behind the letters,' said my informant. 'Probably they called in the local resistance and asked them to kill the SCIRI people.'

Day-to-day survival in Baghdad meant taking life-or-death decisions for mundane reasons. By the end of March it was beginning to get hot in the city and people normally go shopping at this time of year to buy summer clothes. But as temperatures soared the streets of shopping districts like al-Mansur remained eerily empty. Many shops were closed because the owners were too frightened to leave their homes. But staying in your own house also brought problems with it. In the torrid summer heat people need air-conditioning to make life tolerable. But Baghdad was getting only three or four hours of electricity a day. Almost everybody had a generator, large or small, depending on what they could afford. The government price of petrol was heavily subsidized by the state and, despite a much-resented price rise before Christmas, was still cheap. One friend, Muhammad, complained: 'Either I wait seven or eight hours in a queue to buy fuel [at the official price] or I get it on the black market. But black market fuel means that I could have to spend $7–8 a day to run my generator and I simply can't afford that.' Muhammad added that that he had just spent ten hours, 5 a.m. until 3 p.m., queuing to buy a single bottle of gas which he, like most Iraqis, used for cooking. The beginning of summer on the Mesopotamian plain – one of the hottest places on earth – should have been good news for Muhammad's brother, who had a job in a company selling air-conditioning units. But the brother had just lost his job. The company he worked for was owned by a Kurd. His life was threatened and he shut down the company before moving to Jordan with his family.

'The battle for Baghdad has already started,' said Fuad Hussein, the chief of staff of the Kurdish leader Massoud Barzani. 'The fighting will only stop when a new balance of power has emerged. Sunni and Shia will each take control of their own area.' He pointed to districts like al-Dohra and al-Ghazaliyah in the capital where the insurgents or the Sunni political parties were tightening their grip. In the first half of 2006 Iraqi political leaders, whatever they said in public, were increasingly pessimistic about Iraq holding together as more than a loose confederation. 'The army will disintegrate in the first moments of the war because the soldiers are loyal to the Shia, Sunni or Kurdish communities,' one senior official said.

A few weeks later at the end of April there were ominous signs that these predictions of street fighting, as in Beirut thirty years earlier, were beginning to come true. Adhamiyah, the ancient district centred on the Abu Hanifa mosque, is one of the few solidly Sunni areas in Baghdad east of the Tigris. Its people regarded the police and paramilitary commandos as little different from death squads. Over several days in the middle of April Adhamiyah resounded with the sound of gunfire and exploding rocket-propelled grenades. American and Iraqi soldiers claimed insurgents had tried to ambush them. Local people said that, on the contrary, the young men of the district had fought off an invasion of their streets by Shia bent on killing and kidnapping. Sunni gunmen raced from house to house calling for each family to send at least one of their sons to join the battle. 'Go for jihad! Defeat these aggressors,' exhorted the loudspeaker on the roof of a mosque. As the shooting became more sporadic after two days' fighting, frightened residents of Adhamiyah began to pack their goods into vehicles in preparation for flight.

Sectarian cleansing was mainly confined to Baghdad and the nearby provinces – although these had a population of at least six million. But there was violence all over Iraq, aside from the three fully Kurdish provinces in the far north. After three years in Iraq I thought I had become all too inured to violence. I no longer responded to bloodshed, except with the usual words of regret, unless people I knew well were killed and injured. But in Iraq, just as I was imagining I had seen the nadir of savagery, I would hear of something worse. On the third anniversary of the overthrow of Saddam Hussein, the day his statue was famously toppled in Baghdad, I visited Kirkuk where the Kurds were trying to tighten their grip on the oil city. I had entered the city on the day the *peshmerga* captured it with such ease. Three years later it had become a far more dangerous place. I slept on the floor of the house of Rezgar Ali Hamajan, the hospitable head of the provincial council, in a heavily defended Kurdish enclave. Battle-hardened as was this former *peshmerga* he had been shocked by a recent event in the city. It struck me likewise, when he told me about it, as epitomizing all too well the savage hatreds which now boiled across Iraq and from which nobody was safe.

In the centre of Kirkuk there is a building that seems imposing compared to the ramshackle houses all around it; this is the Republican Hospital. It is here that most of the casualties from gun battles, bombings and assassinations were brought. In 2005, some 1,500 people were killed or injured in Kirkuk province. Large numbers of those taken to the hospital died, and there turned out to be an extraordinary reason for the high casualty rate. Sometime earlier the hospital had recruited an enthusiastic young doctor called Dr Louay Omar al-Taie who was always willing to help. What the doctors did not know was that Dr Louay, an Arab, was a member of a cell of the Ansar al-Sunna group, one of the most feared and effective insurgent groups. He tended wounded guerrillas in caves outside Kirkuk but his main job was to ensure that the injuries of police and troops were always terminal. Over a five-month period from October 2005 he murdered no less than forty-three patients who would otherwise have recovered. His victims were anti-insurgent policemen, soldiers or officials. 'I used to cut off the oxygen or the electricity supply in the operating room or reopen the wounds,' al-Taie said calmly in a taped confession.

The murders were easy to carry out because many of the

injured were bleeding when they arrived at the hospital and, according to Colonel Yadgar Shukir Abdullah Jaff, a senior policeman, Dr Louay 'would inject patients he wanted to kill with a high dose of medicine that made them bleed more'. Iraqi hospitals are invariably short-staffed and there is seldom time for autopsies. The doctor might have been able to carry on with his killings indefinitely but at the end of February 2006 Kurdish security forces in Sulaimaniyah had arrested the leader of his cell, Abu Muhijiz, whose real name was Mallah Yassin. He confessed that Dr Louay was a member of his cell, describing how the doctor, recruited after expressing sympathy with the insurgency to a patient, had at first treated wounded guerrillas. Later he agreed to finish off the victims of attempted assassinations and soldiers and police injured by insurgent bombs. These men presumably imagined that, even in Iraq, they were out of danger of enemy attack once they reached a bed in the emergency ward of a hospital.

The outcome of the parliamentary election on December 15, 2005 did nothing to halt the slaughter. Instead it froze in place existing divisions. The four-and-a-half months it took to choose a new prime minister showed the strength of the resistance to the Shia victory at the polls from the US, the Sunni, the Kurds and most of the Arab world. On the surface the dispute was about Ibrahim al-Jaafari and whether he should remain prime minister. There was no doubt about his failure in the job but his pre-decessors post-Saddam, Paul Bremer and Iyad Allawi, had also failed dismally. The Shia parties stuck with Jaafari so adamantly and for so long because they feared his opponents were bent on rolling back the Shia electoral victory and dividing the Shia coalition. In this they were largely correct. It was only in April 2006 that the seven parties grouped in the United Iraqi Alliance, having largely won the battle to prevent the dilution of their power, grudgingly agreed to replace Jaafari with Nuri al-Maliki, his hard-faced deputy in the Dawa party.

The furious arguments about who should be the next prime minister underlined the degree to which Iraqi leaders were out of touch with their own country. 'It is a government of the Green Zone only,' a senior official told me in exasperation. 'I swear to you there are some ministers who have never seen their own ministries, but just call their director generals to bring them documents to sign.' Nor were Iraqi politicians alone in their isolation from life in Iraq. The foreign media spoke of the inability to form a new government as creating 'a vacuum of authority', as if this had not been true of Iraq ever since the start of the occupation. Nevertheless the row over Jaafari is significant because it revealed the real motives and interests of those vying for power in Iraq.

The interim government, formed after prolonged negotiations following the election on January 30 2005, was a Shia–Kurdish coalition. A year later the US, Sunni and Kurds were both deeply unhappy with its performance. The US had been nervous about the prospect of a Shia government of Iraq ever since the First Gulf War in 1991. It disliked the close relations between Jaafari's administration and Iran, particularly after the election of the militantly anti-American president Mahmoud Ahmadinejad in August 2005. Worse still, Jaafari allied himself to the young nationalist cleric and American bête noir Muqtada al-Sadr, whose Mehdi Army militiamen had fought the US military twice in 2004. Sadr had proved his popularity running as part of the Shia coalition in the December 2005 election when his candidates won thirty-two seats. It was these votes which narrowly secured the renomination of Jaafari by the Shia coalition in the face of a challenge from Adel Abdel Mehdi, a former Marxist turned free-marketeer from SCIRI who was the candidate most acceptable to Washington.

The arrival of Zilmay Khalilzad as US ambassador to Iraq in the late summer of 2005 had given a new and more effective twist to American policy. In a bumbling way US officials had for long cultivated Sunni and Baathist notables in the hope of dividing or influencing the resistance. Khalilzad supported the Sunni in negotiations over the constitution and extracted some not very meaningful concessions for them. This was of dubious benefit to the US because the Sunni political parties won only fifty-five seats in December. There was also no real evidence that they could act as interlocutors for the insurgency. It was never like Sinn Fein and the IRA in Northern Ireland who were both parts of the same organization. 'Who exactly are we supposed to negotiate with?' Hoshyar Zebari used to ask me impatiently when people suggested that the government talk to the resistance. The Sunni community, unlike the Kurds and to a lesser degree the Shia, lacked a single effective leadership.

President Jalal Talabani led the charge against Jaafari, demanding his replacement and accusing him of reneging on deals agreed with the Kurds before he became prime minister. There was a personal edge to the dispute. Talabani was an old friend of Adel Abdel Mehdi, with whom he had marched in leftist demonstrations in the 1960s. Jaafari was accused by his enemies of running the prime minister's office as if he was still in charge of a secret cell of the Dawa party under Saddam. Above all the prime minister had neither delivered on Kirkuk – reversing Saddam's ethnic cleansing of Kurds – nor moved towards the promised referendum that was to decide whether or not the oil province would join the Kurdish region. The Kurds were particularly enraged when Jaafari paid a surprise visit to Turkey without even telling his own Kurdish foreign minister, Hoshyar Zebari. Given the permanent Kurdish fear of Turkish military intervention in Iraq Jaafari could not have done anything more likely to anger and frighten them.

For a brief moment the Kurdish parties debated the possibility of abandoning their strategic alliance with the Shia parties. But the situation was complicated because the Americans and British were trying to foist their old friend Iyad Allawi on to the new government. Though he had won only twenty-five seats in the December election, they demanded that he should play a prominent role, perhaps even as a super-security minister. It was never a sensible plan. Allawi did not have a political base aside from this foreign backing. An amusing piece of television film shot during the December election campaign showed the portly Allawi running hard out of the Imam Ali shrine in Najaf pursued by angry worshippers hurling their shoes at him. 'Iyad Allawi is not part of the solution,' Fuad Hussein, chief of staff to Massoud Barzani, said to me. 'It is only the Gulf Arabs, the US and UK who want him.' At the end of the day the Kurds decided that they had to maintain their alliance with the Shia religious parties. 'For the Kurds it would be suicidal to side with the Sunni and Iyad Allawi because you would alienate [the Shia] 60 per cent of the population,' remarked another Kurdish government official.

To win this prolonged battle over who should be prime minister all the Shia religious parties had to do was dig in and wait for the Americans and the Kurds to discover that there was no practical alternative to them. A split was possible but unlikely because Sistani and the Hawza wanted Shia unity and the Iranians, their influence always considerable, also supported it. In addition no Shia political party wanted to be the first to break ranks. When Jaafari finally agreed to step aside in April his replacement Nuri Maliki, his party colleague, was an ideological mirror image. 'This is someone with whom we can work,' said the US Secretary of State Condoleezza Rice greeting the appointment enthusiastically. The US and the Kurds had gained little out of their prolonged confrontation with the Shia parties and the formation of a government provided no solution to Iraq's ever-deepening crisis. 'Lack of a government does not make Iraqis hate each other,' remarked a minister to me gloomily. 'They hate each other and therefore do not have a government.'

Everywhere Iraq was filled with grim evidence of the occupation's failure. Many Iraqis supported the invasion or stayed neutral in 2003 because they were desperate to end the state of hot and cold war in which they had lived since 1980.

Disillusion came fast. Among the Sunni it was total. The US military never came close to crushing their resistance. Insurgent forces seemed able to concentrate and attack at will. Three years after the overthrow of Saddam Hussein, on March 21 2006, a hundred insurgents armed with automatic rifles, rocket-propelled grenade-launchers and mortars were able to capture a police headquarters and stormed a jail in Muqdadiyah, sixty miles north of Baghdad. They killed nineteen policemen, freed thirty-three prisoners and captured enough police radio equipment to make the rest of the police network insecure. On the day Nuri Maliki was chosen prime minister mortar shells rained down on the Ministry of Defence in the Green Zone, killing seven Iraqis.

During the American presidential election campaign in 2004 the White House and Pentagon claimed that most of Iraq was at peace. Selected Iraqi politicians confirmed this rosy view of their country. Eighteen months later a US State Department map with commentaries for each province was leaked to the press; it revealed a far bleaker picture of security. In an assessment of stability one province, Anbar, was listed as being in a 'critical' state, and six others were in a 'serious' condition. In fact the situation was even worse than it would appear to a casual leader unfamiliar with the political geography of Iraq. Baghdad, Basra and Mosul, the three largest cities in Iraq, containing over a third of the population, were all portrayed as seriously unstable. In the eight Shia provinces south of Baghdad, commended as being moderately stable, the most powerful military forces were often the Shia militias and their allies in the police and army. According to the State Department one provincial council, that of Babil south of Baghdad, had dealt with its notoriously dangerous northern region by simply abandoning 'responsibility for this area, claiming to have ceded it to Baghdad province'.[26]

In the debate abroad about how far the conflict in Iraq had graduated to being 'a civil war', I felt that non-Iraqis seldom realized the anarchy, the state of utter lawlessness in which Iraqis were forced to live in Baghdad and much of the country. Official attempts at reassurance unwittingly revealed the true appalling situation. For instance Sami Mudhafar, the Higher Education and Scientific Research Minister, announced in 2006 that he wanted to lay to rest exaggerated figures circulating for the number of university professors murdered over the previous three years. 'I have exact and accurate figures,' he said comfortingly, 'and the number of university professors who have been martyred does not exceed eighty-nine.' Mudhafar denied reports that Iraqi intellectuals were being specially marked down for assassination, saying they were just being killed at the same rate as other Iraqis. The minister added that somebody had recently tried to assassinate him and the government had no idea who was behind it.[27] Nobody was safe. In the four-month period up to March 2006 no fewer than 311 teachers and sixty-four pupils under the age of twelve had been murdered.

Even for people trying to flee, the course taken by many after the Samarra bomb, the way out of the country was not without its dangers. I had a Sunni friend living in a dangerous district in west Baghdad who wanted to get his family to Syria. He took his mother and two sisters to central Baghdad to procure them passports. The next I heard from him was an anguished e-mail reading: 'Hi Dear Patrick, God saved me this morning when I was with my family in the main office of passport issue and there was a car exploded and my sister injured in the right leg.' Some twenty-five police were killed in the road outside the passport office. My friend's plan to leave Iraq was postponed because his sister's leg turned out to be broken and she was in a private hospital. His mother, terrified by her recent experience, refused to return to the passport office to pick up her passport. On April 27 I received another sad message. 'Yesterday the cousin of my step brother (as you know my father married two) killed by Badr troops after three days of arresting and his body found thrown in the trash of al-Shula district (sic),' my friend wrote in slightly shaky English. 'He is one of three people who were killed after heavy torture. They did nothing but they are Sunni people among the huge number of Shia people in the general factory for cotton al-Qhadamiyah district where they worked. His family couldn't recognize his face but by the big wart on his left arm.'

The US never took on board the deep unpopularity of the occupation among Iraqis. Robespierre, no shrinking violet when it came to violence, warned his fellow French revolutionaries that 'nobody likes armed missionaries'. The illegitimacy of the occupation in the eyes of Arab Iraqis – the Kurds were a different matter – was the most important political fact in Iraq after the invasion. It gave the guerrillas a more than adequate popular base in the Sunni community. Before it became too dangerous for a foreigner to linger in the streets of Baghdad I had often watched crowds dancing with delight among the burning remains of a US Humvee blown apart by a roadside bomb. It was by exploiting the solidarity of the five-million-strong Sunni community in the face of the occupation that the anti-Shia suicide bombers were able to carry out their murderous work with impunity and bring Iraq to the brink of all-out civil war.

Hostility to the occupation was not confined to the Sunni. The Shia grudgingly accepted the US presence so long as it did not impede them taking over the government. Polls showed that a high proportion of Shia approved of armed attacks on occupying forces. The British army, more sensitive to local feelings than the American military, still found itself boycotted by local police in solidly Shia southern Iraq. Its soldiers were increasingly confined to their bases. When a British helicopter was shot down by a missile over Basra and four crewmen killed on May 6 2006, crowds of local people erupted in joy. They hurled stones and bottles of gasoline at British soldiers who arrived at the scene, setting fire to three armoured vehicles. During the fighting rioters chanted: 'We are all soldiers of al-Sayid [Muqtada al-Sadr].'

Iraqi politicians trusted by US officials in the Green Zone were, *ipso facto*, not trusted by Iraqis. Men like the past president

Ghazi al-Yawer, prime minister Iyad Allawi or speaker of parliament Hachem al-Hassani, all lauded in Washington and London, won few votes in elections back in Iraq. Their nationalist credentials were suspect because they were too close to the Americans. It was this lack of effective local supporters which doomed the occupation politically and militarily. 'However clever Ambassador Khalilzad's efforts at divide-and-rule may be, few of his options are good,' commented Graham Fuller, the former vice chairman of the National Intelligence Council of the CIA, adding, perhaps a little prematurely, 'The sad truth is Sunnis and Shiites have come to vie with each other in pushing to get rid of the Americans.'[28]

The danger from the American point of view was that the war with the Sunni insurgency was continuing and the marriage of convenience with the Shia was strained and close to breaking. 'We agreed with the Americans only at the point of removing Saddam Hussein,' Sheikh Abu Muhammad Baghdadi, a Shia cleric in Najaf close to Sistani, was quoted as saying on the same day as the British armoured vehicles were blazing in Basra. 'The relationship ended at that point.' Probably there would be no general uprising against the occupation by the Shia without the permission of Sistani and the Hawza. But the feeling on the street was changing across Shia Iraq. 'There is an anger,' said another clerical spokesman. 'You can hear it in the slogans at Friday prayers: "Death to America." They're burning American flags. They're saying, 'The Americans won't leave except by the funerals of their sons."'[29]

Aside from Iraqi Arab hostility to the occupation the US faced a number of problems of its own making. The war had been staged primarily as a demonstration of US power. President George W. Bush pursued in 2002-2003 exactly the opposite diplomatic course of his father in 1990-91. He spurned international legitimacy or the support of the UN. But once Saddam was gone the US was in desperate need of some sort of international force to take over in Iraq. Otherwise the invasion would appear to Iraqis, with good reason, to be a colonial venture little different from the British occupation in 1917. But Washington seemed to revel in creating the conditions for its own long-term defeat. Imperial hubris had run rampant in the US after the easy victory in Afghanistan in 2002. Governments of several countries neighbouring Iraq – notably Iran and Syria – were curtly informed that their days were numbered once a stable pro-US government was established in Baghdad. Not surprisingly they did everything they could to make sure this never happened.

Ripples of violence spread from Iraq. On February 14 2005 I was talking from Baghdad on my mobile to my friend and colleague Robert Fisk, who was walking along the seafront Corniche in Beirut. Suddenly there was a crash which I recognized as the sound of a bomb exploding, but the windows of my room in the Hamra Hotel did not shake as was normal. 'Is that here or there?' I asked Robert dubiously. It was there. He ran 400 metres to where a bomb had carved an enormous crater in the road outside the St George Hotel and killed Rafiq Hariri, the former prime minister and most powerful politician in Lebanon. The Lebanese universally blamed Syria and its local allies. At first it seemed that the Syria might have overplayed its hand. Syrian troops left Lebanon. But a year later, secure in its alliance with Iran, the government in Damascus sounded confident that it had survived the US bid to remake the Middle East.

The war created such bitter divisions around the world that it inspired many conspiracy theories about how it had started and why the US failed. The opponents of the war suspected that it was the result of a neo-conservative plot, possibly orchestrated by Israel, to destroy a potentially powerful Arab state. If there was such a plan it was ill-considered. Saddam's Iraq was militarily and politically weak, as the speed of his defeat demonstrated. The Sunni fundamentalist groups, battle-hardened in Iraq, are likely to prove far more dangerous to Israel and the US than Saddam Hussein. The one clear beneficiary of America's invasion and occupation of Iraq so far is Iran, the most vigorous and powerful opponent of Israel and America in the region.

Proponents of the war in 2003 had their own mythical picture of Iraq and the Middle East. As US failure became evident opponents of the invasion and former supporters have also produced their own myths. Venomous exchanges between the US Secretary for Defence Donald Rumsfeld and senior generals now retired suggest that all would have been well if the occupation army had been bigger. Rumsfeld is blamed for sending too small a force. But if the US had fielded an army twice the size of the 150,000-strong force in Iraq after the invasion the Sunni uprising would still have taken place. Nor did the 'blitzkrieg' strategy of sending the US army racing north to Baghdad without capturing provincial cities help the guerrillas to put down roots and flourish. The insoluble problems for the US were always political not military.

Much of this book has been about the peculiarities of Iraq and the mistakes made by Americans when occupying it. But not all the reasons which led Washington to invade were unique to the US. For the two years before 9/11 I lived in Moscow. I had seen how Vladimir Putin had risen from obscurity in 1999 in the weeks after four apartment buildings were mysteriously bombed in Moscow killing 300 people. Putin had presented himself as Russia's no-nonsense defender against terrorism. He used this threat to launch his own small victorious war against Chechnya and manipulated a minor threat to the state to win and hold the presidency. He speedily demolished the free press. George W. Bush followed almost exactly in Putin's footsteps two years later in the wake of the September 11 destruction of the World Trade Center. Civil liberties were curtailed. The same authoritarian rhetoric was employed. War was declared on terrorism. The American and Russian governments, the two former protagonists in the Cold War, latched on to the same limited 'terrorist' threat to justify and expand their authority. Putin and Bush, though neither were ever in the army, started to walk with the same military swagger.

By 2006 part of the US establishment was searching for a scapegoat for failure in Iraq. The American generals had a point in saying that Rumsfeld should have been fired for incompetence but the same charge could be levelled at the whole of the Bush administration, starting with the president. The fact that nobody was fired underlined that the White House's priorities were ultimately to do with domestic politics and not strengthening America's position in the Middle East. This position is far weaker now than it was three years ago. The 'terrorists' with whom George W. Bush is meant to be at war have a base in Iraq that they yearned for but never secured in Afghanistan. Firing Rumsfeld or any other senior official would have been an open admission of how badly the war was going with possibly damaging electoral consequences. This was the pattern throughout the occupation. A series of misleading milestones – the fictitious turnover of sovereignty in 2004, the elections of 2005 – were put in place to give an illusory impression of progress. All the while the Iraqi state and society came ever closer to dissolution.

As for America, the Duke of Wellington was right to warn of the damage a small war can do to a large state. Washington has paid an astonishingly high price for getting rid of Saddam Hussein. America's victorious war to throw Iraq out of Kuwait in 1991 was the start of its reign as sole superpower – the Soviet Union having conveniently collapsed at the same moment – and the occupation of Iraq in 2003 may have marked the beginning of its decline. Saddam Hussein, in a fit of hubris, had far exceeded his country's strength by conquering Kuwait. Propelled by similar arrogance twelve years later, George W. Bush showed the limits of US power by the invasion and occupation of Iraq.

Notes

1   *Guardian*, January 13 2006.
2   John Murtha, CNN transcript of speech, November 19 2005.
3   Statement by Henry A. Waxman, Congressional Subcommittee on National Security, Emerging Threats and International Relations, April 25 2006.
4   *Azzaman*, April 23 2006.
5   James I. Robertson, Jr., *Stonewall Jackson: The Man, The Soldier, The Legend*, Macmillan, New York, 1997, p. x.
6   H.V.F. Winstone, *Gertrude Bell*, London: Jonathan Cape, 1976, pp. 215–16.
7   'War in Iraq: Political Challenges after the Conflict,' ICG Report, March 23 2003, p. 6.
8   UNICEF: Nutritional status survey at primary health centres during polio national immunization days, March 14–16, 1998.
9   ICG Amman/Brussels, December 4 2004.
10 L. Paul Bremer, *My Year in Iraq*, New York: Simon and Schuster, 2006 *passim*.
11 Antony Beevor, *Berlin: The Downfall: 1945*, London: Viking, 2002, p. 321. I owe this comparison between Berlin in 1945 and Baghdad in 2003 to a letter from an alert *Independent* reader who wrote in to the paper.
12 *New York Times*, February 9 2006. The seven measures of public service performance are electricity, generating capacity, hours of power available in a day in Baghdad, oil and heating oil production, and the number of Iraqis with drinkable water and sewage service.
13 *New York Times*, January 24 2006, citing retired Admiral David Nash in charge of the reconstruction effort.
14 Kamran Karadaghi, quoted in ICG, October 1 2002, p. 15.

15 L. Paul Bremer, op. cit.

16 Keith Middlemas, *The Diplomacy of Illusion: The British Government and Germany 1937–39*, London: Weidenfeld and Nicolson, 1972, quoting Crowe on the title page.

17 ICG, February 15 2006, p. 11, n. 88.

18 *Associated Press*, February 25 2006.

19 L. Paul Bremer, op. cit., pp. 358–9.

20 Brigadier Aylwin-Foster, 'Changing the army for counter-insurgency operations', *Military Review*, November–December 2005, p. 4.

21 Council on Foreign Relations, 'Iraq's Reconstruction Ailments,' Q&A, November 9 2005.

22 CBS News '60 Minutes', 'Billions wasted in Iraq,' February 9 2006.

23 Peter Galbraith, 'Iraq: Bremer's Mess,' *New York Review of Books*, March 9 2006.

24 CBS News, op. cit.

25 L. Paul Bremer, op. cit., p. 178.

26 *New York Times*, April 9 2006.

27 *Azzaman*, March 21 2006.

28 *International Herald Tribune*, April 15 2006.

29 *Los Angeles Times*, May 7 2006.

Index